Why Immigrants Come to America

Braceros, Indocumentados, and the *Migra*

Robert Joe Stout

Westport, Connecticut
London

Library of Congress Cataloging-in-Publication Data

Stout, Robert Joe.
  Why immigrants come to America : braceros, indocumentados, and the migra / Robert
Joe Stout.
    p. cm.
  Includes bibliographical references and index.
  ISBN–13: 978–0–313–34830–3 (alk. paper)
1. Alien labor, Mexican—United States.   2. Immigrants—United States—Social
conditions.   3. Immigrants—United States—Economic conditions.   4. Mexico—Social
conditions.   5. Mexico—Economic conditions.   6. Mexico—Emigration and immigration.
7. United States—Emigration and immigration.   I. Title.
  HD8081.M6.S76   2008
  304.8′73—dc22   2007036175

British Library Cataloguing in Publication Data is available.

Library of Congress Catalog Card Number: 2007036175
ISBN-13: 978–0–313–34830–3

First published in 2008

Praeger Publishers, 88 Post Road West, Westport, CT 06881
An imprint of Greenwood Publishing Group, Inc.
http://www.praeger.com

Printed in the United States of America

The paper used in this book complies with the
Permanent Paper Standard issued by the National
Information Standards Organization (Z39.48–1984).

10 9 8 7 6 5 4 3 2 1

For the Kids;
Paul, Emily, Ingrid, Deirdre and Noah

Contents

Preface   ix

Introduction   1

A Place to Work, A Place to Live   13

Through Hell and High Water   29

Mexican Faces, American Dreams   57

Where the Dollar Is King   79

"It's the Law!"   103

A Pox on Both Your Houses!   125

Don't Kill the Cash Cow   149

Notes   167

Bibliography   179

Index   183

Preface

INDOCUMENTADOS, WHERE AND WHY

I suppose I started writing *Why Immigrants Come to America* when I first shared grammar school experiences with newly arrived Spanish-speaking immigrants who'd come to Wyoming to hoe and thin sugar beets and work in the sugar factory that employed my father. Growing up in that rural, agricultural community, I experienced some of what they did, being obliged to plant, weed and pull onions, dig potatoes, and scurry out during storms to cover tomato plants with tin cans to keep them from being beaten to pieces by hail. I bought my first car with money I earned in California almond orchards and made my way through college on the G. I. Bill and savings from sugar factory shifts.

In the fields, in the military, in the factories, I worked with Mexican immigrants. To some degree, they influenced my educational choices: a degree in creative writing and Latin American studies from Mexico City College (now the Universidad de las Americas). Both as a journalist and as an accountant, I lived and worked in areas with large Spanish-speaking populations. I wrote about their problems, misadventures, animosities, and successes for a variety of national and regional publications. *Why Immigrants Come to America* is an outgrowth of experiences, observations, and concerns that this vibrant and controversial shift of populations created for me both personally and professionally.

That I worked in the fields and factories, and speak a relatively fluent if noticeably accented Spanish, contributed to the collection of information included in this presentation. I have attempted to identify by name and

location as many of the persons I've interviewed and spoken to over the
years. Some of the quotes and opinions expressed were included in newspaper and magazine pieces that I wrote during the 1970s and 1980s. (Other
comments and conversations were not published but were included from
notes that I made at the time.) Throughout this manuscript, I've focused
on interviews, conversations, and current newspaper and media accounts
in order to provide readers and researchers with an accurate, human view
of the persons involved and the problems and challenges that they face.

Although there is some overlap, I've presented the material in the following manner:

> First chapter—Where The Migrants Come From
>
> Second chapter—Getting Across the Border
>
> Third chapter—Living Conditions in the United States
>
> Fourth chapter—Work Conditions
>
> Fifth chapter—Law Enforcement
>
> Sixth chapter—The Politics of Both Nations Involved
>
> Seventh chapter—Recent Events

Undocumented—or "illegal"—immigration has been an increasingly
controversial political issue throughout the last half of the twentieth century. Exacerbated by population growth in the sender countries (principally Mexico but also Central America and the Caribbean) and the im-
poverishment of their economies, millions of Spanish-speaking residents
have moved into the United States. Thousands have died. Millions live in
poverty but the majority—more than 90 percent—find employment and
over 60 percent send portions of their earnings to their families south of
the border. Their remittances provide nearly 70 percent of the incomes of
thousands of towns and villages throughout northern and central Mexico
and much of Central America.

These millions of workers are more than mathematical quantities to be
juggled by politicians and academicians. They are real people, with real
fears, and real aspirations. Many have become voting U.S. citizens; millions of others, despite their precarious living and working situations,
make important contributions to the U.S. economy and to the country's
well-being. Solving the problems that their continued and often desperate
migration has triggered cannot be achieved without understanding how
they live, why they come, and what choices they face. It is to help achieve
these solutions that this book has been written.

Thanks are due to the many people who made *Why Immigrants Come to America* possible, particularly the encouragement and participation of those involved with editing and production on the part of Greenwood Publishing Group: Hilary Claggett, Robert Hutchinson, Brian Foster, and Saloni Jain. I am also indebted to Maureen Ryan for countless hours of interchanging ideas and criticisms and to the hundreds of citizens of both the United States and Mexico who openly and candidly discussed their ideas, situations, and beliefs with me as a reporter, a co-participant, and a friend.

Introduction

Immigration and Customs Enforcement (ICE) agents sweep through factories, farms, and construction sites from Maine to California herding handcuffed "illegals" into detention facilities. Immigrants and their supporters block highways, repudiating a House of Representatives proposal to make undocumented entry into the United States a felony. Six-thousand National Guardsmen head toward the U.S.-Mexico frontier where hundreds of men, women, and children die every year of heat stroke, dehydration, and starvation. No issues have provoked such national outrage since integration and opposition to the war in Vietnam crested in the 1960s as the debate over immigration currently is doing. Despite the clamor, the rhetoric, the accusations, and the arrests, few people really understand who the undocumented immigrants are, how they get into the United States and why they keep coming.

The United States and Mexico share a common border nearly 2,000 miles long, making entry and exit much easier and more common than is possible for Turkish workers in Germany or Brazilian workers in Japan. Unlike foreign workers in those countries, and Philippine laborers in the Islamic countries of the Mid-east, migrant Mexican workers have been able to go back and forth from jobs north of the border to their homes in Durango, Zacatecas, Michoacán, and other states where subsistence agriculture has been the norm for centuries. Until the 1970s, the majority of these workers followed a circular migratory pattern, many crossing legally as *braceros* and others without documentation but the majority returning to their homes during slack seasons. Most of them had jobs waiting for them in the United States and most of them returned to employers who had hired them in years past.

Most popular literature about "the illegal alien" problem (and much academic research) has focused on the migrant worker side of an equation. Very little quantitative study has provided details about employers or about U.S. government participation in the recruitment of farm laborers, even though this participation was a major stimulant to the twenty-three million persons of Mexican ancestry who now live in the United States. The U.S. government openly scoured northern and west central Mexico for workers during World War I and, under the so-called *bracero* program, during and after World War II. (*Bracero* derives from the Spanish noun *brazo*—arm; a *bracero* is a "strong arm.") This recruitment, the "pull" side of the "push-pull" theory of migration popularly described by academics, brought as many as 400,000 workers a year into the United States between 1942 and 1965.

Braceros typically earned ten to fifteen times what they could earn in Mexico. Most were men between sixteen and thirty-five and came from large interconnected rural families. Relatives often helped finance their trips and the *braceros*, in turn, sent remittances back home. The traditional subsistence agriculture of western and central Mexico and the increasing demand for temporary labor in the United States combined to form a dynamic that expanded rapidly as the needs for both increased after World War II. An unplanned consequence was expansion of labor-intensive agriculture during a time of rapid technological advancement in other fields. As long as low-wage workers were available, employers continued to rely on them rather than develop more efficient systems of planting, thinning, weeding, harvesting, and packing.

"A temporary migration system rests on a structure of economic opportunities in the place of origin that, while insufficient for the full subsistence of a household, can maintain a family provided that one or more members of the household become labor migrants," the authors of "Transnational Migrant Communities and Mexican Migration to the United States" concur.[1] The temporary employment offered *braceros* and non-*bracero* enrollees recruited by firms like Mills Orchards in California helped both employers and workers to resolve the economic situations in which they found themselves. The migrant workers earned in a day or two what they would have garnered in a month in Mexico and U.S. employers had at their disposal a flexible nonunionized workforce that they could manipulate according to seasonal demands. "Immigration scholars routinely note that the U.S. government recruited about five million farm workers from Mexico during a twenty-two year period" from 1944 through 1966.[2] Non-*braceros* responded to a similar or even larger number of private recruitments. The overwhelming majority of these *indocumentados* worked in agriculture or agriculturally connected production facilities.

During the depression years of the 1930s, the federal government rounded up and deported hundreds of thousands of immigrants (some legal and many not). Twenty-some years later, during the post-World War II economic slump, the United States repeated a campaign of massive deportations. But hardly had "Operation Wetback" concluded when manpower demands during the Korean War increased the need for unskilled and semi-skilled workers, both in agriculture and in industry. Similar needs recurred during the war in Vietnam.

Mexico, meanwhile, suffered severe economic crises in the early 1980s and again in 1994, exacerbating unemployment and triggering massive rural-to-urban and Mexico-to-U.S. moves. NAFTA, China's takeover of the *maquiladora* (assembly plant) market and politically motivated xenophobia in the United States altered the ways that the demand-push equation functioned. Although a majority of migrants continued to return home during non-employment periods, many others became permanent U.S. residents. The "push" they were experiencing emerged from what Manuel Ángel Castillo describes as an absence of opportunities and an option for breaking limiting barriers despite the fact that the migrants have to endure separation from their families and estrangement from their communities of origin as well as being forced to confront an often hostile or culturally difficult and alien environment.[3]

Worker migration, both from Mexico and Latin America to the United States and from Mid-East, Asian, and African countries to Europe, Japan, and Singapore, depends on two principal factors: that those involved have a reason to leave their communities of origin and that they have economic ability to do so.[4] The absence of opportunities and financial hardships of those emigrating has been well documented but less attention has been paid to the economic influences. Few emigrants just "up and go." They need transportation, destinations, a means to survive. "It is no small irony, in light of recent migration control efforts," Cornelius and Rosenblum observe, "that many of today's strongest migratory systems were initiated through deliberate, government-sponsored recruitment of 'guestworkers' during the 1940–1970 period."[5]

As the "pull" from U.S. employers continued to act as a forceful magnet, deteriorating economic conditions south of the border continued to impel migrants northward. That more and more emigrants successfully found employment stimulated greater migration and strengthened both the reasons to leave and the ability to do so successfully. The majority of these emigrants "drawn by the combined pull of a labor market that promises wealth and the push of local economies that promise little" occupied a middle world that transcended borders but lacked roots in either Mexico or the United States.[6]

As more and more immigrants broke the circular pattern of yearly temporary migration and settled semi-permanently or permanently in the United States, a year-round workforce developed that included an increasing number of women immigrants. Workers who decided to stop migrating back and forth to Mexico sought year-round jobs in service-type areas such as gardening, housekeeping, and childcare.[7] As more jobs in construction, services, food- and meat-processing plants, and the garment industry opened up, particularly in areas that previously had hosted little undocumented immigration, urban and semi-urban residents joined the migratory tide in increasing numbers. The authors of "Transnational Migrant Communities and Mexican Migration to the United States" contend that the current economic situation in both rural and urban Mexico favors what they describe as a "permanent migration system."[8] It includes rural residents who've found it impossible to make a living in their home communities and/or who've lost land they formerly owned. They no longer seek seasonal work, but join others in communal clusters that keep them physically and sentimentally linked to their places of origin.[9]

Ironically, U.S. governmental efforts to crack down on illegal immigration has contributed to the establishment of permanent migration systems. As long as migrants were able to cross the border easily, work and return home, they felt little impetus to remain in the United States. As border security tightened, more and more *indocumentados* decided not to risk leaving and reentering and sought non-agricultural jobs in urban areas. The Simpson-Rodino Act (U.S. Immigration Reform and Control Act) passed in 1986, designed to legalize longer-term *indocumentados*, establish penalties for knowingly hiring those not legalized and beefing up border vigilance, unintentionally encouraged immigrants to remain in the country instead of migrating seasonally.[10] That nearly three million Spanish-speaking immigrants gained legal status under Simpson-Rodino further stimulated permanent immigration as residents of poverty-stricken areas throughout Latin America surged northward hoping for employment and for a chance at legal residency. In addition, many immigrants eligible for green card renewals opted for naturalization instead of reapplying for the non-immigrant work permits.

The authors of "Factors That Influence Migration" trace the origins of Mexico-U.S. migration to employer needs for basic labor, particularly during stress times when high production was necessary and a shortage of manpower existed.[11] Immigrant workers responding to this "pull" paved the way for family members, relatives, and neighbors to join them north of the border. As linkages between communities south of the border and migration grew, subcultures that encompassed a hierarchy of workers, agents, employers, smugglers, and remittances developed highly efficient communication systems that included knowing what jobs were available when, who one could trust to guide a group safely across the border, and who had been injured, who had given birth to twins, and where one could find the best places to buy everything from boots to hamburgers.

Residents of rural Mexican communities frequently had better information about what jobs were available throughout the United States than either U.S. residents or state employment agencies. Migrations from those communities were well planned and paid for and those leaving knew they had jobs waiting for them once they arrived at their destinations. The networks set up in the United States not only made it easier and less expensive for *indocumentados* to find work and housing, they lowered the risks of apprehension during border crossings. Few emigrants left Mexico or other Latin American countries without having decided, singly or as family or community groups, that the entering the United States illegally was worth the effort. In many parts of northern and west central Mexico migration became so much a part of community life that from infancy both boys and girls assumed they would go to "The Other Side" to work. By the time they reached forty years of age most men from those areas had made at least one U.S. trip and many families had experienced four generations of migrating members.

Nevertheless, as Cohen points out, a large percentage of any Mexican community remains at home. These residents may choose to do so out of necessity, or fear, or obligation, or satisfaction with a lifestyle that though economically deprived provides social and personal satisfactions.[12] And they may or may not become involved with or benefit from the migration process but they recognize its existence and accept it as part of their social environment.

Escobar Latapí and his co-author affirm, "The U.S. need for flexible seasonal workers persisted after legal recruitment ended, and Mexican workers had become dependent on U.S. earnings, so the migration continued."[13] The decision by one migrant, one *bracero*, to emigrate became multiplied first by ten, then by a hundred, then by a thousand, then by tens of thousands. The process became self-sustaining as immigrants built upon their own and previous experiences to set up social structures and support systems that encouraged more of their countrymen to emigrate.[14] Not only does emigration become a means of economic advancement, it becomes a way of life. Residents of even the smallest hamlets discuss which *coyotes* to trust and which to avoid, where to obtain counterfeit documents and which means of sending remittances are best.

For many employers the need for low-wage labor corresponded to immigrants' need for employment. Unlike businesses and industries that developed a stable work force through training, promotion, and responsibility, these employers required a constant flow of workers who would accept bare minimums and not expect advancement.[15] Frequently they hired through immigrant field bosses and contractors and often did not know—or care—where their workers were coming from. Using immigrant intermediaries to hire and supervise workers not only lowered the cost of recruitment but guaranteed the employers efficient worker teams, many of whom were related to each other or who had come from the same communities in Mexico.[16]

Krissman, among others, complains that immigration literature does not sufficiently deal with employers and how they profit from migration networks, the glut of low-wage workers and the apprehension and deportation activities of the *migra*. Many of these employers are faceless corporations run by U.S. managers who in turn hire immigrant supervisors and recruiters. Since these employers do not actively engage in recruiting, hiring, or certification of legal documents they are not legally responsible for abetting undocumented immigration, even though they promote it through their employment policies and benefit from it financially. In recent cases, their companies have cooperated with law enforcement agencies by opening personnel records and allowing ICE agents to raid and deport workers. ICE charges the immigrant workers with possessing falsified documents but the employers go scot free whether or not they knew about the false documentation or, in fact, helped workers to obtain it.[17] Krissman calls this "plausible denialability" and urges more research on how those who create the undocumented worker demand function and interact with the migration systems.

Once the pattern of dependency on flexible immigrant workers is set, employers find it virtually impossible to revert to native workers without massive changes in technology, wages, and job structure. A number of California employers have told me that they would increase pay, housing, and benefits but can't afford to do so unless their competition does likewise.

Competition dictates keeping wages low in order to achieve a desired profit margin and competition among low-wage jobseekers prohibits pressuring for higher pay or benefits. No one involved wants to break the cycle, so it continues. Cornelius notes that invariably in receiver economies the least attractive jobs go to immigrants; consequently, entire sectors of advanced industrial economies become dependent on immigrant labor. The flexibility of being able to hire and dismiss as work demands ebb and flow greatly benefits employers. They are not inclined to develop permanent work forces and "continue to recruit new immigrant workers in an effort to stave off meaningful labor market reform."[18] In fact, when low-wage workers are not available and employers have to pay more for the same work, a strong incentive to find laborsaving substitutions is created.[19]

When that happens, as happened with tomato producers in California in the 1960s, the industry involved undergoes drastic changes. California tomato producers who turned to mechanized harvesters could undersell their competitors, many of whom, unable to afford the expensive equipment, sold their interests or turned to other forms of agriculture. "This experience suggests that dependence on immigrant workers is a one-way street and that market force alone will increase the employment of migrants."[20]

As the United States attempted to close the border, making undocumented immigration more difficult, an increasing percentage of emigrants sought professional help from so-called *coyotes*, or *polleros*. Decried north of the border as vicious criminals who prey on susceptible would be immigrants, *coyotes* became an indispensable cog in the migration process for most undocumented aliens entering the United States after 1970.[21] Many of these *coyotes* guaranteed door-to-door delivery from towns in Mexico to jobs in the U.S. and their fees generally were paid by receiving relatives in the United States.[22] The authors of "Factors That Influence Migration" report that 71 percent of those attempting to cross the border in 1994–1995 employed *coyotes* compared to only 50 percent during 1990–1993 and that in 1994–1995 over 70 percent made it on their first attempt without being apprehended.

Despite anti-immigration rhetoric in the United States, immigration from Mexico and Latin America has had little negative impact on the salaries of already employed U.S. workers. Migration primarily affects the well-being of the immigrants themselves and, by extension, their families and communities. "Only on very rare occasions has it been demonstrated that immigrants deteriorate working conditions or social services."[23] The September 11 attack on the World Trade Center in New York and the Pentagon building in Washington, D.C. brought a new dimension—terrorism—into the immigration picture despite the fact that undocumented immigrants presented no apparent terrorist threats. As numerous *indocumentados* have told me, "They want the work we do, but want us to be invisible after doing it."

The need for inexpensive labor has existed since the beginnings of recorded history. The Babylonians, Egyptians, Greeks, and Romans recruited or enslaved less technologically advanced populations in order to construct everything from tombs to highways to aqueducts. (And, as mercenaries, to man their armed forces and, as servants, to fulfill domestic roles.) By the late sixteenth century, Mexico was importing workers from the Philippines; a century later slave ships ferried captured peoples from Africa to the Western Hemisphere to work in agriculture, construction, and mining. Invariably these recruitments impacted local mores and altered demographic patterns, creating class distinctions and legal restrictions.

For the most part the governments of the countries that needed cheap labor fostered these forced or stimulated migrations. Employers within those countries took advance of the influx to produce goods at reduced cost, often casting the workers aside when they were too old or feeble to be of further use. As political situations within the importing countries changed, governments ejected or absorbed those who had entered as immigrant workers. Where racial differences existed, as they did in the United States, governments often legislated against immigrants and their descendants, limiting citizenship, ownership of property, and education.

Generally speaking, the migration of low-wage workers increases during times of expansion and contracts during times of cutbacks or recessions. The governments of the countries concerned either stimulate or retard migration as the expansions and regressions occur. As most capitalistic governments embraced globalization in the 1970s and 1980s, creating a greater need for an abundance of low-wage labor, the U.S. government responded to internal pressure and tightened control of undocumented entry. Unlike most countries of western Europe, the Arabian states, Singapore, and Japan, the United States did not originate or develop a planned importation of workers. (The *bracero* program already had been terminated.) This created a totally paradoxical situation "in which, in a world more interconnected that it ever had been, where the flows of money and commerce had been liberalized, the flow of persons, by contrast, confronted barriers that actually seemed to exclude international migration from the globalization process."[24]

This served many U.S. employers well. The restrictions served to reduce the cost of labor by putting the onus of illegality on the workers rather than on those who recruited and hired them. *Indocumentados* have few legal rights or privileges; as a result they accept low wages and substandard working conditions.[25] The system that has functioned in the United States during the past three or more decades has featured demand north of the border, a push toward migration south of the border and a law enforcement intermediary that forces the worker flow underground but only in isolated cases has restricted employers from taking advantage of those who sieve through to fill the low-wage jobs available.

The Mexican government vocalized objections to U.S. law enforcement's treatment of *indocumentados* but purposefully did nothing to retard emigration. Money sent home by the millions of Mexican-born workers, both legal and undocumented, kept the country solvent by acting as a safety valve for jobseekers and permitted federal and local governments to reduce spending on domestic programs. Not only has this had a destabilizing effect, it has exerted a downward pull on local economies. The "safety value" provided by emigration has left a vacuum behind it.

Neoliberal economic policies pushed for free trade agreements that would open frontiers for commerce. Their proponents, most of whom were connected with exporting nations, insisted that once they were in place they not only would increase the flow of manufactured goods and raw materials but they would create jobs in both industrialized and developing nations as well. U.S. presidents Gerald Ford and George G. W. Bush advocated such accords but it was President Bill Clinton and Mexico's globalization advocate President Carlos Salinas de Gortari who finally signed the North American Free Trade Agreement (NAFTA) in 1993.

NAFTA turned out to be disastrous for Mexico. Theoretically, Mexico was supposed to develop a raw materials industry to supply NAFTA-stimulated manufacturing but the *maquiladoras* financed by foreign firms did not develop rapidly enough or pay well enough to meet employment demands. At the same time, while the U.S. government continued to subsidize agricultural products, Mexico pulled most of its subsidies, forcing prices higher and driving over 1.4 million small-acreage producers out of business. Escobar Latapí, et al., estimate that 600,000 of these farmers became NAFTA-caused additions to the normal flow of *indocumentados* seeking employment in the United States.[26] Mexico's population has doubled since 1970 and includes 38 million persons between fifteen and thirty-four years of age. Mexican economists say the population explosion is certain to push more Mexicans across the border, further intensifying the United States' already heated immigration debates, unless Mexico's economy dramatically improves.[27] Instead of stemming undocumented immigration, as both Clinton and Salinas de Gortari prophesied, NAFTA stimulated the push northward of hundreds of thousands of Mexican nationals.

The sudden devaluation of the peso when President Ernesto Zedillo took office on December 1, 1994, further devastated small landholders and small business owners. "The peso devaluation, by raising the peso value of wages earned by Mexican migrants in the United States by about 40 percent, increased the prospect that vast new numbers of Mexicans would seek illegal entry into the United States."[28]

Layoffs occurred almost instantaneously, with over 250,000 losing their jobs. Businesses that had debts in dollars closed (Bean and Cushing estimate as high as 10 percent of businesses in some cities shut down within two months after the devaluation), electricity, gasoline, and commodities prices soared, Mexican banks raised the interest rates on credit cards by 60–100 percent, creating a huge number of forfeitures and bankruptcies. While wages and salaries remained the same inflation pushed prices up as high as 40 percent. The numbers of those emigrating without documentation increased dramatically. So did the numbers of families depending upon remittances send by workers in the United States.

Castillo insists that *remesas* are not a substitute for the loss of human capital. Migration beginning with a circular flow of temporary workers does not continue indefinitely but at some point roots itself in the receiver country.[29] Meanwhile, instead of developing resources and means of self-support, many communities in the sender country that have become dependent on money flowing to them from their emigrant population fail to develop internally. The only product they incubate are new, young emigrants to be sent away to perpetuate the dependency cycle.[30] As immigrants develop stronger community ties in the United States and their children receive U.S. educations they tend to lose some of their ties to the home country and consequently send fewer remittances. Nonetheless as part of the larger migrant community, they often help newcomers from their former communities to emigrate, creating a new generation of remitters.

However, communities with tighter ties to their emigrant expatriates have benefited by edging away from dependence on subsistence farming and developing cottage industries and retail services. Cohen describes communities in rural Oaxaca which have opened retail outlets and numerous family-run small businesses, including print shops, hair salons, bakeries, and car repair shops.[31] Nevertheless, the vast majority of the remittances received are used for paying basic necessities, such as food, clothing, and housing, and not for any kind of investment purposes.[32]

Many Mexican economists and emigration investigators support some form of "guest worker" program. Castillo points to the successes of a Canada-Mexico accord which guaranteed transportation to and from the sender country and regulated wages paid to the imported workers. For a guest worker program to be successful, he insists that four qualifications need to be met:

- For workers, fair pay and the right to live and work in the receiver country;
- For employers, an adequate supply of workers;
- For the sender country, the opening of employment for an important segment of the population; and
- For the receiving country the balancing of employment between imported and native workers.[33]

Guest-worker programs have not functioned as well in the United States as they have in Europe and other receiver nations because of the border the United States shares with Mexico. It is much more difficult and expensive for undocumented Brazilian workers to reach Japan or Portuguese hopefuls to reach Switzerland than it has been for Mexican nationals to cross into the United States. Nevertheless a number of immigration researchers have suggested that reducing the disparity between wages paid to workers in the United States and those paid to workers in Mexico would strongly affect the latter's decision to emigrate. By the same token, should the U.S. government enforce minimum wage laws and/or drive wages paid to native workers higher, employers would be more likely to hire them rather than face legal sanctions.

To a certain extent both employers on the "pull" side of the equation and emigrants on the "push" side face similar decisions: Are the risks worth taking? To date the answer from both has been a qualified *yes*. As numerous *indocumentados* have told me, "If I can work only three weeks, or four or five before I am deported I will have earned more than I could in six months in Mexico." And as employers have told me, "I can survive a few fines, a few raids. What I can't survive is paying out so much that I can't stay competitive anymore."

A Place to Work, A Place to Live

WATCHING, WAITING

Ismael Teyo has no idea what the United States is like. He never has been there. Dwarfed by the hillside behind him, a scrub-brush tangle of parched rocky soil dotted with browning saguaro, he braces his elbows against his knees and squints at the trail he will follow once it becomes dark. Tonight is the night, he has decided: He will make a run for *The Other Side*.

If he fails, he says, he will try again. He will try until he makes it past the gangs of Mexican *cholos* who rob and rape prospective emigrants, past the North American *migras* who swing heavy clubs and pursue border crossers like Teyo with helicopters and SUVs, past the bleak hills into green valleys or bustling cities where work awaits him.

He knows that whatever he encounters could not be worse than the dying hills of Oaxaca, where he and his family lost their land and ran out of money and food. And he knows it cannot be worse than living in a ramshackle jungle of cardboard and corrugated metal shelters propped on torn tire casings on the outskirts of Tijuana where he had been staying. He knows that to cross the desert means risking his life but he also knows that life is worthless without enough to eat, without a place to live, without something to do with his hands and mind. He has to cross, he says. There is no other choice that he can make.

Over twenty million Mexican men, women, and children already have made the decision he has been struggling to make. Over six million of them now live illegally in the United States. Through amnesty granted by the Simpson-Rodino Immigration Reform Act of 1986 and through naturalization another ten or eleven million Mexican-born immigrants have legal status or citizenship. And as many or more have jostled into cities on the Mexican side of the border where they live and work and rear their families. Many of them still hope to make it to *The Other Side*.

Ismael Teyo wants to become one more of the more than twenty million who now reside in the United States. Squat and stubborn, his *indigena* temperament reflected by the calm set of his dolphin-like jowl, he does not relate to movements or theories or political goals. Without land, without a livelihood, with only a vague concept of where he is going or what it could be like when he arrives, he watches and waits. In the year and a half preceding his arrival on the border, a million *indocumentados* have done the same thing that he is doing. In the year and a half to come another million will make the attempt. Many like him will come from Oaxaca and speak little or no Spanish. Others coming from the shredded hills of Chiapas will speak even less. Every month thousands head toward the United States from Mexico City where they no longer can afford to live, and thousands more forge northward from Central America and from Colombia, Ecuador, and Peru.

At some point the migration will reach a saturation point. The surge will reside, boundaries will change, counter-migrations will take place. New generations of Ismael Teyos, finding the circumstances of their lives insupportable, will strike out in new directions.

They will have to. Things never stay the same.

WHERE THEY COME FROM

The border separating the United States and Mexico meanders for 1,933 miles from the little Gulf port of Brownsville to the sprawling city of Tijuana and the suburbs of San Diego that nestle against it. Until well into this century, this frontier was unmarked, unnoticed, and unpatrolled by anything except stray livestock and vultures. Thousands of Mexican citizens fled the revolution that began in that country in 1910, creating a cheap labor pool throughout the U.S. Southwest. During World War I, the United States suspended literacy tests and granted legal status to Mexican workers as long as they stayed with the employer who hired them. Police in the cities that straddled the border often exchanged wrongdoers guilty of drunkenness or petty crimes. Even legal deportations were handled by local authorities until the Border Patrol was formed in 1924.

Many who emigrated during the revolution returned to their home country after the fighting ended but by the mid-1920s recruiters from the Midwest were drawing workers northward. Not only did these *enganchistas* promise better wages and working conditions than the Southwest farmers were offering, but they provided free transportation to the job centers. Packing plants, canneries, sugar factories, highway construction, and railroads considered Mexican labor essential. In 1923 alone, the *enganchistas* brought nearly 35,000 laborers to Illinois, Ohio, and Pennsylvania. By 1927, between 75 and 90 percent of sugar factory workers in the Midwest were of Mexican origin.

Migrant employment continued to increase until the Great Depression threw hundreds of thousands of people throughout the United States out of work. Among the first to feel the impact were Mexican workers and their families. They began to drift back in the late 1930s and early 1940s. During World War II, the Roosevelt administration instituted the *bracero* program which granted temporary work visas to thousands of Mexican farm and factory laborers. The program was well-enough publicized within Mexico to attract skilled and semiskilled workers and the wages being offered were high enough that many small landholders left their corn and melon crops in the hands of sons, wives, and cousins in order to earn more in a few months than they would realize from their own farms in several years.

One of those who enrolled was Aguascalientes postal worker Jorge Valencia. A tall, lean father of five, Valencia combined vacation time with a leave of absence every fall during and after World War II to work in a Hamilton City, California, beet sugar factory. A high school graduate and dedicated worker, Valencia learned to operate machinery and became one of the more highly paid seasonal workers. He told me that his sugar factory earnings had enabled him to enlarge his house in Aguascalientes from four to nine rooms and to buy several adjacent pieces of property.

"In Aguascalientes I am considered quite . . ." he laughed, touching his work boot as he copied a phrase he'd heard " . . . well-heeled."

Unlike Valencia most *braceros* came from agricultural backgrounds. Like him, however, most of them were either heads of families or mature older sons and came from states in the interior of Mexico, principally Michoacán, Zacatecas, Guanajuato, and Jalisco. Luin Goldring, in a presentation made at the Problems and Challenges of Migration and Development in America conference in Cuernavaca, Mexico, in April 2005, termed these temporary workers "target earners."[1] Many owned small farms or rural businesses that their families or relatives could maintain during their absences. They intended to live Spartanly, save as much as they could, and return to their Mexican homes after three to six months with money enough to buy land, construct houses, or purchase farm machinery. As *braceros* their transportation to and from their homes in

Mexico was guaranteed, housing in the United States was provided, and they were paid the same wages that U.S. residents doing the same work were paid.

Ernesto Galarza noted in 1964 that besides providing war-strapped U.S. agriculture with a small legal workforce the *bracero* program greatly stimulated illegal immigration.[2] Thousands who had not applied headed for California's citrus groves and central valley farmlands, Texas cotton fields, and the grain lands of the central West. Fred Krissman notes that recruitment of *indocumentados* exceeded that of legal *braceros* throughout the post–World War II period.[3] Margulis and Tuiran insist that U.S. employers welcomed the availability of both *braceros* and their undocumented counterparts because they only had to pay salaries, not retirement, union, or other costs that U.S. workers demanded.[4]

A lifetime migrant named Celedoñio Perez told the Sacramento *Bee* in 1991 that he had been recruited to work in the United States in 1944.[5]

"A man from the government came to our town," he remembered, "and was charging eighty pesos, and he would tell us where to go if we wanted to be contracted for work. We paid him and he gave us a voucher that we took to Mexico City. There we would go to the contracting center which they had at the main bullring. People would sleep there so they could be there when they were called. They shaved our heads, our armpits, everywhere. They thought we had fleas.

"They took us to a place called Los Baños Juarez . . . They made us go into a huge shower stall, all of us naked . . . All of a sudden they turned on the steam, and it got so hot, a heat I had never felt before. And right when all of us were drenched in perspiration, they turned ice cold water on us. There was no place to hide. Before we knew what was happening, we were on the train the next day for Texas."

As Goldring notes, the great majority of the *braceros* and *indocumentados* who crossed in the 1940s were "males, family heads, not so poor that they couldn't afford the costs and risks of migration but not so affluent that migration was unattractive." Until well into the 1960s and 1970s, many of Mexico's colonial cities, like Zacatecas, were very insular and depended upon the surrounding areas for the products that they used and sold.

Those who remember Zacatecas as it was fifty and sixty years ago describe a regional capital that overevaluated its gentility and refinement, had some light industry that manufactured clothing, furniture, pottery, and prepared foods for local use. The city's youth promenaded every Sunday night in the city square, the *chavos* going in one direction, the *señoritas* in the other, flirting as they passed under the watchful eyes of parents and chaperones. There were a few wealthy families but the majority of both workers and tradesmen earned just enough to get them from one *quin-cena* (payday) to another. Government-guaranteed prices for corn, wheat, and beans, plus government-supplied seeds and fertilizers, enabled most of the *ejidarios* and small farmers to buy a few extras for their houses and families and to celebrate important occasions like Christmas and Easter but seldom to get far ahead financially.

When the first *braceros* returned in 1943 and 1944, they brought money with them—money that they and their families utilized to buy things that previously they hadn't been able to afford. As a former city councilman explained to me years ago, "Those of us in Zacatecas at the time had little actual spending money. Prices for everything were low, people built their own houses a few bricks at a time, what you didn't have cash for you traded for." A returning worker who'd sewn 60 or 70 percent of his three-month's earnings into his coat lining or shoe sole had enough to buy almost anything he wanted—a used car, several hectares of land, a well-digging machine. His wife and children who had agonized over his absence and the difficulties of getting along without him felt marvelously affluent. Friends and neighbors considered that he had done something successful and important.

Between 1942 and 1947, 32,000 to 62,000 workers legally crossed each year to work on U.S. farms and in U.S. sugar factories. Another 130,000 were recruited to lay and replace ties and rails and do other railroad maintenance.[6] The railroad program was terminated in 1946, but the agricultural program continued, the number of admittances declining during the immediate post-War years then soaring when the Korean War began. Nearly 200,000 *braceros* entered the United States in 1951 and 1952; by 1955 that number had doubled. Participation remained high—over 400,000 through 1959, declining to 195,000 in 1962 and 177,000 in 1964. The program was terminated in 1965.

The Mexican government decided initially to contract *braceros* only through Mexico City, and in 1944 through Guadalajara. At that time the states in the central part of the country were experiencing greater unemployment and subemployment than the states further north. The returning *braceros*, paid fifteen to twenty times what they could have earned in Mexico, wedged new spaces in the traditional social structure of the towns and smaller cities in this depleted area. But few spent much of their earnings on luxuries.

"My dad had grown up on his land in a little stone house, two rooms maybe, the kitchen outside, no electricity, no running water," an immigrant from Durango who now lives legally in northern California told me. "All his life he worked to make the house and the land better. To raise more chickens, more hogs, clear more space to put in tomatoes. Everything jumped ahead after he went to the United States to work as a *bracero*. He became, for that area, rather prosperous. He was very proud of himself—so much so that he bragged, too much I think, to his neighbors."

The year following the return of those first *braceros* saw a rush of applicants wanting to duplicate their success—far more than what the program could accommodate. By 1943 and 1944, many of those who could not acquire *bracero* status had decided to cross the border and find work on their own. At that time penalties for being caught were not severe—one faced deportation but once deported one could turn around and cross the border again.

Many of those who left to seek jobs followed known paths, crossing into areas of southern Texas and New Mexico which for many years had had predominantly Mexican populations. Unlike the *braceros*, those who did find work were poorly paid and "barely accepted as human beings by bigoted landowners and foremen," as one of those migrants who later became a legal U.S. resident told me. Many were turned over to U.S. authorities for deportation once their jobs had played out. Others followed Texas and New Mexico acquaintances of Mexican descent northward into the grain-producing states where farmers and ranchers were so desperate for employees they were forcing bums off freight cars into the fields and sugar factories and the Army was bringing in prisoners of war to plant, thin, and harvest.

Even migrants who had suffered through whipping dust- and rainstorms, who had huddled on the banks of irrigation ditches to sleep, and who had been cheated of their earnings seemed to forget the hardships they had endured as celebrations of their success passed from one *ranchito* and one rural community to another. What little money they earned, and what little they returned with, vitalized the economies of these remote areas. Every centavo of it was extra, brought in from outside, and brought an equal amount of affluence to the communities.

Return to Aztlan describes how migrant networks developed during the *bracero* years.[7] Journeys that would have seemed inconceivable to rural residents of west-central Mexico became commonplace. "The institutionalization of the migrant networks during the *bracero* era considerably reduced the costs and risks associated with U.S. migration and made it accessible to everyone, young and old, male and female, poor and rich."[8]

Each year after World War II more workers crossed the border, many winding up in fields and sugar factories as far away as Michigan. They did not go there on their own—they were recruited, either with signed contracts as *braceros* or, later, informally as farmers, and small industries connected with agriculture sent *paisanos* to bring them northward. In many cases, the recruiter sought relatives and friends from his home region.[9] Escobar Latapí and his coauthors report that between 1942 and 1964 the governments of both the United States and Mexico permitted private firms to recruit non-*bracero* workers for seasonal employment.[10]

Neighborhood and familial ties kept the worker groups together. Their connections with their home communities remained strong, a benefit both to their families and to their employers who could rely on a fairly stable worker flow that could be increased or decreased without great difficulty. "All that is necessary for a migrant network to develop is for one person to be in the right place at the right time and obtain a position that allows him to distribute jobs and favors to others from his community."[11] By putting worker recruitment in the hands of one of his migrant employees, a farm or business owner not only solved his labor needs but relieved himself of the bother of hiring, firing, and dealing personally with his employees.

This affluence, as limited as it was at first, changed how communities throughout the cradle areas of migration regarded both the temporary absences of able-bodied males and their own consumption and spending values. Many *braceros*, particularly those like Jorge Valencia who had some education and experience, wired money to their families in Mexico via Western Union. Over time this became an accepted and safe way for emigrants to send remittances but many *braceros* and the majority of early *indocumentados* dealt only with cash.

Returning from a Christmas trip home to northern California from Austin, Texas, in the early 1960s I found myself seated by a trembly Chicana grandmother who talked throughout the night because, she said, she was afraid to go to sleep. I asked her why but she only could respond that traveling alone frightened her, especially on a bus when she was surrounded by strangers. When the Greyhound arrived in El Paso, the grandson who was at the station to greet her thanked me for befriending her and explained that she was transporting hundreds of dollars in cash from another grandson who worked near Stockton.

On another occasion, I met a father in San Luis Río Colorado, Sonora, a few miles south of Yuma, Arizona, who had come with a cousin by bus from Hermosillo to accompany a son who was driving his car from California.

"He has the *dinero*," this sturdy gray-mustached parent affirmed, "and we have the *pistolas*." The *dinero*, he assured me, wasn't going to get waylaid by either robbers or police before it got to Hermosillo.

For an increasing number of immigrants, legal and undocumented, crossing the border was only one of a series of migratory steps. The decline of the cattle industry and the closing of family-owned mines drove many rural residents toward the cities during the 1930s. As one migrant described the conditions on his parents' *ranchito* near the pueblo of Símon Bolivar, Durango: "There were twelve in my family and really there wasn't enough work for all of us to do. We hunted, collected and sold firewood, and tried to fix things but there was no real way to make money so one by one we left. I went first to Durango, then to Hermosillo, then to Ciudad Juarez, and finally El Paso. My brothers also left. Finally even my parents moved. That is a problem with big families. Everyone needs to work but when there is no work to do one must leave and find something else."

The first move for many rural migrants was to the nearest larger center of population. Most of Mexico's colonial cities had established business and residential sections that were not accessible to marginal newcomers, so the new arrivals were forced to wedge their way into shantytowns on or near the cities' outskirts. Many of them envied the returning *braceros*; others sought employment with them, or information on how to shirttail their successes.

Members of poorer urban families also began to consider "heading for the dollar." Living and work situations for many of them were similar to that of rural residents: big families, crowded quarters, everyone working but nobody earning very much. Fewer urban migrants returned to the homes they had left, however, and many of them induced women family members to make the trip north, presumably because urban emigrants were more likely to wind up in cities like Los Angeles, El Paso, and San Antonio where there were opportunities for domestic and food service employment.

Not everyone returned with money to spend. Many did not return. Others never made it across the border, or were deported, or were robbed or cheated out of their earnings, or they drank it away, or they decided to stay and work in one of the border cities. But in towns and small cities throughout the central part of the Republic, a new society, powered by *bracero* earnings, had begun to form. It was destined to transform the economic and social life of much of Mexico.

As more men from the individual communities migrated and returned—the "target earners" that Goldring defines—more and more residents absorbed the benefits of this new earning power. Life and industry in many of the sender communities became increasingly matriarchal. Women and children ran small businesses, farmed, and worked as artisans making pottery, hats, shawls, and huaraches. Children accepted as normal that their fathers and older brothers had gone to *The Other Side* to work and that the money the migrants brought home would provide cash needed to invest in land, animals, seed, and fertilizer. The women left behind by city emigrants typically took jobs in the "informal" sector, particularly in the shoe and garment industries.[12]

"There was a lot of movement among families," immigrant Blas Tamayo told me. "Over half of the people I knew grew up with someone besides their parents."

School-aged boys were shuffled off to work on an uncle's ranch, a daughter would be sent to do housework for someone who lived in the next largest town, a married daughter would return to her mother's house with her baby after her husband left. Many girls married or began having children when they were thirteen, fourteen, or fifteen and often left their babies with others while they worked in the fields or in cottage industries, tanneries, or canneries. Young and old women, accustomed to helping their husbands and fathers in the fields and with livestock, took over planting, picking, feeding, and even butchering.

That changed, sometimes drastically, when the men returned. Alcoholism ran high in many rural areas and many of the men, after six or eight months of robust work and personal deprivation, became abusive. Not all of the wives and mothers were willing to give up the control they'd accrued during their husbands and sons absences and many of the latter were unwilling to settle back into rural routines. In most cases, the majority of both men and women worked out ways to compensate for the changes this new way of living brought but the *ranchitos* and rural communities never returned to their premigration rhythms.

The wife of a *bracero* who later emigrated illegally with him to northern California recalled that her husband returned to their home in Durango for shorter lengths of time each year. Left to manage their small acreage, she planted less corn, chilies, and peas each year and sold the goats and "the little roan horse" that her husband had liked so much but that became difficult to feed and care for.

"For him," she explained, "our home had become a place to come to in order to rest, to visit the children who hardly knew him anymore." Eventually, unable to secure entrance to the United States legally after the *bracero* program was disbanded in 1965, her husband returned to northern California and a year later she followed.

"My heart always will be in Durango," she told me, "but it was live there alone without my husband or live here [in California] with him so I chose to live here."

Those leaving their hometowns and villages relied on a network of informants and acquaintances to find work, places to stay, and transportation. Many would return after completing a particular planting or harvest cycle or cannery or lumber camp season but others would shift from one job to another, usually in the company of friends or relatives, and continue to send varying amounts back to their parents, brothers, sisters, and children. Surveys taken at the time indicated that most temporary workers, legal or undocumented, sent 35 percent of what they earned to their immediate or extended families. The same surveys indicated that these remittances provided the only income that 65 percent of the families of these workers received. As more migrants sent more money home, more brothers, cousins, nephews—and later daughters and sisters—joined this migratory workforce.

Business cycles adapted to the new major source of income. Money loaned was to be paid back when the worker returned; sales of business materials and purchases of livestock were based on instructions from afar. Migration "widows" temporarily merged their families with other migration widows in order to work or reduce expenses. In all of these towns, one sensed a lingering apprehension: "Is he all right?" "How much is he earning?" "When will he come home?" "Will he come home?"

This temporary migration system drew more and more people in as the networks described in the introduction formed and became self-perpetuating, reinforced "by a structure of opportunities in the place of destination that provide(d) temporary work opportunities"[13] and an increased dependence upon more and more participants in the process. Durand, Massey, and Parrado note " . . . migrants lacked strong incentives to prolong their stay once a savings target or short-term income goal had been reached.

"The various privations and sacrifices endured while working abroad were justified ultimately by the dream of a better life at home."[14]

Reactions and changes in individual towns throughout the wide swath of sender communities varied depending upon the number of absent target earners. In many of these communities the local production of goods diminished in importance because a smaller percentage of residents needed to depend for their livelihood on meager corn and vegetable crops or raising goats, sheep, or other livestock. Though many migrants continued to return to their homes during off seasons, others remained in the United States or returned only as far as the Mexican border cities. Women from the areas a long distance from the border often did not try to cross alone but went north to join their husbands in Reynosa, Nuevo Laredo, Ciudad Juarez, and Mexicali. Some stayed only temporarily, then returned to their homes when their husbands reentered the migratory workforce. Others found jobs in the bustling border cities and remained permanently.

By 1970, post–World War II economic patterns based on the consumption of goods within the producing countries was giving way to focus on production for external trade.

"In developing nations, state bureaucracies were slashed, government-owned firms were privatized and social barriers were dismantled to expose formerly protected, insular economies to the full force of global competition," Durand, Massey, and Parrado assert.[15] The progressive diminishment of federal subsidies in Mexico stimulated migration to cities and to the U.S.-Mexico border, where tax-exempt *maquiladoras* were hiring production-line workers. It also stimulated emigration to the United States, where the new economic focus was creating an immediate need for unskilled labor.

The impact of these economic changes—globalization—on hundreds of thousands of small landowners and cottage industries was immense. "Households were left with little more than a decision of whether to emigrate or revolt."[16] Most chose to emigrate, leaving many of the sender communities in Mexico with financially dependent populations. Emilio Maldonado, who I interviewed at a Gridley, California, migrant housing project, remembered, "At first all I wanted was to bring money back to my family. I didn't think I would be a *bracero* forever. After I don't remember how many years I started to feel that I wanted more of what the people up here [in northern California] had. Just bringing money home and living in that dusty little depressed town wasn't enough anymore."

Thousands of circular immigrants duplicated Maldonado's experiences, particularly after Mexico's presidents de la Madrid and Salinas pushed neo-liberal reforms. The passage of the Simpson-Rodino Act in 1986 changed forever the migration model that had been in effect since World War II. The Amnesty provisions of that Act required that those applying for permanent residency live in the United States while their applications were being processed. As a result, Durand, Massey, and Parrado note, "all undocumented migrants with a potential claim for amnesty ceased circulating immediately and began preparing their petitions."

CHANGING WORLDS

The *bracero* agreement limited participation to farm workers and seasonal sugar factory employees. But non-*braceros*, the majority of them *indocumentados*, began to discover that many small industries and businesses—furniture makers, garment manufacturers, tanneries—were willing to hire temporary workers. This opened the doors to wider and less-defined migration. Women were wanted as seamstresses, housecleaners, nannies, men for all kinds of basic manual labor. The wages paid to them far exceeded what these immigrants could earn in Mexico. Surveys taken during the late 1960s and early 1970s indicate that nearly two-thirds of immigrant undocumented workers had been employed before they left their places of origin. The border, after the Operation Wetback crackdowns during the Korean War, had become relatively porous; short-term visitor visas were easy to obtain and many construction firms, private contractors, and manufacturers in California and Texas hired by the day or week in order to cut down on employee overhead.

San Diego, Los Angeles, and El Paso already had sizeable Mexican populations by 1955. Many emigrants, like Maríbel Diaz, had come from small towns in the interior and worked on the Mexican side of the border before migrating. ("I just went shopping one day," she told me, "and I found a job and didn't go back.") Others like Joel Aguilar had been working but were unable to earn enough to support themselves and their dependents. A shoe factory employee in Leon, Guanajuato, Aguilar told me that he barely earned enough to provide for himself, the wife from whom he was separated, and his teenaged son. When the brother of a workmate showed up in Leon with a car, talking about the construction work he was doing near La Mesa, Texas, Aguilar bit.

"He offered to give me a ride to El Paso. I couldn't imagine ever earning enough in Leon to buy a car, so I said 'yes.' A few weeks later I was pouring cement, making eight or ten dollars a day and spending only three or four. When I wasn't working I crossed back [to Ciudad Juarez] and lived there. I was a border rat but it was better than being stuck in Leon."

Statistics show a fairly high rate of employment throughout Mexico in the late 1960s and early 1970s but most of the economic growth was on the higher end of the pay scale: professionals and service employees, refinery and unionized assembly plant workers, importers and government employees. But even the newly financed assembly plants and petroleum-associated industries underwent layoffs, slowdowns, and strikes. High birthrates and large family sizes pushed more and more young people into the workforce, keeping wages low and limiting opportunities for promotion. Droughts that parched much of the north-central part of the Republic thrust more and more rural families into the cities and their rapidly expanding *colonias populares*.

"It wasn't whether one had a job or not," Aguilar explained, "it was whether one could earn enough money to get ahead." In the United States, he said, one could make the same kind of economic leap that the *braceros* had made during the previous two decades. Work, live Spartanly, save money, buy a car, a house, eventually a little business of one's own. Like the *braceros* most of these emigrants did not intend to become permanent U.S. residents. According to Mexico's National Center of Labor Information and Statistics most migrants during this period stayed less than 160 days in the United States. "Half-a-year there, half-a-year here" was the motif of these "birds of passage."

After Ken Light photographed living conditions in Oaxaca in the 1980s, he commented, "People literally have the clothes on their backs and a wooden shack, a bucket of corn and that's it . . . so the idea that someone can come here and make that [$3] in an hour is an incredible draw. All you need is for one person who has gone north to return. He'll tell people that in California they can earn a lot of money—enough to buy a car, or a house with a flush toilet. Who wouldn't want to come here after hearing that?"[17]

"Back in our town in Mexico, there are nothing but women," Guadalupe Hernandez, who migrated back and forth from Mexico to California for over seventeen years, told the Sacramento *Bee* in 1991, "All the men are here [in the United States]. Women or old people are back in our towns . . . The only time Mexican men go back to their country is when they are no good for anything anymore. They are either old or hurt or both. There is nothing left for them. That's when they stop."[18]

Like the *braceros* and the undocumented farm laborers, women migrated in greater and greater numbers because a need existed for what they could provide. U.S. involvement in Vietnam pulled thousands of young men out of the workforce. Integration and the feminist movement opened employment in business and industry to many African-Americans and women. In addition, high production costs in the northern and northeastern United States triggered a southward and southwestern shift of many businesses and industries. The economies of San Diego, Los Angeles, Houston, and Dallas boomed and the boom created needs for all kinds of domestic, food service, childcare, and sweatshop workers.

Typically women entered this workforce through a series of intermediate steps. The oldest daughter in a family of seven children would marry and go with her husband to Ciudad Juarez or Tijuana. A younger sister would visit, or move, north to take care of her sister's children while the sister worked. An aunt or sister-in-law would join them. One or another would find out about work on *The Other Side*, usually as a domestic servant. Over the years each one of them would move back and forth, working on one side of the border then the other, their permanency dictated by family attachments, boyfriends, health, homesickness. Many of these women never had finished primary school and most had started working before they hit their teens.

In 1965, the same year that the *bracero* program officially was terminated, the first *maquiladora* opened in Tijuana. Stimulated by Mexican government tax and property concessions underwritten by the Programa de Industrialización de la Frontera, and by the availability of hundreds of thousands of unskilled workers for whom the minimum wage was one-eighth of what it was in the United States, the *maquiladoras*—assembly plants that specialized in electronics components, music cassettes, toys, and textiles—spread from Tijuana to Reynosa. Although designed to help ease unemployment in the border cities, the *maquiladoras* almost exclusively hired women between the ages of sixteen and twenty-four. Many assembly plant managers refused to hire women with children and immediately terminated the employment of any who tested positive after required pregnancy tests.

"It was all repetitive hand labor—eight to ten hours of performing the same little task over and over again," Maríbel Diaz described the assembly line conditions. Many women worked only a few days or weeks before quitting or being fired. Others mollified the monotony by anticipating how they would spend their salaries. To be paid $19 or more a week was a fortune for minimally educated women who'd never earned more than a few pesos a day before. Not only could they buy clothes and bijouterie, they could send money home, they could improve their living conditions, they could help support lovers, husbands, children, and family members.

Few of the *maquiladoras* provided any employee benefits. Some did offer training courses for employees but all operated on distinct production standards: each woman installed so many zippers per hour, assembled a minimum number of so many cassettes, soldered together so many wires. Women could get laid off or fired without explanation and any health problems incurred while working were discounted.

"There [in a textile *maquiladora*] I left part of my kidneys and my eyes," Norma Iglesias quoted a Tijuana resident.[19] "I never earned a fixed salary, they paid me by the piece...[but] the dresses we made were precious! They sold them in the most exclusive shops in the United States and they cost $200 to $300 dollars. And us? We earned forty-five pesos [about $4.00] for each dress we made. Incredible!"

Despite the difficult working conditions, low pay, and job uncertainty there were no shortages of young aspirants to choose from. Word spread rapidly from daughter to sister to cousin to aunt to niece throughout the northern and central part of the Republic: *"Come to the border, there is work, you can earn money!"* Those who didn't work in the assembly plants took over childcare for those who did. *Ambulantes* (roving merchants) were everywhere, selling candies and fresh-cut flowers and tamales and figurines and lottery tickets. Prostitution increased. So much did the demand for women workers increase that a distinguished Nuevo Leon don confided: "For centuries here in Nuevo Leon a new father cursed his luck if a daughter was born, for a daughter was useless. Now he curses if a son is born, for a son is a do-nothing liability. 'Had it been a daughter,' the new father exclaims, 'she could have gone to a *maquiladora* and supported me! A son? What can he do except marry?'"[20]

Although Mexican state and city government officials welcomed the employment that the *maquiladoras* promised, they were not equipped to handle the demands that both the new industries and their employees placed on community facilities. Many of the places in which the newcomers lived lacked water, electricity, sanitation. Barren fields filled with shanties; broken-down buses served as residences. Two, three, and more families shared cramped quarters in which they had to sleep in shifts. Newly arrived workers scrambled to find what had been garages, chicken coops, and sheds in which to live.

The *maquiladoras* themselves weren't much more luxurious. "The factories, from the street, have an inoffensive appearance, nevertheless," writes Iglesias, "the pungent odor of chemicals and burnt solder permeates the air; the noise of the machines mixes hellishly with the music of the radios that each one brings . . . smoke, vapor and fibers turn everything gray and the green, blue or yellow smocks that one sees the workers wearing are to protect, and not contaminate, the work materials [not the workers who wear them]."

Although the *maquiladoras* offered both income and independence, most assembly line workers stayed relatively short periods of time at any one plant. They could be fired for tardiness, slowness, temporary ineptness, illness, conflicts with other employees or with supervisors, or unsatisfactory personal appearance. Many would quit because they couldn't stand the pace, others because of family or personal problems, pregnancy, or a preference for other types of work. "For many," commented historian E. H. Hutchinson, "the *maquiladora* was a bridge between rural Mexico and 'the good life' in the United States."[21] Thousands crossed that bridge, quietly and unobtrusively, as thousands more trundled toward the border seeking a way out of poverty.

Border crossing was not a one-way proposition. The towns on the frontier were getting pushed from both directions. The number of *indocumentados* deported by U.S. law enforcement increased from just over 55,000 in 1965 to over 900,000 in 1977.[22] Most deportees were turned over to

Mexican authorities in the border cities, a reverse flow of unemployed and needy men and women crammed into an already congested environment. In addition, many others who'd illegally entered the United States returned to the border cities. Audrey Singer and Douglas Massey estimate that 27.9 million *indocumentados* entered the United States between 1965 and 1986. Of those, approximately 84 percent—23.3 million—returned to Mexico on their own volition. (These figures, like those of INS, do not reflect persons making multiple crossings, but they do highlight how the migration pattern worked when the border was essentially porous and target earners could migrate for short periods, earn desired money, and return to their homeland.)

Not everyone who moved to Tijuana, Ciudad Juarez, and the other border metropolises was poor, of course. As Jeffrey H. Cohen points out, by the 1990s successful emigrants were returning to Mexico and city dwellers were moving to rural areas for tranquility and safety.[23] Meanwhile, industry and commerce brought entrepreneurs, doctors, investors, educators, and a whole range of high- and mid-level professionals to capitalize on the burgeoning prosperity of the border cities. These newcomers built skyscrapers and freeways, world-class hotels, bullrings, and nightclubs, libraries, auditoriums, and universities. By the 1980s, over 10 percent of Mexico's population lived within twenty-five miles of the United States. Another five to nine million Mexican-born emigrants had used those same border cities as a springboard to reach the United States.

Through Hell and High Water

EASY DOES IT

Pablo Angulo clearly remembered the first time he left Mexico and entered the United States. He still was in his teens when his employer told him, "Come on, we can get a good prices for the horses. But I need you to go with me. I can't take them alone."

"We put five of them, all just a year old, in the horse trailer and started to drive," Angulo grunted in the raspy, singsong way he had of speaking Spanish. "After a while I asked him where we were going and he told me, 'Houston.' It seemed like a funny word but there were lots of towns with funny names so I didn't think anything about as we kept driving and driving. When we reached a place called Matamoros my employer told me to check on the animals. I carried them some water and while I was in the trailer my employer closed the tailgate and drove on without letting me out.

"I didn't think much of it, but then we stopped I heard my employer talking to a guard of some kind. The guard came around to look in the trailer and saw me and I heard him ask, 'What's he doing in there?'

"'He's with the horses,' my employer said.

"'Where's his papers?'

"'What papers?'

"'Identification papers.'

"'How can he have identification papers? He can't even read. He's just with the horses. I sell them, I bring him back. I can't sell him, he's not worth anything.'

"'Go on,' the guard laughed and in that funny way he had of speaking Spanish he told my employer, 'get the hell across.'"

Angulo didn't stay in the United States—he told me he didn't like it there—but he made several other trips with horses to be sold at Texas auctions. He claimed he'd never had difficulty crossing although eventually his employer did get papers of some kind for him.

Immigration agents were stricter at other crossing points although an immigrant named Felix Maytorena told me it was the U.S. customs agents who hassled border crossers the most.

"I think they didn't like anybody who wasn't a rich tourist," he said. "The customs agents liked doing strip searches, you know, like making you bend over and spread your cheeks. They would take away things they said were illegal, like books written in Spanish that they said might be pornographic. Sometimes we would swim the river just to not have to deal with them."

For many the problem was not crossing the border but what to do before and after one crossed it. Buses ran from the interior to almost all of the frontier cities but the bus stations were havens for con men and thieves. Some would pose as taxi drivers and offer to take the new arrivals to a border crossing or hotel or safe place to stay, then rob them. Labor contractors would assail newcomers, offering job opportunities or easy transit across the border. Children as young as eight and nine would tug at hands and arms, *take you to a hotel! a restaurant! a barbershop!* Would-be *indocumentados* traveling in groups had a better time of it than those who arrived alone but even for them it wasn't easy and it didn't get any easier once they crossed the border.

Most emigrants relied on contacts within the Mexican and Chicano communities to find housing and jobs but many spent night after night sleeping under freeways, in drain pipes or culverts and eating what they could buy (usually tortillas) for a few pesos. José Lucero, a Tijuana schoolteacher who often visited relatives across the border in National City, remembered persuading police in that border town to release a young migrant from Michoacán who had been living off the carrots and radishes he pulled from neighborhood gardens.

"He was very careful not to step on any of the other plants," Lucero told me. "And sometimes he even weeded around those he didn't eat."

An *indocumentado* who I met in Nuevo Laredo in the early 1960s described successfully crossing the Rio Grande at night, then getting lost from his companions after reaching *The Other Side*. The road he followed led away from the river and he walked all night and most of the next day "seeing nobody, just a couple of cars that passed and didn't stop." Exhausted, hungry and frightened, he finally stumbled into a farmyard "where the dogs almost killed me" and begged the owners to turn him into the police.

"They telephoned but the sheriff wouldn't come for me so I walked another whole day and when I finally got to a little town the police wouldn't believe I'd walked that far. They said they didn't have time to arrest me so they printed up a sign for me, WANT TO WORK! and I sat outside on the street and after a long time a farmer picked me up and I stayed in a shed behind his place for two months feeding and killing chickens and helping butcher hogs. He didn't pay me but I got the leftovers from his table and a place to sleep."

The arrival of more and more migrants in the border cities created new occupations for those who knew their way around. Job brokers and guides—the first *coyotes*—commandeered newcomers and escorted them into the United States. Most of these intermediaries spoke enough English to deal with U.S. farmers and sweatshop owners and had lived in the United States long enough to be able to jam the *indocumentados* into some kind of slum housing. Migration had a price and at the end of the long journey those who'd left farms and villages hundreds of miles way were willing to pay it.

OPEN FLOODGATES

Between 1965 and 1977 more than four million Mexican citizens entered the United States. Six hundred thousand entered legally—that statistic can be verified.[1] The estimates for illegal entries and the statistics for deportations don't take into account multiple actions by the same individual. As Felix Maytorena bragged during one of our conversations, "Look at me! You see just one man but I am fifty!" He was exaggerating but by his own count, he had gone back and forth between California and Mexico six to eight times a year each year during the early 1970s. During one three-week span he was deported twice, reentered three times, worked five different jobs and got drunk "well, *really drunk*, just once."

Even for non-agricultural workers, crossing to *The Other Side* was temporary and seasonal. Layoffs were frequent, particularly in the food service and construction industries. Canneries, packing plants, beet sugar factories, and lumber mills hired only when they were in full production. In addition, particularly during the 1960s and 1970s, many single men headed for the United States to fulfill specific financial needs. Antonio Valencia (no relation to Jorge Valencia, mentioned in the first chapter), wanted to further his education.[2]

Although Valencia grew up in the northeastern part of the country he had been living in Mexico City since he was seventeen. He had a scholarship to the national Politécnico university but couldn't afford housing or books after moving out of his brother-in-law's apartment to make room for his sister's new baby. He spent a week or two visiting a schoolmate in Guadalajara and the two of them decided to head for Tijuana to earn enough money to return to school. At the last minute his schoolmate reneged but Valencia, finding Guadalajara no more lucrative than Mexico City, boarded a bus for the border city.

As he stepped off in Tijuana he was besieged by brutal voices shouting, *"Va para Los Angeles, compadre?" "A Los Angeles?" "Va para la pasada?"* He pushed past, brushing off the hawkers but several of them followed him, repeating offers to take him to Los Angeles. A young woman blocked his exit. "Come with us...Los Angeles ..." he heard her say as he ducked away to escape the confusion and noise.

The street in front of the station was almost as hectic. Taxi drivers whistled to get his attention. A frenetic young man not much older than Valencia grabbed his shirtsleeve. "Safe...easy ..." he intimated "... Los Angeles...not expensive ..." An older man in a ratty sweater leaning against the door of a grimy barbershop urged, "Go, *chavito*, go. Better now than later. Better you get out of this place."

Unlike most young jobseekers arriving in Tijuana, Valencia was not naïve to city ways. He threaded his way through the commotion, bought a couple of tacos and a few chunks of spiced fresh coconut and went to look for a place to stay on the fringe of Tijuana's Zona Norte—the red-light district. Through a temporary job cutting and loading rebar for a construction site he met a sailor who'd become stranded in Tijuana and who had decided to cross the border. He had crossed once before with a *pollero* and felt that he could duplicate the trip on his own. He persuaded Valencia and one other man to go with him.

Their few clothes and personal items crammed into backpacks they rode together as far as a local bus would take them. Squatter villages— jammed together shelters of lamina and cardboard, car parts, and stacks of ripped up tires—marked their advance along the barbed wire barrier that separated Mexico from the United States. For more than an hour as the sun was setting they trudged along the International Highway as though they were hitchhiking or headed for some distant rancho, then the ex-sailor led Valencia to the battered remains of an old delivery van turned on its side. It reeked of defecation and urine: Countless emigrants before them had huddled there waiting for an opportunity to cross.

Twice as they made their four a.m. dash across the highway and along the fence to a place where they could squeeze through, the three men flung themselves face forward on the ground to avoid being seen by the drivers of cars flitting along the highway. The trio scoured through thorny dry growth and thick sand, holding onto each other as they waded into the murky water of a canal that separated them from a highway visible half-a-mile away. Clouds of mosquitoes hovered above them, the attacks so pervasive the three men could hardly resist flailing their arms and cursing.

For most of the following day they huddled out of sight, sleeping fitfully and wishing they had brought more with them to eat, then they hiked all night through the darkness, paralleling the road at a safe distance so as not to be seen by passing cars. Just at dusk they caught a ride in an old truck driven by a *compa*—a Chicano who laughed at their appearance but said he'd gone through worse tribulations ten years before. Not until months later did Valencia make it to Los Angeles, enriched, he claimed, by his experiences but scarred by them as well.

Estimates vary widely on the percentages of crossers apprehended compared to those who slipped through. Border patrol officials in Tijuana suggested that they apprehended one out of three in 1979 but other researchers guess that four out of five crossed successfully for every one that was caught. Even border patrol veterans admitted that trying to catch illegal entrants was "a cat and mouse game" and, as one reassigned *migra* confided to me, "I was always glad to be the cat."

Although many *indocumentados* like Valencia were able to cross without assistance most arrived at the border knowing they'd need help to get past the *migra*. Felix Maytorena claimed never to have recruited *amigos* to leave Mexico but he admitted that several of his compatriots became solicitors for *contrabandistas*. These solicitors would exaggerate what great opportunities existed in the United States, explain how much it would cost to arrive safely and put the recruits, with their money, on the bus to Tijuana with instructions about how to contact the person who would then contact the person who would take them across the border. Often these rural recruiters would make the bus trip north with their *pollitos* to protect them from criminal gangs who would waylay travelers or pick up unsuspecting emigrants in Tijuana or other border cities and rob them, for it was common knowledge that many of those heading for the border were carrying substantial amounts of cash.

Getting that money before the *coyotes* could get it competed with car theft and drug smuggling as a criminal activity. The *coyotes* themselves could become victims. Their cash-only business made them vulnerable if they were unprepared to defend themselves. Some carried pistols and most of them set up networks of contacts to decrease their exposure and to conceal their identities. A prospective client had to go through several intermediaries before he could meet the person who actually would conduct him across the border.

Herman Baca in 1981 the president of the Commission for Chicano Rights, noted that the Border Patrol's hard-nosed policies prompted more immigrants to seek help from smugglers and brokers in cities south of the border. The Mexico City daily, *Excelsior*, reported that these *polleros* earned more than $22 million dollars in 1978.[3] According to *Excelsior* approximately 100 separate bands, some of them with gangland connections, were overseeing nearly 20,000 guides, each of whom earned hundreds of thousands of dollars a year.

"Transporting people," a Calexico border official admitted, "has replaced the drug traffic as a profitable enterprise. Not only is it safer, but few guides go to jail, even when they do get caught."[4]

The *coyote*, of course, divvied part of his earnings with the feeders who brought him clients and often had employer contacts in the United States for whom he supplied workers. For that reason few *coyotes* would make excursions with fewer than five or six *pollos* and usually they preferred between eight and twelve. A Chula Vista, California, woman, now a legal resident in California, told me about crossing Otay Mesa, east of Tijuana, at night with another woman who suffered an asthma attack just as Border Patrol agents were approaching with flashlights.

"There were eight of us," she described the scene, "and our guide told us to spread out in different directions. My husband and I managed to dive into a culvert and we lay there shivering and trying not to cry for what seemed like hours until the *migra* finally went away. I think they apprehended all of the rest except the guide, who like us escaped."

As noted in the Introduction, most Spanish-speaking immigrants did not regard *coyotes* as criminals but as necessary intermediaries whose business was to get them safely across the border. Many immigrant communities in the United States maintained close contact with communities in Mexico and the two shared their knowledge of who could best facilitate crossing. Escobar Latapí, et al., refer to these interconnections as "microstructures of migration"—persons from the same communities or same trades who grouped together to help each other and to help others with similar backgrounds to migrate.[5] Once established in the United States these interconnected groups maintained contact with *coyotes* they could trust. And the *coyotes*, for their part, took special care to accommodate groups they had worked with before and from whom they could expect prompt and accurate payment.[6]

These *coyotes* "do not just feed off or prey upon the migrant stream," insists David Spener. "Rather, they themselves are an integrated part of it. These enterprises are structured around tightly bound, transborder networks of trust that link Mexican immigrants in the U.S. interior to friends and kin in . . . the migrant sending regions in Mexico's interior."[7]

A baby crying, a sneeze, a panic attack, a dropped backpack, a displaced boulder could lead to discovery and deportation. Some *polleros* wouldn't accept women with children because they felt children were too difficult to keep quiet. Others charged higher prices to take women across because women slowed a group down when it became necessary to run for cover. Once inside San Diego or Los Angeles the new arrivals became parts of the Hispanic communities there and risked deportation only if they were apprehended for some misdemeanor or infraction.

Crossing the Rio Grande into Texas presented different problems. The river was shallow enough in some places that *indocumentados* could wade across, or swim, and paddle from one shore to the other on inner-tube rafts. Even so the waters could be very deceptive. The first time that a would be emigrant named Abraham Aguilar made his attempt; he tied his clothes, water, and some food in a plastic garbage bag and with it fastened to one wrist, he edged into the water. The current was stronger than he'd expected and the water colder. He paused to catch his breath, then he pushed forward, slipping and sliding as he tried to keep his footing and not be forced downstream by the current.

As he twisted around to make sure he was following a route directly across the river, he stepped into a hole and lost his balance. He was able to push himself erect but halfway across the river, already exhausted and not sure how far downstream he'd detoured, he fell again and panicked because he could not touch the bottom. He tried to swim but the plastic bag attached to his wrist impeded him. Blubbering and plunging again beneath the surface, he managed to release the bag and, half-swimming and half-crawling, make his way back to the Mexican shore.

Wrapped only in a couple of half-rotten gunnysacks that he scrounged along the bank, shivering and coughing the dank water he'd swallowed, Aguilar followed the river until he came to a little cluster of cement-block houses. The residents of one of them laughed at his condition, gave him some raggedy old clothes and commented that he was lucky not to have washed up on the "Playa de Muertos," where the bodies of unsuccessful *espaldas mojadas* sometimes were found.

Twelve weeks later Aguilar tried again, this time in the company of six others. One of them, an experienced ranch hand and horseman, showed them how to tie themselves together with knots they could yank loose if they were being pulled under the current. They fastened plastic bags holding their possessions to the rope in order to have their hands free. Two of those crossing wore old life jackets they'd acquired in a Reynosa *segunda* and all of them went naked into the water.

Fighting the current, as Aguilar had done on his previous attempt, they forged across slowly. To Aguilar's surprise the water in the middle of the river seemed shallower than it had closer to the bank. But just before they reached the U.S. side they slid into water above their heads where the force of the current had gouged a channel. Swimming and tugging each other they groped along the washed out bank trying to find a place to pull themselves out. Aguilar managed to grab a clump of mesquite and cling to it while one of his companions looped the rope around a knobby stump beside it. They dried themselves off as best they could, tugged on clothes and stumbled through coarse mesquite and chaparral until they were far enough from the river not to be detected by any passing border patrol vehicles.

Even having crossed the river they still had a long way to go. Traveling only at night and diving out of sight when they saw approaching headlights, the seven *indocumentados* skirted the border patrol checkpoint outside Falfurrias, over hundred miles north of Reynosa, and finally made it to San Antonio. The several among them who'd crossed the Rio Grande before jested to Aguilar, "It's the first time that's the hardest. It gets easier after this," a concept that he found it very hard to believe.

Some farm labor contractors recruited workers for cotton, citrus, and grain plantings and harvests, and transported them to the areas where they'd be working. Other independent "contractors" solicited clients by arranging safe transportation for them to areas where they would be likely to find work. The *transportista* would cram between eight to twenty— sometimes more—men, women, and children into a windowless van or delivery truck. José Cortés, a government health worker for the state of Tamaulipas in Mexico, described one group who traveled over 300 miles in a truck compartment which the driver covered with manure.

"The manure was damp," he told a Reynosa newspaper reporter, "and soon permeated the compartment. Over half of those being transported got sick and vomited the food they'd brought for their lunches."

Other migrants jammed into pickup camper shells, converted school buses, trailers, and rental moving vans. The trips became longer as more and more jobs became available in construction industry and food service in other parts of the country. Instead of a twelve-hour ride to Dallas or Houston, trucks and vans filled with migrants stayed on the road, often without stopping, for twenty to thirty hours before unloading their human cargo in Milwaukee, in Chicago, in Minneapolis, in Washington D.C. By the mid-1970s transporting *indocumentados* had become big business. So had hiring them for half of what non-*indocumentados* could be paid.

LAND OF OPPORTUNITY

According to official INS statistics, U.S. authorities deported 952,200 Mexican *indocumentados* in 1978.[8] That statistic is inflated because it does not include multiple deportations of the same individual. It does, however, reflect stepped up law enforcement action on the part of U.S. authorities who had been under increasing pressure from politicians, labor unions, and various citizen groups to effectively close the frontier. The U.S. Congress poured money into border control personnel recruitment throughout President Jimmy Carter's administration (1976–1980) in what they announced was a "get tough" policy against undocumented aliens.

Construction crews erected barbed wire-topped walls on the U.S. side of the border to make Tijuana crossings more difficult. Helicopter patrols and electronic surveillance devices alerted border patrol units to possible infiltrations. INS (Immigration and Naturalization Service) spokespersons asserted that entering the United States illegally was a federal offense and that agents no longer would mollycoddle those they apprehended. A border patrol agent shot and killed two men while they were handcuffed together a few hundred feet from the border near Tijuana. Several other would be immigrants died of gunshot wounds and countless others, including an ill-fated group of Salvadorans whose bodies were recovered from Organ Pipe Cactus National Park in July 1980, perished from thirst, starvation, and exposure.

Despite the increased ratio of migration throughout the 1970s the rate of employment remained relatively high within Mexico. Oil prices were up and the federally owned monopoly, Pemex, had extended its capacity by constructing "floating city" platforms to pump crude from beneath the waters of the Gulf. Most workers and business and industry owners and investors were unprepared for the financial collapse that occurred at the end of President Jose López Portillo's administration. The "Crash of 1981" and consequent floating of the peso against the dollar triggered soaring inflation and thrust the median incomes of hundreds of thousands of Mexicans well below the poverty level.

Factories and businesses laid off employees they no longer could afford to pay or they simply closed their doors, leaving hundreds of thousands

out of work. Even those who managed to maintain some kind of employment or business incomes saw their savings depleted by as much as
1,000 percent and small business owners, farmers, and the employees of
companies that had been dealing in dollars collapsed into bankruptcy. The
tightened anti-immigrant policies instituted by the Carter administration
and expanded by President Ronald Reagan's first years in office made it
harder for *aspirantes* to slip into the United States but did nothing to discourage those affected by the Crash from trying to get across the border.
Crossing attempts increased rather than decreased despite the "get tough"
program.

The Crash also lowered the cost of labor for firms doing business on the
U.S.-Mexican frontier. The number of *maquiladoras* operating in Tijuana,
Mexicali, and Ciudad Juarez quadrupled as Korean and Japanese companies set up new assembly plants, many of them associated with the electronics industry. Most of them, like the U.S.- and Mexican-owned estab-
lishments, hired only young single women and set stiff production quotas
for them.

That *indocumentados* would work for less than minimum wage, and
were less likely to complain about either how little they earned or working conditions, encouraged more and more marginal enterprises to rely
on them. The majority of places that offered new employment were in
the northern Midwest (particularly Chicago) and the East and Northeast.
Few emigrants could get there on their own; almost all of them needed
help. Supply and demand elevated those who could import and transport
immigrants to elite status. Few earned as much money—or ran continual
risks—as the *coyotes* did.

By 1970, according to Cerrutti and Massey, over 60 percent of first-time
aspirantes contracted *coyotes* to get them into the United States. The percentage rose to nearly 80 percent by 1986 when the Simpson-Rodino Act
went into effect. It has remained that high—or higher—since.[9] As border
enforcement has stiffened and become more sophisticated, the prices *coyotes* charge have risen from $150 for a simple Tijuana to San Diego jaunt
forty years ago to as much as $2,000 for Mexico-to-Chicago or other U.S.
city delivery in 2005.

Benigno LaBouyer told me that he paid $800 for the trip from
Brownsville, Texas, to Washington, D.C. with eighteen other immigrants
in the back of a U-Haul truck in 1979. The descendant, he claimed, of
a French soldier who'd come to Mexico in the mid-1860s with Emperor
Maximilian, Le Bouyer had lost his position as a primary school music
teacher and couldn't pay off what he'd borrowed to finalize the purchase
of the house he'd acquired in Tampico. He resisted "maybe a dozen" job

broker offers before accepting one that gave him names and contacts in Washington, D.C. that he could telephone to verify that he would arrive safely and have a job waiting when he arrived.

"We had nothing to eat but some vegetables that the driver bought us. For a toilet, we had a bucket that we emptied at night. Two brothers with us on the trip—they were youngsters, maybe fifteen, sixteen—got very scared and we had to put gags in their mouths and hold them against the floor whenever we slowed down, or stopped to get gas."

LeBouyer stayed in the District of Columbia only six months. After he returned to Matamoros, he learned that the *coyote* who had transported him across the United States had been arrested. Although persons convicted of bringing illegal immigrants into the United States faced up to five years in prison for each person they imported, convictions before 1986 were rare. LeBouyer said his *coyote* was "back at work" within six months. The *Atlas World Press Review* quoted Alfonso Fuentes Ruiz, the Mexican consul in San Isidro, California, as saying in 1978 that 15,000 "guides" were arrested but barely 1 percent were punished, and all of those convicted were freed on bail.[10]

Many immigrant brokers capitalized on the publicity given to the arrests and deportations to discourage would be emigrants from attempting to cross on their own. Their contact people exaggerated horror stories about *migra* violence and unjust detention to enlist recruits. They also described the risks non-escorted *aspirantes* faced from being shaken-down for payoffs or bribes by Mexican police and the dangers to which they would be exposed if gangster bands detected them trying to cross the border on their own. They pointed out that getting to the border was as dangerous as trying to get across it.

Some of these gangster bands were well organized and included members of municipal police forces but most were wildcat gangs of young delinquents who'd given up trying to get into the United States and/or who had criminal records on one or both sides of the border. Some had their own informants (or the same informants, or "heels," who directed newcomers to the *coyotes*.) They learned which *coyotes* chose which routes, what vehicles they used, how they operated. Sometimes the members of these bands would intercept emigrant groups and extort money from them; others chose more violent methods, particularly when they came across emigrants in isolated areas.

Just as a nineteen-year-old migrant named Luis Pulido and the group of eight other men and three women left the van that had taken them to a deserted spot east of Tecate, they heard a series of loud whistles.[11]

"Back! Back to the van!" their guide shouted but before they could turn and stumble through the loose sandy soil four men dressed in black jeans and black sweatshirts cut them off. Two of them flashed knives and another pulled a gun from his belt. They ordered the men to step forward one at a time. While the one holding the pistol watched, the others frisked and stripped each of the migrants of money and valuables. They then forced them to get back into the van but wouldn't let the three women accompany them. One of the women's husbands twisted away and lunged at the pistol carrier but the other assailants threw him against the back of the van and kicked and beat him. They slashed the van's tires and three of them forced the women to go off with them while the other stood guard with the pistol. Pulido and the other migrants could hear the women screaming and crying as the assailants raped them, then the four attackers fled, leaving the group to get back to Tijuana, moneyless and devastated, as best they could.

Despite that experience, Pulido later made it across the border after borrowing money from his relatives and paying a different *coyote*. Between those two crossings, he made two other attempts and was caught both times. The first time he and several dozen men and women decided to cross Otay Mesa, east of the San Diego suburb of Chula Vista, during the night. Knowing that it would be almost impossible to make it all the way into and out of the canyons and barrancas lining the mesa without being detected by the border service helicopters that patrolled the area, they agreed that as soon as they were spotted three or four of the men would break out of concealment and split in different directions while the others threaded their way upward, trying to stay hidden as best they could.

They were nearly halfway across the mesa when the helicopter appeared, its huge floodlight blanching the hillside and its rotary blades flinging dust, brush, and debris in murky swirls beneath it. Sighting the men dashing ahead of the other aspirants, the helicopter veered sharply above two of them, a loudspeaker giving staticky warnings that were impossible to understand. Headlights appeared on the hilltop as first one, then another Border Patrol all-terrain vehicle bumped along a makeshift road toward two of the men who had stopped running. Pulido rolled beneath a patch of dense brush as the helicopter swerved back and forth overhead.

One border agent came so close to the place Pulido was hiding he could hear commands being issued on the *migra*'s walkie-talkie but the officer's attention was diverted and he rushed away without seeing Pulido. Hours later the young migrant made it to a highway that he thought would take him into Chula Vista but he'd lost his sense of north and south and headed in the wrong direction. A passing truck driver radioed the Border Patrol; two officers picked Pulido up and, after ascertaining that he didn't have identification papers, drove him back to Tijuana and released him to the Mexican side of the border without booking or fingerprinting him.

A few weeks later, when Pulido was apprehended trying to cross again, the arresting officers took him to a detention center, fingerprinted him and told him he would face criminal charges if he made another attempt to illegally enter the United States. For that reason, he explained, he chose to borrow money and make his next attempt with a "professional." This time he was successful, although the trip turned out to be nearly as hazardous as his previous efforts.

The *coyote,* a tall fidgety man who kept looking at a huge watch strapped to his wrist, crammed his charges into the back of a minivan and drove slowly out of Tijuana. He pulled onto a rutted unpaved path and turned off his headlights as the vehicle bumped toward the border. It was so dark that Pulido, on his knees on the floorboard between the driver and front seat passengers, couldn't see either the road or anything on either side. Now and then he heard the van slap against some kind of brush and was aware, from the driver's muttered grunts, that other vehicles were in the vicinity but, like the van, were driving without lights. The tightly packed passengers groaned as the van lurched into depressions or banged over rocks. The driver sat rigidly hunched over the steering wheel, twisting it this way and that as he maneuvered past what to Pulido were unseen obstacles.

Flashing lights to their right splayed the mesa with patches of red and blue as the driver accelerated and the van careened forward, almost tipping over twice. Pulido could hear sirens and, behind them, the roar of an approaching helicopter as the van vaulted onto a graveled straightaway, barely missing another car, and sped forward. Twenty minutes later the driver swerved into what appeared to be an abandoned barnyard and shoved his charges into the camper shell of a pickup that would take them into Chula Vista. To the thanks they offered he responded only, "Bah! Like shooting cats in barrel."

Photographer Ken Light spent time on the border in the mid-1980s and reported, "On some nights there were so many people coming across that the patrol was overrun." He witnessed a single *migra* arrest forty-eight *indocumentados* at one time. "Those forty-eight could have jumped him but they didn't." Although desperate, they weren't violent; they merely wanted to get through to places that they could find jobs.[12]

Estimates made in 1982 indicated that one out of every twenty-five *indocumentados* living in the United States had entered legally but no longer had legal documentation.[13] Some were ex-*braceros* who'd never returned to Mexico after the program was disbanded. Others had been granted work permits or student visas and had let them expire. Still others had come legally as tourists and never returned to Mexico.

Many residents of Mexican border cities work in U.S. cities and even more residents of Mexican border cities purchase clothes, small appliances, and other items north of the border. Many *indocumentados* like Maríbel Diaz simply "went shopping" and never returned. "As long as you didn't look like a farm worker they [the Border Patrol], didn't bother you," a long-time *indocumentado* who later acquired legal residency through the Amnesty provisions of the Simpson-Rodino Act told me in 1989.

Southern California, in particular, hosted hundreds of thousands of residents who had been issued short-term passes to visit family members, shop, or participate in business dealings. These permits, called "white cards" or Forms I-186, enable Mexican border residents to spend a maximum of seventy-two hours in the United States. When they first were authorized for issue in 1952, they restricted the bearer from traveling more than 150 miles from the border. That limitation was lowered in 1969 to a maximum of twenty-five miles, which allows those crossing from Tijuana to go as far as San Diego, but not legally to Los Angeles. Throughout the 1970s and early 1980s, white card holders frequently shrugged aside this restriction, however; despite Border Patrol checkpoints set up at San Clemente and Temecula, they seldom were hassled and often, if questioned, were told simply to return to within twenty-five miles of the border.

Those possessing white cards cannot work in the United States but "green card" holders can. Green cards were and are highly prized possessions. Rumors circulating during the mid and late 1970s hinted that there were three times as many cards in circulation as had actually been issued. Probably that is an exaggeration, but they often were loaned, sold, copied and counterfeited. Jorge A. Bustamante, the former president of the Colegio de la Frontera Norte in Tijuana, asserted, after a detailed investigation that only 10–15 percent of green card holders actually used them to regularly cross the border to work.

With *braceros* no longer available after 1965 many U.S. agriculturalists petitioned the U.S. government for help and thousands of "Form H-II" admissions were authorized. Form H-II workers could be hired only if they didn't displace jobs that could be held by U.S. citizens. More than 12,000 of them were rushed across the border to salvage citrus, sugar beet, olive, and onion harvests in each of the years 1965, 1966, and 1967. The admissions declined after that; between 1,000 and 2,000 entered the United States each year during the 1970s and early 1980s.

Few Mexican emigrants seeking work in the United States knew anything about the H-II program. Most of those who participated lived close to the border and referred friends, relatives, and acquaintances to whoever was accepting applications. After the desperation harvests of the mid-1960s most U.S. farmers were able to contract enough workers on their own, rather than go through the Department of Labor for H-II help. A northern California olive grower told me in 1980 that "illegals" were easier to hire and manage than H-II employees because "you can just write their names down and send 'em out to the trees" instead of "filling out paperwork up the bazoo."

White cardholders, green cardholders, H-II importees, tourists, and immigrants possessing fake or counterfeit documents swelled the ranks of those who had become permanent or semi-permanent U.S. residents. For many entrants having a legal document—any kind of legal document, visa, social security card, driver's license, work permit—made both employment and residency easier. In some cases these legal documents were shared by more than one person. An immigrant I met through friends while I was in Los Angeles in the early 1980s jokingly passed off references to a "double identity," then explained that he was one of four or five—or perhaps twenty or thirty—legally admitted "Jorge Loredos." A dark, squat porcine fellow, he'd grown a thick mustache and plastered his hair straight back from his forehead to resemble the Mexican passport and U.S. visa photos the real Jorge Loredo had let him use for what, he said, was a "hefty" price.

"We fat Mexicans all look alike to you gringos," he laughed, defining his entrance through immigration as "casual and cursory" although, he admitted, customs inspectors had made him disrobe "checking to see if all my fat was really me." Using the acquired documents as verification, he'd obtained a California driver's license and a social security number. He said he carried a photocopy of the visa in his wallet, confident that he could explain that the original document was at his work place, in a safety deposit box, or had been lost if he was called upon to prove his legality.

Counterfeit documents of all kinds could be purchased in Tijuana or across the border in Chula Vista, San Diego, and Los Angeles. Some of these fakes were better than others but most served as "legal" identification for an agricultural or sweatshop employer who only needed to see a photocopy in order to hire the bearer. Beneath the inscription *Resident Alien* across the top of the card, the I-151 bears a photo, fingerprint, birthdate, card number and expiration date. To produce fake cards the counterfeiter only needed the basic equipment that any fast-photo or Kinko's-type copy shop would use.

Social security cards were equally easy to duplicate. Those printing fake cards usually took the pains to make sure that the numbers they put on them corresponded to numbers being issued to people about the same age as the recipient. Periodic raids closed some shops but invariably others popped up and the crackdowns north of the border only stimulated business on the Mexican side. Police raids there netted similar results: the counterfeiters were arrested and the equipment confiscated but there were few convictions and fewer prison sentences meted out. The pseudo Jorge Loredo that I met in Los Angeles insisted that the Tijuana raids were shakedowns to force the operators to pay bigger bribes. He compared them to drug busts, where the authorities only muscled the little and mid-level dealers, not the "big guys" who could pay huge *mordidas* for protection from police commissioners, mayors, governors, and Army generals.

Despite the ease with which some *indocumentados* crossed the border with white cards or tourist documents, 70 percent of those surveyed in 1999 and 2000 claimed they'd gone through experiences that put their lives in danger while trying to enter the United States, either from extreme heat or cold or the lack of water, food, and exertion that caused insurmountable fatigue.[14]

CRACKING DOWN

Forty years of benign neglect apparently ended on November 6, 1986, when the U.S. Congress passed the Simpson-Rodino Immigration and Control Act. The Act provided amnesty for *indocumentados* who'd arrived in the United States before 1982 and could prove continual residence and for migrant workers who had worked in agriculture for more than six months each year between 1982–1986. It also stipulated that not-documented aliens who'd entered the country after 1986 should be deported and that employers who knowingly hired illegal aliens could be fined and/or given prison terms.

Newspaper headlines throughout Mexico and Latin America warned that massive waves of deportees would flood their frontiers. Mexico's chief of migratory services Eugenio Calzado Flores spread the alarm that the three million *indocumentados* thrust back into Mexico would overrun the country, creating near-starvation conditions, massive unemployment and an acceleration of violent crime.[15] Ciudad Juarez's municipal president Alfredo Urías predicted that the city's law enforcement would not be able to deal with more than 400,000 deportees arriving "without more than the clothes they're wearing, starving and disposed to criminal acts."[16] The alcaldes of eighteen small cities in the Altos of Jalisco predicted "economic, political, and social chaos" when thousands of evicted *deportados* whose remittances had been the area's main financial support swarmed back into the highlands.[17] Guatemala's *Prensa Libre* bemoaned the impact those forced out of the United States would have on that country's newly elected moderate government.[18]

United States immigration officials noted a "significant increase" in the number of Mexicans, apparently *indocumentados*, crossing back into Mexico from Texas during the first three weeks of December. Municipal authorities in Ciudad Juarez set up *albergues* to accommodate the disenfranchised hordes but most of the returnees passed up those accommodations to head further south. By the end of December the deluge had dwindled to an inconsequential trickle. The Red Cross estimated that the increase of December returnees in 1986 was scarcely 10 percent greater than each of the three previous years and most of those passing through the city were returning voluntarily, as they did each year, on their way to spend time with their families.

Statistics from Mexicali and Tijuana showed a dip in apprehensions but by February 1987 the border patrol was corralling as many or more *aspirantes* per month as it had throughout 1986. Amnesty didn't change conditions in Mexico. In the mid-1980s inflation was at its worst, the peso was practically valueless, drought had harrowed huge swaths of the Mexican countryside and unemployment and under-employment had driven thousands of Mexican families into oppressive debt. While Simpson-Rodino (termed "The Anti-Immigration Act" in Mexico and Central America) eventually did legalize the residency of nearly three million Mexican-born U.S. residents, it did nothing to stem undocumented immigration. To struggling families looking northward, "Amnesty" added one more proof to the already prevalent myth that life on the other side of the border brought happiness and financial gain. Three million had succeeded—why not three million more?

Thousands of farm workers eligible for amnesty found that they lacked documentation to prove they had worked in the United States for six or more months. Some merely ignored the omissions and continued working as *indocumentados* for farmers who would hire them. Since the only requirement for proof of temporary employment in agriculture was a letter from a labor contractor or employer saying the migrant had worked for more than 90 days each of the required years, it was easy enough for workers to get real or apocryphal documents. Estimates varied, but most indicated that over half of the 1.1 million workers legalized under the farm worker provisions of Amnesty actually did not qualify.[19]

Many farm workers who didn't qualify for Amnesty drifted back to the border cities. There these returnees were pushed by newcomers arriving from previously low-sender states, particularly Oaxaca and Veracruz, and from Central America. Squatter communities spread for miles outside of Tijuana and Mexicali, along the river and inland from San Luis Río Colordo, across the desert outside of Nogales and along the Rio Grande outside of El Paso, Piedras Negras, Nuevo Laredo, and Reynosa.

Just as Mexicans entering the United States without proper documentation became, by definition, "criminals," Central Americans illegally entering Mexico to get to the United States were considered to be lawbreakers. Anyone could report them and have them arrested; consequently anyone could shake them down. Mexican journalist Jorge Reyes Estrada of the Mexico City daily *Uno Más Uno* noted that neither the Mexican military nor municipal, state, or customs police legally could detain undocumented foreigners but few of those fleeing unsupportable conditions in Central America realized that. What money they hadn't paid their *polleros* they handed over to uniformed agents to keep from being arrested, beaten, and incarcerated.

Like the U.S. Border Patrol, Mexican police found it easier to apprehend *indocumentados* than to go after the smugglers. Police throughout Mexico are notoriously poorly paid and in most places supplement their meager salaries by collecting *mordidas* from traffic violators, unlicensed businesses, after-hours liquor sales, pimps, and bar owners. Some Central Americans being transported through Mexico reported that their guides, instead of trying to avoid police, contacted them for protection. In some towns along the so-called "Refugee Route" local administrators would grant temporary "visiting permits" which the *indocumentados* had to pay for.

Seldom if ever did violations result in arrest or punishment. The Central Americans had no access to the criminal justice system. "It's as though they come into the country with a sign plastered across their forehead, 'I am a victim. Abuse me!'" a former Ciudad Juarez business manager told me. After a torturous trip of weeks—sometimes even months—the *indocumentados* still faced enormous challenges and hardships when they arrived within sight of the United States. For every twenty or thirty who slipped cross the border successfully two or three hundred more piled into border cities like Matamoros, Tamaulipas behind them.

The sprawling city, which was doubling in size every four or five years, had no places to put the new arrivals, no services to offer, no money to give. Criminal bands of vicious young *cholos* on the Mexican side of the river lay in wait and raided, raped, and killed. Even Matamoros residents who at first had been sympathetic to the plights of the refugee Central Americans began to blame them for turning what had been a pastoral retreat of shrimp fishermen and citrus growers into one of the most violent border cities in the world.

Not only had Matamoros become a clogged funnel for desperate immigrants, it had become a focal point for cartel drug exports. Motor launches slipped in and out of its river harbor, small planes took off and landed from the airport a few miles southwest of the city, Suburbans with blinded windows cruised through town. Clinton administration rhetoric blended drug dealers with *indocumentados* but offered very little proof that any connections existed between the two. Even cartel big shots like Chapo Guzmán spoofed at assertions that the drug lords used migrants to get their illicit goods across the border. "We cannot use the *indocumentados*," he was quoted as deriding, "because they are too dumb. If they weren't so dumb they wouldn't be *indocumentados*."[20]

By the 1980s the drug trade through Mexico had become tightly controlled, with a rigid chain of command. Much of what was being channeled through originated in South America and was moved in bulk by airplanes, boats, or trucks with concealed storage compartments. In all likelihood now and then a migrant would be paid to carry a small amount across for a street vendor or small-time dealer but overall cartel investment was too great to trust sending significant amounts with inexperienced and likely-to-be-apprehended novices.

Nevertheless hangers-on and discards from drug trafficking—users, small-time street peddlers, informants, petty thieves—slid into the impoverished shack cities overflowing with unsuccessful and would-be migrants. Gangs formed. Most of the gang members who preyed on incoming *aspirantes* had come to the border as *aspirantes* themselves, or as children of men and women seeking to cross the border. Unable to restrict the spread of shantytowns around the border cities, or control the increasingly better organized and better armed gangs, Mexican police often became predators instead of protectors. Jorge Bustamante asserted on Mexican national television that he doubted that anyone could find a police commander who hadn't gouged undocumented workers for payoffs or bribes at one time or another.

Ethnic differences contributed to a pecking order that keyed one group against another. Emigrants from Oaxaca who spoke primarily the Mixtec or Zapotec languages knit defensively to resist assaults from those who regarded them as *indio* inferiors. Central American arrivals, many of whom hoped to receive asylum as political refugees when they reached the United States, clustered in nationalistic little communities. Bordello owners coaxed, bribed, or bought many younger women into prostitution. Stragglers who had hadn't been able to cross the Rio Grande successfully, or who had gotten lost in the Sierrita Mountains on their way to Tucson, or who had surrendered at gunpoint on Otay Mesa, passed themselves off as experienced *coyotes*, collecting what they could and abandoning their *pollitos* as soon as they could pocket the money and run. Deaths became more common and the prices charged by tried and true "professional" *coyotes* went up.

In September, 1996, the *Sacramento Bee* published a three-part series written by S. Lynne Walker that traced the illegal entry to the United States of a 21-year-old *aspirante* named Luis Muñoz whose mother in the little village of Chichimequillas, Guanajuato, told him that it was time for him to follow his father's and brothers' footsteps and go north to Chicago to earn money that would give him a better life.[21]

"She has raised twelve children in a three-room adobe house with no running water. None of them has had an education, and many days they have gone without food. She wants more for them, and she knows there is only one way for them to get it. Still, she wept when Luis left. 'Every time one of you leaves,' she told him, 'a piece of me dies.'"

Her son's first attempts to cross the frontier, similar to the first attempts made by Luis Pulido, resulted in failure. In Muñoz' case the arresting officers were Mexican police who busted him, his *coyote*, and several fellow *aspirantes* as they tried to scramble over a fence leading to the border east of Tecate. He was released after twenty-four hours and, like Pulido years before, had to seek the help of another *coyote*.

Twice his next trip was aborted, the first time because there were too many *indocumentados* in the group and he couldn't go with them and the second because Border Control agents were clustered near the place the *coyote* wanted to cross. Two nights later the *coyote* led them through dense fog to a shallow tunnel that other emigrants had dug beneath the 10-foot high steel fence. It was just deep enough that the members of the group could mole under it one by one. Crouching on the other side, they waited until the *coyote* ordered them to run, then together they bounded through mesquite and scrub cedar thickets toward a stagnant creek bed. The vegetation there was so dense the migrants couldn't be detected by a helicopter roaring overhead and the fog was thick enough that the *migras* had turned off the infrared night vision scopes set at intervals along the border to detect moving figures.

From the creek bed the *aspirantes* scrambled up a steep hill, slipping in greasy mud and diving under trees when the helicopter passed overhead. Finally reaching the crest, they paused for a minute. "From the ridge," Walker wrote, Muñoz "sees the silhouettes of children's swing sets in the back yards, and television sets flicker in distant homes. A great city stretches out before him, glowing in radiant light."

A glimpse, no more, for their journey wasn't over. The *coyote* led them down the hill to the outskirts of San Ysidro and pried open a huge metal grate. Holding onto each other the *indocumentados* followed the *coyote* through a huge rat-infested drainage pipe in darkness so dense they could see nothing. Gagging and trembling they tromped underground for over a mile, then finally emerged undetected. "The first leg of his trip to Chicago has come to and end." Walker ended the second installment of the *Bee* series. "He [Muñoz] is standing on U.S. soil and no Border Patrol agents are in sight."

The driver hired by the *coyotes* to take Muñoz to Los Angeles reeked of whiskey when he picked up the group of immigrants a few hours later. Detecting a car following him the driver accelerated past one hundred miles an hour, swerved toward an exit ramp and smashed into a compact car. He roared away before police arrived, cutting back and forth from freeway to freeway, and finally dropped the young man off at another safe house. That night, tucked into a secret pickup compartment, Muñoz was ferried past the Temecula checkpoint to Los Angeles where money wired to him from his brother in Chicago was waiting. As his *coyotes* advised, Muñoz spent part of the money getting his hair styled and buying new traveling clothes, a counterfeit green card and an airplane ticket from Ontario to Chicago. (He was less likely to be detected as a possible *indocumentado* at the smaller Ontario airport than at the more rigidly controlled LAX.) The day after arriving in the Windy City, Muñoz went to work scouring pans in a restaurant, a six-day-a-week job that paid him $1,000 a month, a "fortune for Luis," wrote Walker, "and a house for his mother."

The hair styling and new clothes became a typical ploy for evading Border Patrol detection. A *coyote* named Cedric Calderon described dressing up *indocumentados* to look like college students and driving through the Temecula checkpoint in a late-model car with them in the passenger seats.[22] Most Border Patrol agents, he claimed, pictured immigrants as dirty, shaggy, and scared and wouldn't pull clean-cut types over and ask them for IDs.

The average cost for one individual to leave his or her home community in Mexico and reach his or her destination north of the border is four to seven times the annual household income of the average rural Mexican family.[23] In Muñoz' case, described above, the immigrant's brother paid for passage—but as a loan guaranteed by the dishwashing job the *indocumentado* had waiting for him. In many cases it is the employer who pays the *coyote* and deducts the costs from the worker's first paychecks. Some of the worst examples of this twenty-first century indentured servitude have occurred in the Gulf Coast states, particularly Florida, and are described in more detail in seventh chapter.

While they don't actively participate in the process of bringing unauthorized immigrants into the United States, many legal and/or naturalized immigrants provide services to new arrivals, including meals, transportation, and safe houses. In most cases they do this to help members of their own particular communal or ethnic groups. Over time these mutual assistance networks have spread to include hundreds of associates, each providing some type of support: job and travel information, temporary housing, etc.

Krissman describes an Amnesty-legalized immigrant who travels back and forth to Oaxaca imparting information and advice on emigrating, making loans to pay passage, and sometimes driving *aspirantes* from his home community to the border. A cousin of his who lives near the Temecula checkpoint drives through to see if the *migra* are stopping cars, then phones the information back to the waiting *transportistas*.[24] So interconnected are most immigrant communities that such services are supplied as a matter of course. "It's the least we can do," a Chico, California legal immigrant told me. "It's something we pass along. Others helped us, so we help the newcomers. And they'll help those who come next."

For all the interconnections that exist, and all the support and help that they provide, crossing the border continues to be a hazardous experience. The "cat and mouse game" has become more intensive and more dangerous. Helicopters, high-powered all-terrain vehicles, infrared night-vision scopes, television propaganda, and steel walls make detection easier and apprehension more likely. Border patrol agents patrol major thoroughfares, radios tuned to reports of possible *indocumentado* intrusions. Their willingness to indulge in high-speed chases has triggered several spectacular accidents.

One of the most notorious occurred on April 17, 1998, after two panel vans cut past the Otay Mesa Mexican customs post by swerving into the inbound lanes at six o'clock in the morning and racing into U.S. territory. Mexican customs fired pistols at them but missed and two U.S. Border Patrol cars and a helicopter picked up the pursuit. The smugglers' vans roared west on Otay Mesa Road then swerved north on the 805 freeway toward Chula Vista and National City, the two Border Patrol cars' sirens shrieking as they followed. As the smugglers cut in and out through the early morning traffic, trying to outdistance the *migra*, one of the vans turned sharply onto a side road. As it did the driver lost control of the speeding vehicle and crashed into a concrete wall, ramming the thirty-four passengers who'd been jammed into the van against each other, the sidewalls and the roof. The Border Control agents and passerbys tugged bloodied, shocked, and weeping *indocumentados* out of the crumpled vehicle until paramedic-manned ambulances arrived. They transported the twenty-five most seriously injured passengers to nearby hospitals.

The agents called off pursuit of the second van after it detoured off Interstate 15 onto narrower but still heavily trafficked County Road 76 but a Canal 8 television helicopter, in the air to report traffic conditions, notified the Patrol where the driver and his twenty-nine passengers had abandoned the vehicle.

Like Muñoz, the two vanloads of *indocumentados* had had to evade police on both sides of the border. And like him the risky high-speed entry hadn't been their first attempt to cross. The same year that the accident occurred, the American Friends Service Committee reported that it wasn't unusual for *indocumentados* to report having made eighten or nineteen attempts to cross before successfully getting into the United States.

Given those statistics, Muñoz probably was lucky. He'd made only one unsuccessful attempt and had had others cancelled. Fortunately for him his *coyote* ring was well-organized. He was sheltered in safe houses in Tijuana, San Diego, and Los Angeles, and conveyed past Border Patrol installations in three separate vehicles, in two of which he'd lain cramped and hidden in concealed compartments. He paid out over $1,200—all of it borrowed money—and he understood that should he be stopped for any kind of infraction in Chicago he would be handcuffed, jailed, and deported. But he knew that, should that happen, he already would have had sent lots of money to his mother. And after all, that's why he had undertaken his dangerous journey.

The "cat and mouse" game has forced *aspirantes* to try to cross at more dangerous and difficult points but they have continued to cross in increasing numbers. Cornelius reports that not only did the number of undocumented farm workers increase yearly throughout the 1990s but so did the numbers of immigrant service employees and construction workers. "There is no evidence that the strategy [of tightened border enforcement] has produced shortages of illegal immigrants to agriculture, construction, low-level service occupations, or the supply of day laborers for landscaping and construction work."[25]

MORE AND MORE PERIL

"We apprehend people who are wandering out here for days," Border Patrol spokesman Jim Pilkington told another Sacramento *Bee* reporter, Mareva Brown, in September 1997.[26] He was talking about eastern San Diego county, where over a hundred Mexican migrants died every year during the mid-1990s trying to enter the United States. Fifteen froze to death in January 1997 after snow and freezing rain swept through the Cleveland National Forest and the San Ysidro mountains. Survivors told the Border Patrol that their *coyote* had led them to believe that they were within a few miles of roads that would take them to San Diego. One of the survivors had carried his twenty-year-old wife on his back while he desperately sought help and didn't realize that she had died while he was carrying her until searchers found him. Four others, abandoned by their *pollero* because they couldn't keep up with the rest of their immigrant group, froze in a rugged canyon.

The Clinton administration's decision to close the border east of Tijuana by erecting over thirty miles of solid steel fences and adding thousands of newly trained *migra* to patrol every foot of the fence line forced emigrants further east, where their choices were the trails that led around or through heavily wooded San Ysidro mountains and the Cleveland National Forest or the blistering deserts closer to Mexicali. Both are desolate, unpopulated areas where landmarks are indistinct and hiking difficult, particularly for persons unaccustomed to twelve to sixteen hours a day of forced walking. Most of those who died, like the four men mentioned above, were left behind because they couldn't keep up with the rest of their groups.

Since penalties were much heavier for someone caught smuggling *in-documentados* than for merely entering the United States illegally, most *coyotes* felt their first obligation was to save themselves and protect their employers. This was true for both those who led groups across the border and those who transported them past checkpoints and hauled them across the country. Often guides had to postpone or abort trip after trip in order to take advantage of fog, moonless nights, or security lapses. Frequently they fled at the first hint of Border Control approach.

Postponements could make *indocumentados* testy and impatient. Crammed into shantytown safe houses, tense and exhausted from days or weeks of uncertainty and travel, they would chafe at delays, accuse the *polleros* of deceiving them, of not delivering on their contracts. To prove their creditability the *polleros* would consent to riskier missions than they might otherwise have chosen. One was through the San Ysidro mountains and Cleveland National Forest, a four-day jaunt.

Just getting across the scrub-covered dunes east of Tecate to the first pines and cedars cost enormous effort. The mountains looked closer than they were and the emigrants had to start out at night. Once onto the rutted lower slopes they rested during the daylight hours then, at dusk, followed their guide along little used hiking trails. Progress was slow and tiring as they weaved into and out of gorges clogged with ocotillo and salt cedar. Many migrants complained if the *coyote* restricted how much water they could drink or if he shortened their rest periods. They would dive for cover every time a startled wild boar charged through the underbrush or they would scramble into a gully to evade being seen by overnight campers. The altitude, the thin air, the cold, the exertion brought dizziness, nausea, and exhaustion.

Short of sleep, tired, disillusioned, they often would argue, bicker, sometimes even come to blows. Then one or two in the group would start lagging behind. The others would try to help them, sometimes by tugging them up the winding trails as they climbed. Or someone would trip and twist an ankle and he or she would have to try to keep up hobbling on a makeshift crutch. The guide would get tense, nervous, miss a branch trail, and have to detour back in order to take it. By the third day, the group still would be twenty-four to thirty-six hours short of their destination. Finally, the weaker members couldn't keep going and had to give up. "We'll come back for you," the others would promise. Maybe a hiker or forest ranger or border patrol flyover would spot them and call a rescue crew. Maybe . . . or maybe not.

Crossing the desert further east was just as hazardous. Shade and shelter were nonexistent and distances deceiving. A coroner's investigator from Imperial County, which extends from its border with San Diego county to the Arizona state line, asserted in 1997 that a person couldn't carry enough water with him to make it across either the East Mesa or the area south of the Heber dunes. No one knows how many may have died and not been found but each year more bodies are discovered.

Tabulations of migrant deaths do not include those who die on Mexican soil. Every winter scores of would be or rejected border crossers become exposure casualties in Tijuana and Mexicali. Thousands more die of diseases contracted in the frontier cities. Dysentery, flu, and hepatitis outbreaks are common. Malnutrition is ever-present. Beatriz Ramirez in Tijuana reported in January 2000 that the harrowing experiences of migrants by *cholo* gangs along the border included murder as well as robbery and rape.[27]

Border Patrol spokesmen accused *coyotes* of "profiteering" and "taking advantage of these people's desperation" without acknowledging that tightening border security didn't change starving, landless people's feeling that their only hope for survival was getting to the United States. Many *coyotes* had themselves been *indocumentados* who had crossed the border successfully, then helped family members or friends do the same on subsequent occasions. Others were recruited because they knew or could learn the routes quickly. The businesses run by the *polleros* grew as they became more successful. They expanded by hiring more "heels," more recruiters, more guides. Many of these individual guides were teenagers; others had crossed and failed to earn the kind of money as temporary laborers that they could make working for the *polleros*.

By the turn of the twenty-first century not only the bus stations but the airports in Tijuana and Mexicali had become *pollero* hangouts. A sharp "heel" could pick out a prospective customer even if he was well dressed and flying in from Mexico City or Guadalajara. In the late 1990s inflation, cutbacks and factory closings displaced more and more workers, many of them with at least high school educations and technical or clerical job experience. Like most of those who'd preceded them through Tijuana they holed up in near-Avenida Revolución flophouses until they could make their first attempts to cross.

Some, better prepared and financially better off than rural immigrants, could purchase counterfeit U.S. visas for the going rate of $1,500 U.S. and take a taxi to San Diego. Others also caught rides in private vehicles. All along the border, from Tijuana to Matamoros, shade tree *carrocerías* were outfitting vans, pickups, and hatchbacks into individual personnel carriers. A compartment squeezed beneath the backseat of passenger car could accommodate an unseen passenger. So could the false floor in the bed of a pickup or a modification to a camper van. Some *aspirantes* merely hid in a trunk and hoped it wouldn't be opened for inspection.

Entry points become so congested by the mid-1990s that neither the Border Patrol nor customs could check the contents of every vehicle coming across. The driver ran the risk of being arrested for smuggling if he were caught; consequently he charged from $450 to $1,500 for the trip, depending on the destination. Most *coyotes* wouldn't take the chances themselves so they hired someone to drive the specially outfitted cars through the checkpoints. Many *indocumentados*, including Luis Muñoz, claimed their chauffeurs had been drinking or were high on drugs and the smuggling combines complained that the only persons willing to take the risks were drunks or addicts who desperately needed the money.

The authors of "Factors that Influence Migration" attribute the crackdowns during the 1990s (Operations "Hold the Line," "Gatekeeper," "Safeguard," and "Rio Grande") for stimulating people smuggling enterprises. By 1998, 73 percent of *indocumentados* attempting to cross were doing so with the help of *coyotes*. "... we find that smuggling has achieved enough regularity to become an established business with three segments; local agents, local and border smugglers, and border-only smuggling businesses, each with a menu of prices and services. Thus, unauthorized migrants have several packages of services available, and several options to pay for the cost of illegally entering the United States, including working in a coyote-provided or coyote-arranged job in the United States to repay smuggling costs."[28]

Although the Border Patrol and the politicians urging greater intervention touted the success of the operations named above and cited apprehension and deportation statistics to prove it, more than 70 percent of those attempting to cross did so without being caught. Ironically, the billions spent to "secure the border" increased the success rate that *aspirantes* were recording and made unauthorized entry a booming multi-billion dollar business.

Mexican Faces, American Dreams

HUTS, CAR BODIES, AND OLD MOTELS

The World War II *bracero* accord stipulated that employers had to provide adequate housing for the temporary workers. It defined "adequate housing" to include the availability of drinking water and sanitary facilities, heating and cooking units, beds, etc., and charged Labor Department employees with inspecting the facilities. Some of the bigger farms and ranches already had hired hands quarters on their properties. Others erected them, or converted barns or processing sheds into makeshift bunkhouses. In California, government officials reopened depression-era migrant camps for *braceros* to use. Some had concrete block foundations, wooden walls, and tent roofs. Others were more rustic. A camp set up for peach harvesters north of Sacramento included wooden-framed cubicles with tarpaper walls, some of which ripped apart during rain- and windstorms.

A former *bracero* who returned to California as an *indocumentado* remembered getting out of the truck that had hauled him and three other *braceros* from Los Angeles to Woodland. "There was nothing there," he told me, "just rows and rows of tomatoes and field corn. 'Where do we live?' I asked and the farmer pointed toward a truck stacked with two-by-fours and laminated sheet metal. 'There,' he grunted, 'start building!'"

Rundown tourist parks and resort cabins served for migrant housing in various central west and mountain states. Some, like the one in Torrington, Wyoming, were relatively pleasant. The individual cabins, though small, were solidly constructed and shaded by old cottonwoods. A path led down to the North Platte River, where a spillway created natural bathing pools. The beet sugar factory where most of the *braceros* worked was on the other side of the highway and operated twenty-four-hours-a-day. *Braceros* who worked different eight-hour shifts shared some of the cabins, some sleeping while the others worked and vice versa. A number of married couples with school-aged children lived in larger cabins nearby, although most of them had come north from Texas, not from Mexico.

Less comfortable was the bunkhouse on a Montana ranch. After an early fall blizzard roared south from Canada, blanketing the countryside and driving herds of antelope out of the frigid high country, the ranch owners fought through snowdrifts to check on the *braceros* who had been cutting and stacking the last of the alfalfa crop. The bunkhouse was empty except for ridges of frozen snow that had filtered through the window frames and cracks in the walls. Alarmed that the workers might have tried to outrun the storm and become icebound or frozen to death the owners rushed back to their house but were intercepted by their foreman, who informed them that the *braceros* had moved in with the mules and covered themselves with hay. As one of the *braceros* later explained, "We are used to animals. We can survive with them. What we cannot survive alone is the cold."

Despite the primitive conditions few of the *braceros* quit or complained. Paychecks compensated for most inconveniences. Many of the *braceros* had worked as migrant laborers in Mexico and had endured worse living conditions there. Wes Essex, a Montana ranch foreman during the 1940s, remembered refereeing arguments about the value of the dollars his *braceros* were being paid and their delight when they realized how much the thirty cents an hour they were earning would buy once they returned to Mexico.

How often or how well the Department of Labor inspected the farm and migrant camp accommodations is debatable. In most areas it was up to the individual farm owner to take care of details, including maintenance, food, and wages. Department personnel did follow up on more serious complaints but in many cases the season had ended and the *braceros* had returned to Mexico before any action could be taken.

Even with the shortage of department manpower, the program ran more smoothly than it did after 1948 when the Department of Labor turned the contraction, payment, and accommodation of workers over to farm owners. The new agreements authorized the department to periodically inspect work areas and work conditions, which included housing. Department representatives occasionally angered some farm owners by insisting that the owners improve working conditions and living quarters but in many areas the "adequate housing" consisted of hastily built shacks, shanties, crowded bunkhouses, and jerrybuilt shelters put up by the *braceros* themselves.

Most labor camps and other types of subsidized housing didn't differentiate among legal *braceros*, *indocumentados*, and Spanish-speaking migrants who were legal U.S. residents. During the 1950s and 1960s, caravans of migrants wended their way from southern California to Oregon, Washington, and Idaho and from El Paso through New Mexico and Colorado through the Central West to Wisconsin and Minnesota. Although many of the workers were single, others took families with them. The wives and children worked beside the men in the fields, the children often beginning this labor when they were five and six years old. Seldom did the migrants stay in any one place for more than a few weeks. Some had cars or old trucks; others traveled by Greyhound and often walked long distances to get from a highway stop to a campground and from there to a work place.

In the late 1950s, south of Sacramento on the road that leads to Brannan Island beside a deep rapidly flowing irrigation canal, I came across a little shrine made of painted cinder blocks and imbedded with tiny quartz stones. Faded artificial roses lay in a recessed cavity. Residents of a nearby migrant camp told me the parents of a seven-year-old who had slipped on the muddy bank, fallen into the canal and drowned had placed it there.

"It was cemented together with the mother's tears," one of the camp's residents told me with poetic matter of factness. She went on in Spanish to relate stories of broken legs, an amputated hand, a baby who'd died because her parents couldn't get her diarrhea to stop, a man crushed beneath a truck when he tried to adjust a jack under its axle. She, her husband, and two of their three children lived in a heavy canvas tent they'd bought in a Bakersfield army surplus store. The oldest child, a 10-year-old, had gone ahead to Yuba City with another family that had had room for him in the back of a pickup. He had work there, she explained, and as soon as her husband finished his job thinning sugar beets they would join him.

The camp, at first glance, seemed to be a scattering of old cars, canvas, and burned out *fogatas*. But as I entered it I realized that it extended for nearly half-a-mile along the side of the levee. Shelters built solely of brush shaded tied-together bedrolls and five-gallon tubs, several of which had been bent into primitive cook stoves. Army-type pup tents lay collapsed over their owners' possessions. Sheets of canvas pegged to a truck bed turned on its side and fastened to a pair of shovel handles driven into the sand formed a protective pavilion that housed at least two families.

I asked the woman who'd told me about the accidents how many lived in the camp and she shrugged. "We come and go," she told me. "It's hard to count."

In a plastic bucket, she scooped water out of the canal to cook a pot of beans. "It's all that we have to drink," she commented with the same shrugging acceptance she'd used describing accidents and death. "Sometimes it makes us sick but eventually we get used to it." She told me the men would arrive soon "with food and beer" and they would laugh and eat and drink and curse and fall asleep hoping that it wouldn't rain or the wind wouldn't blow or the canal overflow before morning.

A majority of single workers returned to Mexico during the winter but by the 1960s more and more migrant families stayed in the United States until they could begin work again in the spring. Those who'd followed crops into the northern Midwest usually returned to Texas where Spanish-speaking communities had expanded in and around Dallas, Ft. Worth, San Antonio, and Austin. Those who'd ended their work seasons in Washington, Idaho, and Montana retraced their routes to California, where the Sacramento and San Joaquin valley climates were less severe than they were further north.

Some migrants lived year-round in the reopened Dust Bowl labor camps. Both the men and the women sought pick-up jobs doing housecleaning, making tamales, or setting out smudge pots in the almond and orange groves. Because they had to scrimp to make their meager savings last until farm jobs opened in the spring, they often could not dress their children in more than homemade or used clothing and often sent them to school without lunches.

For many of these children the school experience was far from positive. "I hated school!" The hurt was still apparent for Amelia Rodriguez thirty-five years after she first stepped into a Tracy, California, third-grade class. "I had on an old dress and old shoes and the teacher couldn't understand my name and kept asking me to repeat it and each time I did I felt like I was shrinking and I tried to spell it but I couldn't remember how to pronounce 'g' in English. My vocal chords stopped working and I couldn't make any sounds at all. The kids around me were laughing and I turned because I wanted to run away and I bumped into a desk and fell down and they laughed even more."[1]

Although she spoke some English, she didn't speak well enough to keep up with her schoolmates. Just sitting in class made her so tense she screamed and almost fainted when someone touched her. She developed a tic in one eye and on her way to school discarded the lunch her mother packed for her because it contained tortillas and beans and "other things the regular kids didn't eat. I remember being glad when we left to go back out to work again. It took months before I felt like myself, like who I really was."

The expansion of farm production during the 1950s and 1960s increased the number of temporary workers needed to plant, thin, hoe, and harvest. As more workers joined the migrant caravans, places to live became even more difficult to find. Some of the more experienced migrants began to rent living quarters the year round. Emilio Maldonado remembered that the old Dust Bowl migrant camp outside of Gridley, California, sported several sturdy "garden homes" surrounded by patches of corn, tomatoes, melons, and fruit.[2] In addition, a number of jerrybuilt shanties and cabins were spotted under the sycamore and walnut trees and cattywumpus shacks teetered on their foundations across the unpaved roadway from a field of star thistles. During the height of agricultural production only a few residents—"grandmas and little kids and a few men who'd been so badly injured they no longer could work . . . "—remained in the camps to watch over all the residences, a woman who grew up in one of the camps remembered. She then added, "It was quite a thing for any of us to feel like we had a home to go back to."

HUSTLE, HATE, AND HOPE

To Carmelita Muñoz the Sacramento Valley was an endless expanse of sunshine-lit trees and distant frame houses set beyond her reach like shiny Disneylands. For five years, she moved among towns like Stockton and Corning and Modesto without ever entering one of those houses or ever going alone into a store, café, or school. She cooked, cleaned, cared for her husband, brother-in-law, and grown son, recited her prayers, and fulfilled all the traditional roles she had been brought up to honor in her native Michoacán. She was totally dependent on the men around her and on other migrant wives in the camps and towns in which she and her relatives lived. Until she fell sick and had to be taken to the emergency ward of a large hospital she never directly had spoken to anyone who didn't speak Spanish.

"I was so embarrassed!" she exclaimed during a May, 1989 interview. She covered her face with her hands at the memory of trying to deal with receptionists and nurses and doctors. "I was so ashamed!"

Thousands of immigrants remember experiences like hers. Isolated in a land that seemed foreboding and inhospitable, they entered a Spanish-speaking subculture that brushed against the dominant English-speaking majority only briefly and superficially.

"They live in fear of the things they can't understand," a California pub-lic health nurse told me.[3] The nurse, a Costa Rican immigrant who'd come to the United States when she was fourteen, described women coming from miles away to contact her because she was the only bilingual per-son they knew. Even in cities like Sacramento in the 1970s, immigrants were turned away from state Department of Health clinics because no one working there spoke enough Spanish to understand them.

Many young mothers, like Carmelita Muñoz, postponed getting medi-cal care for their infants because they neither could explain symptoms to medical personnel nor understand what they were being told. Years ago, I encountered a distraught mother outside an emergency room cradling a whimpering baby. I spoke to her in Spanish and she told me she was waiting for her husband to bring a friend's school-aged son from a town twenty miles away so he could translate what the doctors and nurses had tried to explain to her. "I just nodded *yes*, I thought I could figure it out," she whimpered, "but I couldn't." She showed me a prescription and a note written in English with instructions how to apply the medications and what kind of nutrition the baby should receive. I translated them for her and she seemed relieved; even so she asked me to wait with her un-til her husband arrived. The hospital environment seemed so alien and frightening she didn't want to be alone.

Crowded, unsanitary living conditions triggered camp epidemics throughout the 1960s and 1970s. A University of Colorado medical inves-tigator compared labor camps in that state to refugee camps in Biafra. He found children suffering from advanced cases of scurvy and kwashiorkor, diseases normally related to protein deficiency and starvation. Typhoid epidemics felled thousands of migrants in Florida in 1973 and struck oth-ers in New York a few years later. Contagious diseases frequently disabled the majority of camp occupants who shared unhealthy drinking water, crude sanitary facilities, and insect- or vermin-ridden food supplies.

Most *indocumentados* tried to avoid confrontations, friendly or not, with any persons with authority. In the 1970s, less than 5 percent of farm work-ers eligible for income tax refunds filed for them, in many cases not only because they did not understand that they should prepare tax returns but also because they did not trust any dealings with the government.

"It constantly is impressed upon us that entering the country without proper papers is unlawful," an applicant for the 1987 Amnesty program told me. "We are by definition criminals even if we do not feel that we have committed any crime. When we are together, *mexicanos, compañeros*, in each other's company, in our communities, we are okay, there is a bond-ing, a sense of security. But outside of our groups we run away from milkmen because their uniforms remind us of the *migra*. Just applying for a driver's license gives us heart attacks. Many of us do not argue about our paychecks even when we are being cheated because we are afraid to call attention to ourselves. We always are afraid there is an evil shadow hanging about our heads. Never do we feel quite safe."

As work became available in cities throughout the Southwest, West, and Midwest, both legal and undocumented immigrants moved into them, competing with newcomers from Vietnam, Korea, and the Middle East for below minimum-wage jobs. In 1990, the Midwest counted more than 1.2 million Mexican-born residents, almost half of whom lived in Chicago. Spanish was the dominant language in immigrant neighborhoods. Many residents seldom left the area in which they lived. They rehabilitated trades they'd learned before emigrating; others invented or learned how to become beauticians, cooks, small appliance repairmen, mechanics, plasterers, roofers, cab drivers, kindergarten assistants. They added Big Macs and pizza to their diets, but beans and chilis, tortillas and *carne asada* remained staples. They sang Mexican songs, danced to Latin music, hung portraits of the Virgin of Guadalupe over little altars in their livingrooms. Mexican *barrios* in Chicago, in Washington, D.C., in Denver, and Oakland and Los Angeles and other cities were crammed against equally marginal residential areas whose principal occupants were African-Americans, Koreans, Haitians, Puerto Ricans.

"We felt crowded, pushed all the time by everything," a welder remembered growing up in Chicago in the early 1970s. "At home we children shared bedrooms. We had almost no yard. The streets were always filled with people—kids, gangs, women with baby strollers, drunks. You had no privacy. You learned about everything. Sex, because somebody was doing it in the back of a parked car. Drugs, because some overdosed bozo collapsed on the sidewalk, or broke into the house down the street to steal a TV. My dad worked evenings in a restaurant—ten, twelve hours a night. He'd be gone when I got home from school and sleeping when I went to school. My aunt and uncle made *chorizo* in their kitchen. My cousin and I would take it around to stores and markets. You know how people treat ten-year-old kids trying to sell something? Cheat us. Tease us. We were always afraid of getting beaten up or robbed. Even the school classes were crowded. Some of the kids sometimes had to sit on the floor. I can't tell you how many of my teachers quit. In the winter everyone in the class would have colds from wading through the snow."[4]

Most immigrants moving into cities to work hard to make do with apartments in older rundown neighborhoods. Often families doubled up to reduce the amount each was paying for rent. They would cram old washing machines into kitchens, shove rollaway beds against walls, run extension cords from a single outlet to TVs, appliances, lamps, and electric fans. On cold days, they would move space heaters from room to room, or crouch around a kitchen oven. If their gas or electricity were turned off, they would huddle together in overcoats and earmuffs until they accumulated enough money to pay the bills. Staircases were hazards; plumbing often stopped up or overflowed and repairs were accomplished with whatever materials could be found cheaply: particle board, plastic tubing, discarded rug or linoleum scraps, wooden crates. On their way to and from work or school, the members of some families would detour through alleys to scavenge in garbage cans for things that might be of use. Old cars seats served as sofas and the big wooden spools used for winding cable as tables.

Fires were frequent. Many, like the pre-dawn blaze that roared through a tenement on Chicago's northwest side in December 1991 and killed ten immigrants, resulted from jerryrigged wiring. Garments hung out to dry over a space heater in Austin the same year fell and ignited, destroying a duplex. Faulty butane connections on old trailers, lighted cigarettes dropped on mattresses or rugs, gas leaks, thinners, or other chemicals being used for cleaning or repair ignited fires throughout areas where immigrants lived.

Winters in Texas and California were less severe than those that wrapped the Midwest and Northeast in ice, wind, and snow. Housing in most Texas cities was unofficially but strictly segregated throughout the 1960s into the 1970s, with African-American and Hispanic areas separated from the newer suburbs. Those were boom years for Texas' economy; not only did *indocumentados* pour in from Mexico but migrant and seasonal workers from rural Texas and neighboring states sifted into the cities instead of returning to their winter homes.

"In this society we are 'See-Throughs,'" a thirty-year-old junior college student who'd grown up in a migrant family in a small town south of Austin told those attending a 1973 University of Texas forum. "Thirty percent of this city's population is Hispanic. We are everywhere you look— on the buses, in restaurant kitchens, construction sites. In supermarkets, in department stores, in malls. You see us but you don't register that you've seen us. To you we don't have real existences."

Many immigrants—the majority—maintained contact with their home communities in Mexico and solidified the social networks to which they belonged. Family groups and communal groups congregated in the same areas and bonded both socially and economically. Temporarily out of work members lived with relatives or friends. They loaned money to each other, found jobs for each other, ate, talked, played dominoes, and watched television together, sewed and cooked for each other, and shared gardening spaces. By pooling resources many of them were able to start small businesses, particularly those that catered to the immigrant community—bakeries, taco stands, tortillerías, car repair shops. And they were able to pay *coyotes* to bring new family or community members to the places they lived.[5]

By the 1970s, these kinship networks had become self-sufficient operating units that included not only permanent immigrants but all the intermediaries that functioned between them and their relatives and cohorts in communities in Mexico. As these networks grew, they were able to absorb more newcomers and to offer basic accommodations, including employment and housing, as soon as the new immigrants arrived. Also, as these established Spanish-speaking communities grew, so did their accumulation of resources.

"If I don't leave my neighborhood [in Austin, Texas] I don't know that I'm not in Mexico," a mother of two young children told me in Spanish. She said she and her husband rented a two-room "Aunt Minnie" that he and another migrant had built on property owned by residents who had moved into Austin's Montopolis area twelve years earlier. Immigrant families filled parks on weekends, barbecued on vacant lots or on the fringes of Town Lake, congregated to play soccer, even at times sponsored illegal cock fights and quasi-legal boxing matches. There was work in construction, in agriculture, in food service and as domestics, and there was music and dances and celebrations of Mexican as well as U.S. holidays.

Immigrants to San Antonio, Texas discovered "a Mexican city run by *chaboches* [light-skinned foreigners]." Francisco Geraldo, an *indocumentado* who had taught school briefly in Mazatlán and who had slipped across the border thinking that his ability to speak English would help him find work, told a *La Raza* speaker that he had yet to meet a labor contractor who interviewed him in any language except Spanish.[6] Those arriving in East Los Angeles encountered similar experiences. A new arrival there told me, "I saw more Americans where I lived in Guanajuato than I ever see here."

Unlike migrant schoolchildren in rural areas, those who lived in city *barrios* often formed part of a Spanish-speaking majority in their classrooms. They were taught in English—"badly," the cook at one of my favorite East Sixth Street hangouts in Austin told me, "we gave the teachers hell. The best students were the girls and even the smartest ones, they weren't going any place—just, you know, get married. So we learn English but, so what? We still can't get jobs that are worth a damn." He laughed, then added, "But so what? We couldn't get them in Mexico either."

Many immigrant children had become translators for their parents by the time they reached the second- or third-grade. "We were like guide dogs for the blind," Enrique Leon, who became a San Antonio private investigator, remembered quivering with fright as he struggled to vocalize his parents needs to doctors, postal officials, bill collectors. Whenever there was a problem, he said, they would take him with them to mediate.

"There I was, this skinny, trembling kid and I would have to tell my father things he didn't want to hear, things that embarrassed me to say. And when he disagreed I would just about die facing up to somebody big and powerful but I had to do it for my father's sake."[7] Leon finished high school and later went to college on the G. I. Bill but he was an exception among immigrant children.

"Students who entered school speaking only Spanish were destined to drop out," asserted Roberto Martinez, who grew up in rural northern California in the 1960s.[8] Like many college-educated children of undocumented immigrants, Martinez insisted that education was the key to assimilation, a way to break the chain of poverty that for so many migrants had begun in their homelands.

As more newcomers poured into the *barrios* many of the older, more established immigrants gained importance, both financially and as arbiters, labor contractors, rental agents. They set up little stores and repair shops, *guardarías*, beauty shops; they established neighborhood rules; some even taught English classes. They helped arrange transportation, marriages, reconciliations, and funerals. When the wife of a Chicago O'Hare airport porter died, the porter insisted on sending her body back to Fresnillo, in Zacatecas, for burial. One of the more established community members took up a collection to help him with the costs of embalming, casket, and transportation. The porter vowed to reimburse everyone who contributed and to erect something to his wife's memory in Fresnillo, even though it meant giving up his apartment and moving to a rented room where he only could eat cold meals and wash his clothes in a laundromat four blocks away. Rather than argue with him, the go-between agreed to handle the reimbursements by dropping by the porter's room every payday and distributing the money the porter gave him.

"For many of us," Marco Antonio Flores told me, "the church was the tie back to our beginnings." Baptisms, first communions, weddings, *quinceñeras* were performed as they'd always been done in the old country. But when Flores first arrived in Chicago there were few Spanish-speaking priests. Even northern California's Diocese of Sacramento, where

40 percent of the congregation was Hispanic, had no Spanish-speaking clergy until 1970. In 1995, despite the fact that nearly 30 percent of American Catholics were Hispanic, only 3 percent of the priests in the United States spoke Spanish.

As church authorities recognized the growing need to serve the immigrant population they began to offer masses in Spanish in many of the churches that served the newcomer population. Attendance increased but many parishioners still felt estranged because most of the Spanish-speaking priests were not Mexican and didn't mix with the community as the priests they had known in Mexico had done.

Nevertheless, Flores remembered, the church and the activities connected with it provided something solid and unchanging in world that many immigrants sensed was supercharged with uncertainty and change.

A RIGHT TO BE SEEN, A RIGHT TO BE HEARD

By mid-1988, the situation in the Gridley, California, Farm Labor Housing camp had become "a disaster for families." Residents described vehicles careening through their yards and addicts shooting up under the trees. Head Start and Migrant Education teachers stopped going to the camp after one of them was hassled by a drug-dealing bully. Parents refused to let friends of the children who lived in the federally-maintained housing project visit them and mothers from the project kept their children indoors because they feared for their lives.

Calls to law enforcement netted little help. The users merely moved into nearby orchards when they saw a sheriff's deputy approach and the drug sellers moved inside and temporarily locked their doors. Although virtually every family in the project objected to the *droguistas*, the legitimate residents felt helpless to oppose them. The dealers, claiming to be farm workers, sold openly and defiantly, knowing that their neighbors were afraid to confront or report them for fear of attracting law enforcement attention to their immigration status. Few of the residents spoke English and none of the sheriff's deputies spoke enough Spanish to communicate with them.

"Finally we couldn't stand it anymore," remembered resident Amelia Rodriguez. "We had to take a stand for our children."[9] Camp members banded together and Farmers Housing Authority, the federal agency responsible for the housing area, collaborated with an interagency narcotics task force to plant undercover agents in the camp. At the same time a small consortium of educators, parents, and community workers went individually to each of the resident families and urged them, "Hey, this is your home, you can't be silent all the time." In November uniformed officers arrested sixteen "principal heroin and cocaine sellers and a number of ancillaries." A subsequent raid six months later netted five more dealers. A committee of camp residents set up a new governing board and the Housing Authority agreed to hire a private security guard to patrol the camp.

By 1988, both Amnesty and drugs had become part of the migrant experience. Through Amnesty some three million *indocumentados* achieved the right to work and to live in the United States without fear of being deported. But many had more to fear than the *migra*. Gangs ruled huge sections of cities on both sides of the border. Crack and heroin dealers took over entire neighborhoods. As more immigrants arrived, each wave seemingly poorer and more desperate than the one that had preceded it, adequate housing became even scarcer and Border Patrol vigilance more repressive. Immigrants who had managed to establish themselves with transitional housing and semi-permanent jobs resented the newcomer flow. "They give a bad name to Mexicans," I heard former *indocumentados*, legalized through the Amnesty program, complain.

Many of the newcomers were Guatemalans, Nicaraguans, Salvadorans, Hondurans. Not only were they fleeing poverty, they were fleeing war, repression, invasions. They needed to work to make money to send back to their homeland and work was available in the United States, particularly in agriculture and construction. North of San Diego, California, large groups of them moved into the canyons, sleeping and eating under plastic sheeting then scrambling up the hillsides to line up along the highway or in municipal parking lots hoping the driver of the next truck or pickup would jab a finger toward them and say, "You! You! You, c'mon!"

These migrants, contracted by the day and paid by the day, seldom could accrue enough money to rent even the most dilapidated housing. Often they carried everything they owned with them, sometimes burying their few possessions under brush or in caves while they looked for work. Many feared returning to their campsites alone, or late at night, because roving gangs from San Diego, or from eastern Los Angeles, or Temecula, would be lying in wait to assault them. When it rained, or when it was damp or windy or the coastal cities were fog-bound, only a small percentage of those hoping for work in construction or for the flower, orange, or strawberry industries would be selected and those not tapped would shuffle back to their canyon shelters. They'd build little fires to warm themselves and heat the cans of beans or packages of Oriental noodles they'd purchased at one of the convenience stores along the highway.

"We live in cardboard shacks with no running water, electricity, phone service, and with no way to communicate to the outside world," a resident of a hidden enclave called Los Diablos, told a state panel investigating the living conditions of farm workers.[10] Hundreds of immigrants who worked in nearby Del Mar and the surrounding farms and orchards lived there and kept secret the exact location of their dwellings near or in the Torrey Pines State Reserve south of Encinitas and north of San Diego. They posted lookouts to warn of possible encroachments and shared meals, beverages, and medicines depending upon who had earned how much during any given time period.

Drinking water was a constant problem. Many set out plastic buckets to collect rainwater but rain also often brought mudslides and mired the lower levels of the canyons and barrancas with cesspool-like slime. The same buckets served as laundry tubs in which a change of clothes could be soaked with a sprinkling of detergent, rubbed clean, and hung on a tree branch to dry overnight. Periodically the workers would return to the canyons to find their campsites torn apart, water buckets smashed, and clothes ripped—graphic indications that those living in permanent residences around them didn't appreciate their presence.

Some migrants told a *New York Times* writer in 1990 that residents of the coastal towns yelled insults at them, spit at them, and threw garbage at them.[11] The same year a migrant waiting for a possible employer at a Carlsbad supermarket parking lot was bound hand and foot, blindfolded, and put on display wearing a sign *No más aquí!* Immigrants camped in the hills near Poway, east of Encinitas, became the objects of racist venery when "sportsmen" armed with paint pellet guns pursued them through the hills, spattering them and causing more than a few to suffer cuts, bruises, and broken limbs as they tried to escape. More wantonly, a nineteen-year-old hunter who bragged that he "hated Mexicans" shot and killed two migrants, one of which was a U.S. citizen, near San Diego in February 1990. He was convicted of first-degree murder and sentenced to fifty years to life in the penitentiary.

The sentencing didn't deter attacks on migrant campers in the area. An Alpine monthly news sheet, the *Mountain Empire Press*, labeled emigrants camping along Alpine Creek "bugs" and encouraged "sending them a message." A message in October 1992 included an attack by half a dozen assailants armed with baseball bats. The attack left three migrants, all legal U.S. residents, with fractured cheekbones, arms, and skulls.

Despite the immigrant bashing, citizen complaints, and physical harassment, the trucks pulling into the parking lots, the fingers signaling "You! You! You!" didn't decrease. The area's booming economy depended on cheap labor that the migrants could supply. As a San Diego immigrant-aid worker told a citizens' forum in Encinitas, "You want the work they do to get done, but you want them to be invisible after they do it."[12]

In 1991 an estimated 300,000 to 1 million migrants worked at least parts of the year on California farms and ranches. Less than 6 percent of them resided in state-licensed farm labor camps like the one in Gridley.[13] Others, following crops and temporary employment, lived where they could. A California Farm Bureau Federation spokesperson told me that most large growers had stopped providing transient housing, both because of "over regulation" and because "they don't have to, the workers come whether there's housing or not." In 1965, there were over 5,000 state licensed and inspected camps in California. By 1982 less than a third of those remained. And in 1992 there only were 532, even though the number of migrants seeking housing had increased.[14] Barns, garages, and storage sheds, most without either sanitary facilities or safe electrical wiring, had replaced them.

Without the money for conventional housing and a gradual erosion of employer-sponsored housing, low-income immigrants had to take whatever was left. In many cases that meant renting from someone who had no intention of doing more than to collect rent for dwellings unfit for human habitation. Rent often exceeded wages; worker housing in the Sonoma Valley, down a dirt lane from the exquisite mansions of winery owners and Bay Area executives, cost more per month than many workers earned, even though the unscreened and unheated shacks had been condemned by county housing inspectors.

Workers who filed suit against Fresno, California, raisin producer Gerawan Ranches claimed they slept in cramped bunks stacked three high and often refused to use the bathroom because the toilets backed up and everything was covered with cockroaches and flies. In a deposition made after California Rural Legal Assistance filed suit, owner Ray M. Gerawan retaliated that the workers were responsible for the cockroaches and he wasn't about to pay costs for "busted windows, inability to control, can't get people out, whores, fights."[15] He had the camp bulldozed in 1990 rather than to try to renovate it.

By the 1990s rents for even one-room shacks ran $250-350 a month. Many of these structures were converted outbuildings or garages, or semi-rural 1930s-era jerrybuilt houses without foundations. Many depended for electricity on an extension cord running to some other building's outlet and for cooking on a hotplate or butane stove jammed into a corner. Typically more than one family would share the room, particularly if they only were going to be working in the area for a short time. One of two peach orchard workers living in an abandoned tool shed near Raisin City, California, told the Sacramento *Bee* in 1991, "To be able to get a house around here you have to make about ten dollars an hour. If I put the money out for a house I wouldn't be able to eat." He then went on to say, "We really miss our people. Here you feel so alone. Here there are no friends and there is no family. You are only here to send some money back to Mexico. Our families don't know the conditions we're living in. If they did they would be really sad." Both men admitted they would go back to Guadalajara if they could but neither had been able to save up the $200 that the airfare would cost.[16]

Abandoned pickup camper shells, some so battered they couldn't be moved without falling apart, became living quarters. An *indocumentado* named Jose Diaz told me he had slept for three weeks in a huge metal trash bin near Raisin City. Some migrants who worked with him had rented a mosquito net tent for $17 a week and paid a dollar a day to bathe under a hose connected to a faucet outside a barn.

"Abominable," Placer County (California) sheriff's office community outreach worker Annamarie Theis described migrant living conditions around resortland Lake Tahoe, on the California-Nevada border.[17] Thousands of Spanish-speaking immigrants who came to work in the restaurants, motels, ski resorts, and casinos struggled against winter layoffs in crowded campers, abandoned motels, storage sheds, and mountain cabins. Though dependent on cheap labor, the tourist industry, like agriculture and construction, was cyclical and subject to economic ups and downs. The up times provided work for everyone: dishwashers, kitchen helpers, maids, busboys, maintenance men, janitors, car park attendants. But with the first twitches downward came layoffs. Without work neither individuals nor families could pay rent on minimal housing, like an 8'x10' storage shed without hot water and only one electric light bulb for which nine people paid $550 a month rent on the lake's north shore.

While one could camp in a San Diego-area canyon with only a plastic tarp and a couple of layers of clothes during the winter, one needed more in the Sierras. Snows drifting five and six feet deep closed roads and half buried old mobile homes tucked under pines around Kings Beach and Tahoe City. Public health officials there reported frostbite and malnutrition among children and high incidences of influenza, bronchitis, and colds among adults. Burns, falls, and lung problems brought on by inadequate ventilation were commonplace. A faulty connection on the butane heater in a rented trailer ignited and destroyed everything that a family of seven owned, including shoes and clothing. They had to move into a temporary shelter, then share rental space with another family.

As noted in the Introduction and in the previous chapter, the U.S. government's increasingly militant border control strategy corresponds with an increase in permanent settlement by target earners who otherwise would have returned to their home countries during periods of lax employment.[18] Cornelius points out "when the median *coyote* cost was $237, 50 percent of male migrants returned to Mexico after two years in the United States; when the *coyote* cost was $711, only 38 percent returned . . . it is entirely possible that the current strategy of border enforcement is keeping more unauthorized migrants *in* the United States than it is keeping out."[19]

By the early 1990s, the economy had turned from robust to dismal and states like California were wracked by excruciating budget cuts and industry downsizing. In 1993, a San Francisco, California, agency that coordinated a city-run day-laborer program reported that over 80 percent of those showing up for manual labor jobs listed themselves as "homeless."[20] Many who emerged from construction sites, from beneath freeway overpasses, from alley doorways shivering and hungry and finding no work resorted to petty crimes—thefts from delivery vans and restaurant kitchens, panhandling, dealing drugs. Many turned up in city-run hospitals suffering from malnutrition or exposure or dysentery. Usually they would treated and released to the same environment they'd left, no better off economically or physically than they'd been when they entered.

Few *indocumentados* had access to any kind of health care, except for that provided by emergency wards. Many would wait until they became desperate, then stumble in suffering from complications that wouldn't have existed had they sought medical help sooner. In many hospitals, the medical staffs were so short-handed, they could give only brief and sometimes curt attention to incoming patients who had no way of understanding what kinds of documentation they needed. Some of these patients would leave without getting care, others like single mother Cecilia Lopez of San Francisco would pass out waiting in line to get a necessary identification card and be gurneyed to a treatment ward.

Few hospitals or clinics anywhere in the United States offered any documentation in Spanish and many immigrants, particularly *indocumentados*, were leery of signing anything or going to any kind of government office. Men and women working at minimum wage or less-than-minimum wage jobs, being paid by the day, the week, or the job, seldom were able to get far enough ahead financially to be able to afford to be out of work for sustained lengths of time. Six weeks into a job near Fresno, a nineteen-year-old *indocumentado* severely wrenched his back and shoulder lifting filled crates onto a truck. Though in pain he continued working because he didn't want his employers to dock his pay but the following morning he could not raise his arm more than a few inches away from his chest. His seventeen-year-old pregnant common law wife borrowed aspirins for him and he went back to his job site but was so incapacitated the foreman sent him away. Unable to afford either a doctor or food, in pain, hungry, and bitterly depressed, he talked about committing suicide until campground neighbors collected enough money to pay the couple's bus fare back to Mexico.

Neighbors and rescue workers couldn't save the life of Manuel and Catalina Torres' six-year-old daughter when she slipped and drowned while bathing in a lake near Lodi, California. Injured in a farm accident in 1984, Torres was forced to use crutches to walk and watched her disappear. Immigrants Ana Celia Zamora and a friend dragged a ten-year-old girl out of a canal near Austin, Texas a year later. Neither knew how to give artificial respiration nor knew what to do with the blood oozing out the child's nose. Car after car passed as they desperately tried to get someone to call an ambulance. When it finally came the paramedics refused to let either of them ride with the victim to the hospital because neither was related to her or knew her. They later were told that the youngster had died.

A former *indocumentado* who returned to Mexico "because my wife insisted that California was not a place to rear our children" described the small town in Michoacán where they had met as "terribly poor but peaceful, orderly, predictable." There they'd been poor but they hadn't felt as poor as they had in Riverside County where they'd felt constantly pushed, constantly hassled by "purchases, overtime, gunshots, drugs." One of their neighbors had been killed in a bar fight, another in a freeway accident in which his wife had lost a leg. The *indocumentado* and his wife had been robbed twice and the daughter of another neighbor had been raped. Worse than anything else, he claimed, was losing their identity. "We weren't Mexicans anymore. We were nobodies."[21]

Young Juan Mercado wanted to be somebody. Twenty-two years old, naïve but intrepid, he entered the United States as an *indocumentado* in 1989 and made his way, alone, to Oakland, California. Within three years he'd earned enough to pay *coyotes* to bring his parents and his nine brothers and sisters, a few at a time, to east Oakland, where they were able to lease a pizza parlor and operate it as a family, doing all the work, including deliveries, themselves.

"They worked like slaves," a Christian Fellowship minister who knew them told the *Sacramento Bee*, "and they were paid like slaves."[22]

On a delivery with his father in February 1993, the twenty-five-year-old Mercado was shot and killed during a robbery attempt. The five assailants escaped. Neither his father nor his mother could bear to live in the United States any longer. All of the energy and hopes and dreams had ended in a wood coffin and borrowing enough for a funeral and transportation to a quiet little cemetery in a distant Mexican town.

Statistics catalogue migrant deaths that occur on the border. No statistics are available for the number of immigrants who, like Juan Mercado, died after reaching the United States. Nor do any statistics indicate how many infants died at birth or shortly after birth because of a lack of medical attention, or a lack of basic nutrition, or the inability to resist an infectious disease. The statistics do not record pesticide poisonings or loss of limbs, miscarriages or maimings resulting from job accidents. Maricela Ornelas lifts a claw-like right hand she punctured jamming a bodkin through leather linings in an Austin, Texas sweatshop. A thirty-year-old who no longer can walk after months of ten-hour days in a North Carolina tobacco plant navigates her dusty neighborhood in an old wheelchair. There are statistics for the numbers of crimes committed by Spanish-speaking immigrants but not for crimes committed against them by employers, by law enforcement, by vigilante groups like those who attacked young Lázaro Romo in front of a Chico, California Safeway store.

Romo, a legalized immigrant and father of two young children, worked as a host in a local steakhouse. One hot August night in 1993 he and several friends were gathered around a soft drink vending machine outside the supermarket when several locals, led by a nineteen-year-old, drove up to them shouting "beaners" and "spics," then jumped out of their vehicle.[23] Romo's friends dashed back inside the market but Romo didn't make it. A vicious attack left him close to death. He was rushed to a local hospital and survived three-and-a-half hours of neurosurgery but never completely regained his health.

The attack, like many made against legal and undocumented immigrants, was totally unprovoked. The Border Patrol records deportations but there are no statistics that indicate how many prospective immigrants may have tried and failed to cross the border, or how many tried and tired of what my friend Jose Mata called "this battle of the many for the few rewards," or how many tried and were thrust back into Mexico, or how many tried and decided the achievement wasn't worth the price and went back to the country in which they were born. Throughout Mexico and Central America, I've run into men and women who lived in Los Angeles, or La Mesa, Texas, or Orland, California, or Memphis, Tennessee. Some have good memories of the United States, some bad. Some regret having returned to Mexico; others are glad that they did.

When twelve-year-old José Vicente Jara returned with his parents to visit relatives in Villa Guerrero, Jalisco, people who knew his family greeted him, *"Órale pocho, como le va?"* Finally one of his cousins told him what *pocho* signified: half-breed, foreigner, *creado en el norte.* (The dictionary definition is "pale," or "half-ripe," which, when applied to a person, indicates "not quite real" or "less than full-fledged.") No matter how often he went back, he realized, he always would be a *"pocho."* And no matter how long he lived in the United States, he always would be a "Mexican," being, as he stated, "part of two worlds and belonging to neither.

"It's really strange," he added, "fighting for your rightful due when the two cultures that are equally responsible for your identity want no part of you."[24]

WORSE, NOT BETTER

Sons and daughters, grandsons and granddaughters of some of the first *indocumentados* to enter the United States now are judges and county supervisors, Major League baseball players, university professors, surgeons. They remember that their forbears worked long hours in the fields and in other manual labor jobs so that they could go on to something better. Not all of the children of those early immigrants were that successful, however. Some continued to work in the fields as their parents had. Some became rebels and joined gangs, or became criminals and went to prison. Some continued to live in Spanish-speaking *barrios* while others chose to become "Americans of Mexican ancestry" and merge into the dominant English-speaking culture.

As these sons and daughters were going on to whatever their lives in the United States brought, hundreds of thousands more immigrants were crossing the border. Many filled niches that those who preceded them had vacated—minimum wage and below-minimum-wage jobs in agriculture, construction, and food service. They filtered into migrant camps and city *barrios*, impacting both as housing became more scarce. As their numbers increased, they had to scramble harder for jobs, compete both with the thousands arriving at the same time that they had and with those who'd arrived a few years before. From the states bordering the U.S.-Mexico frontier, they followed crops and job openings to Wisconsin and Minnesota, to Chicago, Washington, D.C., even Maine and Alaska and various Canadian provinces. The money they sent back to Mexico—$50, $100, $200 at a time—did more to finance that country's economy than any of its major industries, including at times the exportation of oil.

What had begun in the 1950s as an immigration of younger male workers from central Mexico seeking temporary jobs in agriculture expanded to include men, women, and children from throughout that country. During the 1980s, droughts, clear cutting, and the merging of tiny farming plots into large cattle, cotton, and rice acreages forced hundreds of thousands of small farmers and their families off their land. Many of those arriving at the border came from Oaxaca, Chiapas, and Central America as well as urban centers in Mexico. Living conditions in some areas in the United States had deteriorated to the point that some migrants were treated little better than animals or slaves. But for every horror story brought back to Mexico—assaults by criminal bands, border repression, abominable living conditions, back-breaking work at sub-minimum wages, discrimination— in even the smallest of Mexican communities families were receiving money from relatives in the United States.

Even if one believed the horror stories, one could see that the dollars were coming, linking those who worked in the United States to those who remained in the Old Country. Until the post–World War II migrations, rural Mexican families clustered for generations in the same areas, interconnected through marriage. Bonds remained tight between siblings. Cousins were like brothers and sisters. It was not uncommon for children to shift from one family to another, or for parents to leave children behind when they migrated. Women seldom remained single after they became widows or were abandoned and often merged their families with those of their new partners. These multiple connections tied individuals into large, interdependent extended families. When members of one of these extended families emigrated, they remained emotionally attached—and financially responsible—to those who remained behind.

A few months after I'd interviewed a former Michoacán schoolteacher named Gustavo Castillo for a northern California alternative weekly, I ran into him at a park outside of Corning, a town with a large Spanish-speaking population surrounded by olive orchards. He insisted that I meet the more than twenty people at his family picnic. Besides his wife and two children, they included the uncle who had helped Gustavo come to the United States, the uncle's wife, whom the uncle had met and married in northern California, her two older children and two of their cousins, Gustavo's cousin, the son of another uncle, his wife, and young children, the cousin's wife's aunt and her partner and her partner's father and mother and two of their children. Gustavo called each of them *"tío,"* *"primo,"* *"tía"* without distinguishing between blood and in-law relationships. "We are all family," he explained. "We all help each other." He added that in Michoacán, the family included several "adopted" members, including the Hidalgo-born wife of a cousin who had been killed in a tractor accident three years before in northern California.

During a California legislative session in the early 1990s, an assembly member who was trying to link illegal immigration with drug dealing asked where these *indocumentados* got all the money it took to pay *coyotes* if they weren't dealing drugs. "Their families pay for it," a witness, the son of migrants, replied. He went on to explain that the three most important things in the lives of migrants were shelter, food, and sending money back home. If there wasn't enough money to do all three, the worker did without shelter and food.[25]

"You don't leave the family even when you move far away," northern California schoolteacher Alejandra Casteñeda, the daughter of migrants, told me. "You take it with you. It never goes away."

Where the Dollar Is King

ACE IN THE HOLE

Immigration patterns changed between 1955–2005 but not the work being performed by undocumented migrants. They did what no one else would do at wages that no one else would accept, thus providing a reserve labor force from which agriculture and industry could draw. Designating their entrance into the United States as a criminal act minimized their ability to complain or contest either how much they were paid or the conditions under which they worked. As long as too many from this reserve labor force weren't deported or didn't move into permanent employment there always would be manpower available for seasonal and temporary work.

Since government regulations limited what work *braceros* could and couldn't do, both farm and ranch owners and construction and factory managers filled manpower needs by hiring jobseekers without questioning their nationality or legal status during the 1950s and 1960s. Employers who needed only a few workers and supervised them personally usually didn't require translators or foremen. However, larger concerns needed someone who spoke the migrants' language and understood their customs to recruit, train, and supervise. A number of ex-*braceros* became labor contractors and field bosses, or crew leaders, during the 1960s and afterwards. Most labor contractors spoke English and Spanish well enough to be understood in both languages and knew something about the work they were overseeing.

As intermediary between the owner and the work crew the labor contractor wielded tremendous authority. He could hire, fire, discipline, fine. He could charge work crew members for transportation, water, toilet paper, and other items. He could regulate work hours, set production schedules, and assign the most difficult or the easiest tasks to whom he chose. He was the source of supplies and services, from breakfast tortillas to after-work alcohol. All worker requests and complaints siphoned through him. So did paychecks and worker purchases. As Douglas Massey records in *Return to Aztlan*, many labor contractors brought relatives and *compadres* from their home communities in Mexico to work for them, creating a flow of work and money that linked the receiver area with the sender area.[1] Not only did the labor contractor benefit from his position as intermediary and foreman in the United States, he became a much respected social and political figure in his former home community in Mexico, often sponsoring local projects and events, loaning money, and investing in small businesses and industries.

Most labor contractors were themselves the field bosses but those with larger responsibilities put job supervision in the hands of a crew chief, or "*subjefe.*" According to many farm workers, *subjefes* were worse to work for than either owners or labor contractors. They could make workers' lives as miserable as they wanted, dock them a quarter-of-an-hour for pausing to take a drink of water, demand impossible production results, and skim money on whatever pretext they chose. Often the *subjefe* was a cousin, nephew, or brother-in-law over whom the labor contractor had some kind of family control.

Frequently small-time labor contractors disappeared after two or three weeks, taking with them all or most of what their migrant labor crews had earned. A group of Oaxacans working in the garlic fields outside of Gilroy, east of San Jose, California, in 1991 were defrauded by a contractor named "Juan" who'd given the farm owner a fictitious last name. A few weeks later, another contractor, this one named "Miguel," absconded with another two weeks of wages, leaving the immigrants penniless after more than a month of hard labor.

Labor contractors worked long hours but made good money—as much as $300,000 a year by the early 1990s. My friend Jose Mata of Oroville, California told me that contractors for the tomato harvests in and around Sacramento and Woodland, California pocketed 45 percent of their crews' earnings. Their rationale: They had to send social security payments on each worker to the government; they passed out packaged lunches so the workers wouldn't have to leave the fields to eat; they provided transportation; they had to pay workmen's compensation insurance; they had to hire extra help to run errands, take care of paperwork, and translate for farm owners, truck drivers, and law enforcement.

Few of them, however, found it necessary to offer detailed accountings of these expenses to their workers and many failed to provide housing they had promised. Mata repeated stories told by *indocumentados* who paid for water scooped out of an irrigation canal and who were forced to walk nearly nine miles after working twelve to fourteen hours because the paid-for transportation "broke down." Some Gridley farm labor camp residents remembered sleeping in barns heaped with dried manure that comprised the lodgings their crew chief had promised.

Mata called labor contractors "caciques," comparing them to the rural strongmen in Mexico who wielded control by combining intimidation with force. Some of the contractors, he said, charged the workers for the tools they used as well as transportation, housing, and meals. "The poor bastards would slave all day, the contractor on their backs shouting for them to hurry, docking them everything, even for taking a piss, then rip them off when it came time to pay up."

Many self-employed FLCs (farm labor contractors) operated out of their house or their van and kept minimal, if any, records. They seldom were reported for hiring *indocumentados* since their workers often came from their hometowns in Mexico and depended upon them for everything from food to transportation and work hours.[2]

Not all contractors were villainous, Mata agreed; some were capable ex-field hands who'd proved they could get the needed work done for their employers. But with more jobseekers than jobs, and the jobseekers by definition criminals for being in the country, the contractors could do what they wanted. Besides, he added, many *indocumentados* felt more secure working for a labor contractor than they did for a *"gringo"* they couldn't understand.

"We Mexicans," he added, "respond to authority. Ours is a very patriarchal system. In Mexico the *patrón*'s word is law."

AND THE NEXT DOLLAR, WHERE IS IT COMING FROM?

Asked if it didn't bother her that she was working illegally for an employer who wasn't reporting her wages, an Oroville, California cleaning woman responded, "What is it that work is illegal? Stealing is illegal. Murder is illegal. I get up very early, I go to her house, I scrub, clean, wash, dig, all very hard with almost no rest. I get one dollar per hour. And you say I am doing a crime?"[3]

Relatively few immigrant workers concerned themselves with tax exemptions, social security, or signed time cards. Throughout the latter half of the twentieth century over 45 percent of the economic activity in Mexico was unrecorded, unreported, and untaxed. Doctors, scientists, politicians, translators, taxi drivers, building contractors, prostitutes, and various

Mexican professionals and business persons ran predominately cash businesses. Wages, prices, and commissions were arbitrary, even in government offices. The woman quoted above said she preferred being paid in cash since "the banks they don't like people who don't speak English."

But working "under the table" in the United States has had its disadvantages. Immigrants often took jobs without knowing how or when they were going to get paid. Labor contractors sometimes pocketed all of the earnings of the people they hired and vanished. Employers disappeared. Others shelled out less than they'd promised when the job was finished, or threatened to call law enforcement and have the workers deported instead of paying them. An immigrant from the little town of Tamuín in northeastern Mexico spent two weeks salvaging metal from junked cars in Duncanville, Texas, with nothing to show for his effort but blisters and a worthless check on a cancelled bank account. In Orange County, California, Ignacio Salgado's furniture factory owner closed his shop and disappeared without paying. Salgado filed a claim against the employer and won, but the state left it up to Salgado to find his ex-employer and demand his money.

When state officials closed a northern California convalescent home for health code violations the former owners refused to pay their employees' back wages. One of the employees, a single mother who spoke little or no English, was owed for more than five weeks of work which she was unable to collect. Farm workers in northern California applying for work through the state's Employment Development Department in 1998 discovered that their employers had not reported any of their earnings, disqualifying them not only from benefits but from access to job applications.

Those of us who've lived in Mexico for extended periods of time realize that Mexicans are far more interested in what is happening in the United States than Americans are interested in what is happening in Mexico. By the same token, the "U.S. labor market is proportionately more important to Mexican workers than Mexican workers are to the U.S. labor market."[4] Mexico's labor force includes nearly forty million individuals, five million of whom—over 12 percent of employed Mexicans—are working in the United States, many without proper documentation. Many others earn what they can from irregular jobs like cleaning houses or street sales—cash only, no benefits, no saving for the future.

Instead of discouraging the hiring of *indocumentados*, the sanctions authorized by the Simpson-Rodino Act encouraged employers to embark "on a pattern of systematic wage discrimination against Latinos in general and undocumented Mexicans in particular. Rather than taking the time and trouble to identify which migrants were undocumented, they simply discriminated against foreign-looking workers; and rather than denying them jobs, they simply lowered their wages."[5] The workers, being illegals, had to take what they could get or be fired and the employers, by turning hiring over to labor contractors, absolved themselves of the responsibility of knowing what documents those working for them might possess.

Andruw Korber, a former Los Angeles Legal Aid advisor complained, "that a marginal employer can put on temporary help and offer no benefits, pay no insurance, then dispense with workers with or without paying them energizes the process of hiring illegals."[6]

But it was not to cheat or abuse Spanish-speaking immigrants that many employers chose to hire *indocumentados*. A Los Angeles-area janitorial services operator admitted to me that he hired undocumented aliens because "they don't ask favors, they come to work and they thank you when you give them a chance to scrub latrines." He paid his workers by check, deducting social security and income tax, then cashed their checks for them so they wouldn't have to go through a corner-store operation that took 5 percent.

"The employer of low-wage and unskilled workers ... typically experience a high turnover of American workers because the Americans are dissatisfied with the low wages, hard work, and few benefits ... " Escobar Latapí and his associates confirm. "The immigrants, by contrast, tend to report diligently every day, offer to bring their friends and relatives to fill vacant jobs, and even to train newly hired workers. The loyalty and dependability of immigrants soon makes them ... preferred workers."[7]

In the 1970s field workers could earn fifteen times as much in the United States than they could in Mexico.[8] Migrant children often began working in the fields when they were four-and five-years-old. "The farm owners say their parents use the excuse that they have no one to care for them," northern California Legal Services attorney Lucy Quacinella commented during a 1984 interview. Both Quacinella and the farmers knew that the excuse was a lie. I roamed innumerable northern California olive, walnut, and peach groves during the 1970s and 1980s seeking interviews and saw children under ten picking, hauling baskets, carrying bundles, hoeing. Some that I talked to said they attended school when they weren't working. One eight-year-old told me he didn't know what grade he was in because he didn't go to school that often and when he did the teachers didn't know what to do with him so they let him sit in the back of a class and draw things on sheets of lined paper that they gave him. An eleven-year-old girl refused to go to school in Live Oak, north of Sacramento, because she claimed that her classmates called her a "dirty migrant" and jumped away from contact with her because they didn't want to contaminate themselves. In 1992, the National Child Labor Committee estimated that more than 100,000 children work on farms. Nothing has happened since to alter that statistic.

Farm workers, particularly during harvest times, often were paid by the bucket, barrel, or bag, and everything a child could contribute added to family income. By the time a migrant child was ten, a spokesperson for the U.S. Children's Bureau said in 1979, he or she was expected to produce as much as an adult.

By 1980 an estimated one million migrants were working in U.S. agriculture. The majority were *indocumentados* and many were children under sixteen. (Federal child labor law permitted children fourteen and over to work and children over twelve to work with parental consent.) At that age, they could shuffle for eight- to ten-hour stretches in hundred degree heat filling buckets with garlic. They could wind duct tape around their fingers and strip the fruit from the branches of olive trees. They could dig carrots and sort lettuce and pick peaches and tie flowers but they couldn't rent movies or buy cigarettes or stay out after eight o'clock at night alone because of protections that the law offers children in the United States. They could bath in the brackish water of irrigation canals, eat rancid cheese, and sleep amid cockroaches on the floors of abandoned camper shells but they couldn't enter school without having a social security number and a documents signed by both parents assuming responsibility for their behavior. As Gridley, California activist Cruz Mora exclaimed, "There's something wrong with the laws in this country!"[9]

Now and then a farmer or labor contractor would advise parents not to let inspectors or strangers see their children working but the Children's Bureau admitted that few inspectors actually visited any of the work sites. Not only that, some farm owners and labor contractors actually encouraged the hiring of preteenagers.

"They're more agile and they get to be very good," Texas tomato producer Brian Krueger asserted.[10] Contrary to popular belief, he continued, agricultural fieldwork took skill and experience. A youngster working beside his parents, or with other adults, learned to nab tomatoes off the vines by touch. He learned to pick cherries without pulling the stems from the fruit, to snap off cotton boles without getting husks and leaves, to strip olives from the branches without bruising them, to run up and down ladders in apple orchards. Kiwis, okra, tobacco, carnations all demand special techniques to prune, thin, and harvest. A twelve-, thirteen- or fourteen-year-old field worker was quicker, faster, and more pliable than anyone else "and he's used to the life, he doesn't complain, and he's much less likely to get hurt," the Texas tomato producer added.

That a thirteen-or fourteen-year-old was "less likely to get hurt" is arguable. A migrant worker named Italia Carrillo saw a child fall while hoisting a basket filled with tomatoes onto a truck bed and break her collarbone in a field near Austin, Texas. The crew chief had an assistant rush her to an emergency ward but instructed both him and the child's mother to tell the hospital attendants that the twelve-year-old had fallen while playing. A three-year-old fetching empty bags for onion pickers in New Mexico was struck by a car and killed. A fifteen-year-old from Hamilton City, California, hobbles on crutches after a sugar beet topping machine ripped the ligaments in his right leg.

Until the 1980s, many farmers and field bosses insisted that thinning of sugar beets and other crops be done with short-handled hoes. Hunched over workers would crab along for miles, unable to straighten their backs or relieve the cramps in their legs as they systematically swiped at the dirt between plants, leaving neat rows of individual lettuce or sugar beet sprouts the width of the hoe blade apart. The work disabled thousands of migrants with serious back and circulatory injuries. Tomatoes, asparagus, garlic, onions, and most other products of the vegetable kingdom had to be harvested by workers bending close to the ground. Pruning and thinning often had to be accomplished through clouds of pesticides spread by low-flying biplanes. Some farm owners and labor contractors insisted that migrants prune a certain number of trees per hour without taking either size or tangled branches into consideration. The pressure of complying with these quotas, the unnatural posture with the arms and hands constantly above the worker's head, the pulling and tearing of back muscles aged even the strongest of young workers. Often they would leave the orchards so physically exhausted and in pain that they could barely eat and sleep.

Migrants being paid by the bag or bucket often worked from dawn to dusk with few rest breaks. A moment's carelessness and a pruning knife would slip or an ankle twist or a ladder fall and a worker would be laid up for weeks or months—or a lifetime. A ladder sinking into soft earth in a kiwi orchard near Yuba City, California, fractured the collarbone of a nineteen-year-old migrant in seven places. Francisco Paniagua was pruning pears near Stockton in the same state when he fell and severed a vein in his arm with the shears he was using. A fifty-one-year-old grandfather trying to extract branches caught in a hay bailer in Riverside County lost his right hand. A worker weeding an orchard near Lodi felt his spine pop and pain streak down his legs. None of the four has been able to work at any kind of job since his accident. The nineteen-year-old and worker from Lodi qualified for social security disability payments of approximately

$500 a month—barely enough to pay rent—and Paniagua for workmen's compensation of less than $200 a week. The grandfather accepted a small settlement from his employer's insurance company but the money didn't last very long.

Even so, they were more fortunate than Cirilo Mendoza in La Frontera, Texas. He keeled over in a spinach field complaining that he was having trouble breathing. The labor contractor, annoyed by what he thought was malingering, told Mendoza to rest in the bus until the end of the shift. That evening the contractor drove back to La Frontera and called an ambulance for the semi-conscious Mendoza. The call came to late: Mendoza died shortly after arriving at the hospital.

More than 20,000 farm workers suffered disabling injuries in California every year during the 1980s and 1990s; nationally the figures topped 100,000 every year. In addition, farm accidents killed between 250 and 400 each of those years. Those statistics don't include the thousands of immigrants who didn't report crippling injuries for fear that they would be deported, or not allowed to work any longer. Nor does it include the damage done to lungs, eyes and nervous systems from the more than a billion pounds of pesticides sprayed on crops every year in the United States.

Throughout the 1960s, 1970s, and 1980s the infant mortality rate among migrant workers was nearly 30 percent higher than the national average. Babies were born in the fields, or in camps without running water. Young children would slip and fall into canals and drown, or get mangled by farm equipment or suffocate after being left in a locked car. A Maryland hospital worker described a two-year-old child so covered with fire ant bites that she neither could see, open her mouth, or spread her fingers. She'd been left to sleep on a blanket near the strawberry acreages in which her migrant mother had been working. Throughout the United States, children were maimed after being attacked by vicious dogs, poisoned by battery acid, tangled in barbed wire and scraped, battered, and bruised from falling out of wagons or trucks. They would break out in virulent rashes caused by pesticide spraying and have diarrhea for days—sometimes weeks—after drinking water contaminated by runoff from fields and by untreated sewage. Some were attended by emergency ward personnel but most were not. Like their parents they would have to move on.

Despite the injuries, the hardships, and the deprivations, there were jobs to be had and money to be earned. By living in migrants' camps, work barracks, or skid row hotels, Sonoran-born Felix Maytorena was able to send $300 or more to his wife each month that he was earning. He never felt oppressed or defeated. When I interviewed him in 1980, he lifted a fist that had, he asserted, broken ten jaws and "once in Mexicali I think I killed a man." A deep, diagonal scar creased the back of one hand ("a tractor accident in Idaho; they sent me to the 'Emergency' but afterwards I chewed the stitches out with my teeth") and in damp weather, he said, his chest hurt "from sickness when I was a little boy."

Like many migrants, he found jobs through labor contractors. The year I talked to him he'd dug and topped sugar beets in California's Imperial Valley then had moved northward to work strawberry and onion fields, prune grapes, almonds, and peaches, pick tomatoes and beans, irrigate, thin, load trucks, haul nuts, and finally catch the last fall fruit harvests in Oregon, Idaho, and Montana. No hermit, he had celebrated paydays and holidays as he would in Mexico, drinking and shouting it up with the boys.

"Hey! The Budweiser I throw down like that," he snapped his fingers, "three, four six-packs in a night! And shoot the pool! Ah! The younger ones to me lose all their monies!" As to the hardships of working in the fields, "Hey, those who stay in Mexico, you should see them. Men my age sick, with shriveled stomachs. At least I eat like a man, I work like a man, I drink like a man. And when I go back there is nobody in my village who is richer!"

Ten years later Maytorena might not have been saying the same thing. A young immigrant named Felipe Sotelo told the Sacramento *Bee* that he left a restaurant job in San Jose in 1982 to cut asparagus because he could not earn enough to pay food and $200-a-week rent. For four years he and his young wife lived well by working in the fields and renting a house from their employer for $180 a month. When the employer died the couple lost both their house and income. Wages declined and their new employers became more strict.

"You can never look a boss in the eye," he told the *Bee*, "because he will think that you think you are his equal. And I'm not. I get mad because I have to humiliate myself, but that is life in the field. The one who says, 'That's wrong,' and defends himself, the next day won't have work. He'll get fired. And who will be there to defend him? Nobody." [11]

Indocumentados who successfully entered the United States between 1965 and 1980 were able to support themselves and their families on what they could earn in agriculture. Canneries and packing plants from Texas to California, Oregon, and Washington paid minimum wage and overtime. Field hands worked long hours but often lived in labor camps like the one in Gridley, California, where they paid minimal rent. They were on the low end of the wage scale but they had some stability and their children attended school. Many, like the daughters of former migrant Jesse (Jesus)

Salgado, went on to college. Salgado crossed the border in 1962 and after several years in the fields obtained work as a Sacramento truck driver. He was able to buy a modest home and continued working until all three of his daughters had bachelor's degrees.

But by 1990, the continuing migration diluted the amount of work that previously established *indocumentados* were getting, creating competition and opposition within the immigrant workforce itself.[12] Migrants entering the country risked both their lives and their health competing for below-minimum-wage jobs. Those who worked made ten times what they could have earned a day in Mexico but many times they didn't work full days— or they went weeks without being hired. Even those who worked full-time earned no more than they had ten–twenty years earlier. What had been for years a reliable, if difficult, way of life had become a dead end.[13]

"A dead end in more ways than one," I heard a volunteer with the Association of Farmworker Opportunity Programs in California comment caustically. He said both legalized migrants and newly arrived *indocumentados* were so desperate for work that they sometimes became suicidal. When they did have jobs, he added, they felt they had to push, push, push to get as much as they could. They brought their children with them to work, they did without breaks, for sustenance munching a dry tortilla now and then as they hurried from tree to tree, from vegetable row to vegetable row. Many collapsed at the end of the work day and didn't move until time to go to work again the following morning.

A veteran of more than twenty years picking strawberries in California told *La Jornada* correspondents Jim Cason and David Brooks, "They tell us to become citizens and to learn English but how can we learn English if we can't read and when after working ten hours every day all we can do is throw ourselves on the sofa, turn on the TV, and fall asleep?"[14] Migrant Maria Rulis told the Sacramento *Bee*, "Sometimes you just don't want to face the next day. You're so tired from every day being the same way, and the next day, the same thing, and the day after, the same thing. You get tired, but you can't stop. You have to work."[15]

Grape pickers in California vineyards were paid between twelve and fifteen cents to fill a full tray with unbruised fruit during the 1990s. A picker who could fill thirty to thirty-five trays an hour, haul them to the end of the rows and stack them might earn minimum wage but few could keep up that pace over an eight- to ten-hour day. Olive pickers in the 1990s could make up to $40 a day, out of which $10 went to the contractor, the same as they earned in 1965. Strawberry pickers paid by the box in the fields around Watsonville, California, saw their earnings diminish from an average of $9 an hour in 1985 to $6 an hour ten years later. Pruners in peach, pear, and nectarine orchards could take in $50–$70 if they could prune and tie ten or twelve trees a day without slackening their pace but many couldn't do it day after day.

Being paid by the bag or flat or tub or tree made gaining the equivalent of the minimum wage almost impossible. Overtime pay was nonexistent and farm workers were not included in worker legislation that protected employees in other industries. They were not eligible for workmen's compensation in many states and were exempted from many provisions of health and safety acts.

The tightening labor market affected Texas and the Midwest as well as California and the western states. The Rio Grande Valley's mild climate permitted the growing of winter crops, particularly lettuce, spinach, onions, and melons. Come spring most of the migrants wintering there would head north, through Oklahoma and Missouri and the Ohio Valley to Illinois, Wisconsin, and Minnesota. During the 1970s, they worked long hours every day and pocketed what they considered to be good money. But like the farmers who hired them, the migrant workers were dependent on factors beyond their immediate control. Floods washed away soybean crops, droughts parched cornfields. Gasoline prices forced cutbacks in production and new machines replaced the need for some manual labor. Tomato acreages that might have needed 200 pickers one year would only need 100 the next.

As more *indocumentados* sifted across the border, armies of prospective workers showed up for some harvests. An older migrant, who said he had worked in various locations throughout Texas and the Midwest for eleven years, complained in 1992 that he had been one of over 200 turned away from one of the largest farms in Oklahoma. Only four or five years before there had been so much work on that same farm that even cripples and children had put in twelve- and fourteen-hours shifts. He also said that when there were more workers than there was work the crew chiefs took an even greater percentage of the wages for themselves. Minimum wage laws meant nothing to migrants who were willing to work for half of the established hourly rate.

On the West Coast, agricultural production doubled between 1960 and 1990. (Illegal immigration during the same period, however, increased nearly five-fold.) Most of the agricultural increase was in labor-intensive crops, particularly wine grapes, strawberries, and decorative flowers. All generated a more or less constant need for workers but not a continual need for the same number of workers. Thinning and picking required more field hands, irrigating and trimming less. Unlike migrants like Felix Maytorena who followed a routine of planting, thinning, and picking as they moved their way northward year after year, the workers hired by these more static producers would get paid for three days, then be laid off two or four or six. Some managed semipermanent employment with individual growers who needed the skills that they had developed—like pruning kiwis, grape vines, and almond trees—and were able to make ends meet by collecting unemployment when they were laid off.

Grape field workers in California's Sonoma and Napa valleys often earned less than $500 a month, out of which many paid $400 a month for housing. Some managed to scrape through if the women in their families brought in income as housecleaners, dishwashers, or cooks but few families could afford any luxuries and many went without adequate plumbing, heating, and electricity, and all suffered from rising prices while their incomes remained stagnant.

Farmers, large and small, typically depended upon one good year to carry them through three or four bad ones but farm workers who were barely making it from week to week couldn't do the same. Bad weather wiped out a 1990s cherry harvest in Washington, stranding migrants who had counted on making $1,000 for three or more weeks work. December freezes in Florida and Texas during the same period destroyed winter citrus, tomato, and squash crops, leaving some 35,000 migrants without enough earnings to pay basics like groceries and rent. Not only that, they couldn't afford travel expenses to head through the Florida Panhandle into the Carolinas for the planting, irrigating, and harvesting jobs that might be available there. Of the more than four million migrants who work in U.S. agriculture, 90 percent live at or below the poverty level.

Throughout the 1990s in California employers could hire and fire at will from a farm worker force of nearly 1.5 million competing for less than 500,000 fulltime jobs. The million or more California farm workers without those jobs scrabbled for what work they could find—a few weeks thinning sugar beets, a week or two picking strawberries, a chance to harvest grapes for fourteen cents a tray, three weeks of bloody hands stripping olives from trees. Employers and labor contractors could pick and choose from the hundreds hanging out in parking lots or lining highways seeking work. Anyone who complained wouldn't be selected the next time the crew chief swung off his 4x4 and designated, "You! You! and you!"

The California Institute for Rural Studies reported in 1993 that annual earnings for migrant laborers, when adjusted for inflation, had declined 25 percent since 1978. Immigrants working in the construction, restaurant, and clothing industries didn't fare much better: A U.S. census report listed Mexican-born immigrants who'd arrived in the country after 1980 as the lowest paid members of society. Several migrants in the early 1990s told me that northern California fruit producers told them that they were on the property to work, that they could leave if they chose but as long as they were working the owners and contractors could do with them what they wanted. When one of the migrants objected, "We're not slaves!" the contractor guffawed and said, "No, no you're not. One could sell slaves— they were worth something. You pieces of shit aren't worth anything at all!"

Uri Molina, who worked with migrant programs in California in the 1980s and 1990s after he retired from the Air Force, said he was convinced that major revolutions would have occurred south of the border if the United States hadn't absorbed millions of immigrants during the last three decades of the twentieth century. He insisted that never during his travels through Mexico had he seen working conditions as primitive and cruel as those he'd witnessed in California's San Joaquin and Sacramento valleys.

"The farmers here do not treat the workers as people," he declared. "They treat them like animals."

Worse than animals the U.S. Justice Department confirmed after investigating allegations that a Florida citrus producer imprisoned migrants contracted to pick grapefruit in 1991. According to the investigation the Houston, Texas-based contractors La Pisca promised workers the opportunity to earn $300 a week, minus transportation, room, and board. "Room and board," it turned out, consisted of cramming fifteen to twenty workers each into dilapidated trailers and jerrybuilt cabins and feeding them beans and tortillas. The $300 a week shrank to $25 a week for many workers after costs were deducted. After weeks of ten- and twelve-hour days picking grapefruit, many migrants found that they were in debt to the company. A Florida Rural Legal Services officials described their work and pay conditions as "modern-day slavery."[16] Even U.S. Congressman and later C.I.A. head Porter Goss termed the treatment of the migrants "abuse" reminiscent of that recorded by John Steinbeck in *The Grapes of Wrath*.[17]

La Pisca, which in the early 1990s contracted over 4,000 migrants a year to work throughout the southern United States, wasn't the only outfit accused of making indentured servants of its employees. The Mexican consul in Sacramento confronted state authorities in 1992 with evidence that several San Joaquin Valley dairy farms kept their workers "in slave-like working conditions" by refusing to pay overtime or sick leave, fining workers $50 a day for being sick, firing those who refused to sign waivers releasing the company from any liability if they were injured on the job and over-deducting for company provided housing.[18] The consul complained that neither state nor federal agencies had investigated previous complaints and noted that the "slave-like conditions" existed on many California dairy farms.

Another "slave owner," Edwin Mitchell Ives of Camarillo, California, pleaded guilty on May 15, 1992, to conspiracy, harboring illegal aliens, transporting illegal aliens, racketeering, and wire fraud. Ives and his Chicano foremen didn't depend upon local migrant labor—they imported their own from mountain towns with Mixtec and Zapotec populations in rural Oaxaca. One of Ives' lieutenants, Hector Hernandez, recruited in destitute villages like Santa Ana Yareni and San Isidro Aloapan from 1984 until 1989.

Ives' lawyers claimed he did nothing more than other agriculturalists were doing. He obtained signed contracts, which including advancing workers the costs of transportation from Oaxaca, smuggling them across the border, housing, food, and tools. Some who worked for him returned to Oaxaca with enough money to build additions to their houses or buy appliances like televisions and VCRs. But others claimed that they had worked up to sixteen hours a day cutting and bundling baby's breath and eucalyptus leaves and after five weeks of unrelenting work were told that the expenses they had incurred—including head shaving, toilet paper, and "luxury items" like soap, drinking water, and resoling shoes—exceeded their wages. After six months of intense labor, a Santa Ana Yareni, father of three had accumulated only $200 to take home with him—less than $35 a month. Two others dug their way out of a room in which they'd been imprisoned and reported their situation to the Mexican consul in nearby Oxnard.

Despite the hardships, several of Ives' former employees returned to southern California to work. One of them, Filimon Ruiz, spent three years as a gardener in Encinitas and returned to Oaxaca having saved enough to buy a pair of oxen and breed goats and to plough, plant, and irrigate a small cornfield. His experiences demonstrate why migrants keep coming despite the hardships, the arrests, the discrimination, and the miserable working and living conditions. Just enough *aspirantes* return to their birthplaces with enough money to prompt others to attempt to do what they did. Even so, their situations in places like Oaxaca remain precarious. Should drought or blight wipe out the little cornfield, the oxen die, the goats fail to provide enough meat and milk, a spouse or child be injured or become ill, the former *indocumentado* faces more years of living in caves and cardboard shanties, dodging the *migra in* order to save enough to buy two more oxen, two more goats, some fertilizer, and some seeds.

As I heard an *indocumentado* buying clothes for his children at a San Joaquin Valley, California, K-Mart sidewalk sale twenty-five years ago explain, "In Michoacán there is no work for anybody, never. In *los esta-dos unidos, sí*, this much, at least," and he measured off a quarter inch with his thumb and forefinger. "Here there is always something."

WAITING, WISHING, WORKING

The letter to the *Los Angeles Reader*, typed in response to an article I wrote about undocumented immigrants in 1990, began:

> We have been waiting three days now. Pedro's wife and two small children called from San Diego on Weds afternoon, they had crossed the border safely, and the 'coyote' would have them 'home' in Venice by Thursday noon. It is Saturday after-noon, neither Pedro, nor his relatives in Mexico, have heard a word since.
>
> Pedro works for me. So do 11 other Hispanic men and women from central Mexico and Guatemala. I know that the IDs and Social Security cards they have shown me are fake. They know that I know. We talk about how they came to Cal-ifornia, we talk about their lives back home and the fami-lies they have left behind. These people have such incredible courage.
>
> Gonzalo and his brother in law came two years before his wife Rosa and her sister Blanca. Then Rosa came, leaving their three very small children in Guatemala with her mother. Then Rosa's sister Blanca came with several of the children. Last year Rosa returned to Guatemala for her youngest daughter, who was just three years old . . . her daughter did not recognize her. Rosa was to have returned with the baby in three weeks, but because of illegal detainment in Mexico, she was gone for eight weeks. It took several thousand dollars for Rosa to get through Mexican red tape and home to Culver City. I do not know how Gonzalo managed to come to work and maintain a cheerful front during all those weeks, but he did. We were worried sick. During the time she was gone we all pitched in at work to pick up the slack. Rosa returned to her job. From what I understand, Rosa was lucky.
>
> I own and manage a restaurant in West Los Angeles, about half my staff is Latin and I could not keep my door open with-out them. I don't know of many restaurants that could. No one but Latinos apply for bus boy/kitchen jobs. And the Anglos or

Blacks that do, resent the work of washing dishes and cleaning up, they usually quit within a day or two. I pay more than minimum wage *to train*. Promotions are in house. And the faster a Latino learns English, the faster he is promoted. Most of my staff have been with me for more than a year. In the restaurant trade, that is a minor miracle.

I wish I could sign my name to this letter. As it is I fear recognition for my Latino friends. This town is small when you are hiding.

"If one is an *indocumentado* one has to hide," an immigrant that I interviewed for the same *Los Angeles Reader* article told me. For most of those who were hiding—keeping their identities as undocumented aliens a secret—the fear of being exposed was paramount. Even those who had high school or college educations, or who had professional experience in their home country, could not move into jobs that brought them into extended public contact. They could work in restaurants, small non-union manufacturing plants, construction, but unless they had qualified for and received amnesty, they could not even apply for positions that offered professional training and promotion.

Resentment among undocumented city residents often ran high. Unlike migrants from rural areas in Mexico whose principal work experience had been agricultural, many of those who sifted into the cities expected to do more than clean buildings or bus restaurant tables.

"I didn't think it would be like this here," a Guatemalan immigrant told *USA Today* reporter Sandra Sanchez after a May 1991 riot in Washington, D.C.'s Mount Pleasant area.[19] He and other immigrants claimed that they had come to Washington expecting to find regular work, not catch-as-catch-can temporary jobs, and that they would be able to afford "decent" places to live and to send money to relatives back home. Instead, they found themselves jammed with five to ten others in crowded tenement apartments vying for menial jobs, harassed by landlords, and police, and priced out of any chance for bettering their situations.

While the declining economy in the early 1990s triggered layoffs and reduced work hours, it also created openings for *indocumentados* that hadn't existed before. Small business owners throughout the United States resorted to temporary help to cut payrolls and lower expenses. A Los Angeles electronics manufacturer who fabricated parts for small airplanes laid off most of his permanent employees and moved equipment and machinery to a rented East Los Angeles warehouse. He resumed operations under a different name by hiring unemployed migrants and *indocumentados* who worked from fifteen to sixty hours a week, depending upon sales and production needs. Although he paid no overtime, he gave his employees coffee and lunch breaks and trained them in the use of various types of machinery. He apologized for cutting employee hours when orders diminished but made it clear that anyone who objected or didn't return to work when they were called would be fired.

Many meat and poultry processors began moving from cities like Chicago and Kansas City to small towns closer to the livestock producing areas. As they did many of them restaffed with low-wage immigrant workers, relying "heavily on tapping established ethnic social networks for recruitment purposes . . . numerous communities in Kansas, Iowa, and Nebraska have seen dramatic increases in their Latino populations . . ."[20]

That restaurants, janitorial services, retail stores, and other small business such as printers, laundries and cleaners, upholsterers, and auto repair and wrecking services could add or subtract hours, deduct for lost time or equipment damage, discharge a worker for no cause, and demand unquestioning obedience made hiring *indocumentados* profitable. Technically most of these immigrants were not undocumented—most had documents even though they were forged, borrowed, or counterfeit. Even unions that some immigrants were obliged to join didn't screen for legality and most businesses, like the restaurant owner cited above, only went as far as to assure that their employees presented something official-looking when they first came to work.

Like farm owners, business owners complained about the amount of paperwork required by local, state, and federal governments. In the Los Angeles *Times*, columnist Peter H. King termed the paperwork requirements "irrelevant." He continued:

"A lot of blood and history and paperwork has crossed the border, creating an intractable jumble of naturalized citizens, amnesty cases, undocumented aliens, guest workers, Tijuana commuters, and so on. It's not so simple as brown and white, legal or illegal. In fact, the only thing clear-cut about the border-crossing game is its essential goal: work. This is a plain fact as old as the border itself. No political speech or exclusionary initiative, no fence even, can change it."[21]

Many small business owners and micro-entrepreneurs hiring *indocumentados* were themselves immigrants or former immigrants who catered primarily to the Spanish-speaking population. Greenwood and Tienda note that a study of self-employment in Chicago "showed much higher levels of self-employment among Mexican migrants than revealed by conventional census data."[22] They attributed this to the "invisibility of Mexican self-employment" because many families added to their incomes by street vending, cleaning houses, work exchange, and childcare, and add, "Dense settlement patterns ... are conducive to the emergence of informal activity that caters to the needs of other co-ethnics." But, whereas street sales and nonregistered businesses are commonplace in Mexico, they are not always appreciated in the United States. "Street vendors in Los Angeles have been struggling for a decade to legalize some sort of status for themselves, while the police continue to arrest them and confiscate their goods."[23]

An *indocumentado* I interviewed for the *Los Angeles Reader* told me that after he finished his work days washing dishes in an artsy French restaurant he went door to door selling furry stuffed toys that his wife and daughters made from old rags and wool scraps they got from a tannery. His house was so crowded, he said, that he didn't like going home at night until he was tired enough to collapse into sleep despite TV noise, arguments, and the constant patching and snipping and sewing of the stuffed toy manufacture.

Although *ambulantes* like him hawked everything from cheap watches and framed pictures of the Virgin of Guadalupe to beaded earrings, long-stemmed roses, and lottery tickets, food consistently sold best. A worker who couldn't afford supermarket groceries could afford a curbside burrito, a steaming tamale, a doughnut, or newspaper cone of *chicharón* bathed in salsa. Immigrants crammed three families to an apartment in the barrios tended to spend time in the streets and the busier streets, especially those clustered with strip malls and neighborhood businesses, became places to congregate. In Chicago, in Houston, in Denver, and Los Angeles and Sacramento, and dozen of other cities where immigrants gathered, pregnant women forced out of sweatshops or restaurant kitchens and teenaged mothers with babies on their hips sold tacos and roasting ears and cups of pozole. Talipeds and amputees and children in bright native skirts and nonagenarian-looking grandmothers competed with otherwise unemployed immigrants to augment incomes by hawking popsickles and burritos and hotdogs and popcorn.

"It's always a hustle," a stoop-shouldered legalized grandfather from Sacramento told me. He said he worked for a janitorial service at night cleaning warehouses and workshops and during the day maintained a small photography business taking and developing ID photos. There were other things he could do, he added dolefully, noting relatives and acquaintances who made "ten, twenty, thirty times more" than he did. But they were involved in *la droga* and he didn't want to get involved in that. For one thing, he explained, it was dangerous—people all the time were getting killed. Besides that, few of those who got involved could keep from getting hooked on drugs themselves and they would become thieves, or hang out with thieves, or make stupid mistakes, and get arrested or wreck their cars or their wives would leave them or they'd get mixed up with prostitutes.

It was mostly the younger people, he said, who got involved, the children of immigrants who didn't understand why their parents had risked everything to come to the United States to work. They wanted what they saw on television; they wanted to get out of the barrio but they didn't have educations and they didn't know how to make a good living and while they were working at some go-nowhere job they'd run into somebody flashing money or driving a new car and they'd be tempted and finally they'd give in and once they did they were lost, there was no way for them to get back. No way, he said, except prison or death. It was tragically sad, he added, because their parents didn't know whether to disown them and forget about them or try to help them and keep on suffering and suffering while their drug-addicted kids broke their hearts.

Small manufacturing and service companies that depended upon immigrant labor tended to be only one small step ahead of disaster all of the time. Usually the first sign of impending collapse was a delay in issuing paychecks. Then paychecks would start bouncing. Almost always, the owners would assure the workers that the financial setback was temporary; they would make the bounced checks good the following week. Instead, equipment and office supplies would disappear. Then there would be a "temporary" layoff. When the workers went to check on their return to their jobs and to ask about their lost wages they'd find eviction notices tacked to the employers' door.

Drugs weren't the only danger. Like farm workers, city immigrants lived in constant fear of losing their jobs.

Many fly-by-night sweatshops would skip out on their employees, knowing that as *indocumentados* they wouldn't go to the authorities. But larger and more established firms also went belly up. When Trinity Knitworks in Los Angeles abruptly closed its doors in the early 1990s it owed some 184 employees, almost all of them immigrants, two months back salaries. Many of those thrown out of work had been employed at the plant for over 20 years and owed money for rent, mortgages, cars, and credit cards.

California continued to be the goal of most *indocumentados* throughout the mid 1990s. Thousands of families in northern and central Mexico continued to depend on men going alone to work in California fields and orchards sixty years after the first *braceros* had made the same journey. Those newcomers who had good connections—a trustworthy *coyote*, ranches and farms that paid minimum wage, a room to rent—could earn $200 a week and send half of it to their families back home. Growers with more specialized crops that needed ongoing care preferred experienced employees and kept them working for longer periods of time. Others rehired migrants they knew and who had worked for them before, which gave the migrants a more stable situation than they would have had scrambling from crop to crop every few weeks. It also permitted the workers to take on side jobs washing restaurant dishes, filling in in packing plants, unloading freight cars, or cleaning the trash out of small orchards or demolition sites.

The risk of injury—like the threat of deportation—hung constantly over their heads. A workman staggering into a Woodland, California, health clinic, suffering from stroke-like symptoms admitted that they had been getting progressively worse since he whacked his head against a low-hanging branch while driving a tractor two months before. He didn't want to report it, he said, because he didn't want to lose any days of work. Another migrant severed his thumb cutting florists' flowers and returned to work wearing gloves so the amputation wouldn't be evident.

A 1997 University of California, Davis survey indicated that 11 percent of migrant men and 8 percent of migrant women working in northern California agriculture suffered occupational injuries.[24] Agricultural workers weren't the only ones at risk. A Reno, Nevada chemical plant explosion killed four Spanish-speaking immigrants in 1998 and injured several others, some seriously. An explosion in June of the same year killed four Mexican workers at a grain elevator in Haysville, Kansas. In both cases investigators cited long work hours and unsafe working conditions that previously had been reported but not corrected. Occupational Safety and Health Administration (OSHA) statistics indicate that meat-packing plants, ship scraping facilities and food processing mills rival farm work for causing injuries, primarily to low-paid immigrant employees. (Investigations after the Reno explosion revealed that none of the employees had been taught how to mix the volatile chemicals and instructions for handling and manufacturing blasting devices had been given only in English, which many of the immigrant workers barely understood.)[25]

Immigrants "work long hours for low pay and they know they are very replaceable so they don't want to complain," Joel Najar, immigration policy analyst for the National Council of La Raza told the Associated Press. "We see this a lot in the construction industry. A worker falls off the roof and has to pay everything out of his own pocket."[26] Since most *indocumentados* paid social security on faked or counterfeit cards they were invisible when it came to claims or benefits and they accrued nothing for the future.

Many didn't want to. They were in the United States only to work. A twenty-two-year-old told me that he wanted his two young daughters to grow up in Mexico "with dignity" and not have people abuse and slander them for being Mexican. What he earned as a migrant would keep them secure, fed, clothed in their Michoacán village, and perhaps provide something for his own future. Leaving his home to work in a strange and hostile land, sending almost everything he earned to his family, didn't seem unusual or strange to him. Men from his village had been migrating as *indocumentados* for as long as he or his parents or his grandparents could remember.

Improved economic conditions nationwide in the mid-1990s boosted both agriculture and industry. Unfortunately for most undocumented workers, it was accompanied by increased antiimmigrant sentiments throughout the United States. Welfare reforms targeting "illegals" cut out eligibility for food stamps and medical benefits. Billions of dollars of Federal money pumped into "securing the border" not only made entry more difficult but extended to raids on workplaces and communities where *indocumentados* lived. California's governor Pete Wilson fallaciously blamed immigrants for the state's economic woes and was pivotal in the passage of state Proposition 187 which severely limited noncitizen rights. The propaganda that accompanied these campaigns encouraged individual citizens and citizen groups to lash out against Spanish-speaking residents without distinction to their immigration status. But all the rhetoric, and all the immigrant bashing, didn't change the needs of agriculture and industry for cheap, willing labor. As more than one *indocumentado* told me:

"They only want us here to work. They don't want us here as people."

CLEANING UP

During the Republican National Convention in San Diego in August, 1996, Los Angeles *Times* columnist Peter H. King described a confrontation between a guard at the convention's security checkpoint and a twenty-year-old *indocumentado*:

"Work,' was all the young man said. He offered the word hesitantly, as if unsure of his pronunciation.

"The officer simply pointed, and the young fellow almost trotted down the path. It led to a garage where temporary workers had begun to assemble for their first day on the job. A half hour later, he would emerge with a work detail. He was wearing a new T-shirt with block letters printed across the chest.

"'OFFICIAL CLEANER,' the shirt declared."[27]

Not lost on King was the irony that once the convention speeches started, young men like the official cleaner would become the object of considerable inflammatory rhetoric. But even so his presence would be more than tolerated: It would be needed.

Immigrants who had good connections—a trustworthy *coyote*, ranches and farms that paid minimum wage, a room to rent—could earn $200 a week and send half of it to their families back home.[28] Despite the hardships, the problems, the deportations, and struggles to make ends meet, countless *indocumentados* created new worlds for themselves and their children. Their successes go as unreported as their failures and losses. Throughout the United States one encounters lawyers, doctors, entrepreneurs, artists, professors—and high ranking Border Patrol officials—whose parents entered the United States as *indocumentados* and whose work at low-wage jobs enabled their children to compete effectively in their adopted culture.

I had the good fortune to attend the goodbye celebration for a young Chico, California banker. The son of a *bracero* who settled in California, Rafael Sanchez, then still in his early thirties, was on his way to Mexico City as a Bank of America regional vice-president. By his own admission a "mediocre" junior college student, he'd transferred to California State University-Chico without a major and been persuaded to focus on Spanish. To support himself through college he obtained a teller's job in a local B of A. By the time he graduated, he was fluent in both Spanish and English and the bank needed a Spanish-speaking loan officer. Then the bank needed a bilingual (without accent in either language) vice-president. Then the system needed an experience bilingual regional vice-president in Mexico. Among his parting words, after his goodbye celebration, were: "Now if only I can convince my dad to trade in that '72 LTD he's still driving. But he won't. 'Why should I?' he asks me. 'It still runs fine.'"

Entrepreneurship didn't come naturally to most *indocumentados* but the need to earn additional income prompted many to start small businesses. Taco venders, helped by their spouses and children, equipped a truck or trailer with a butane stove and drove to places where people gathered. There's hardly a town in the United States that doesn't have a home-owned Mexican restaurant. Many expanded into family-owned chains, like Casa Lupe in northern California and *Taquerías Mi Ranchito* in the Houston, Texas area.

The first *Taquerías Mi Ranchito* opened in the mid-1970s when a family of *indocumentados* from Villa Guerrero, Jalisco pooled enough money to start a little neighborhood business. As its popularity increased, the eleven brothers and sisters brought in more relatives from Jalisco and Mexico

City and opened other *taquerías*. They became one of the most popular chains in the area, with most of the outlets managed and staffed by former Vicente Guerrero relatives and friends.

Immigrants usually did not like to borrow money, preferring to work and save to invest instead. As a result, fledgling businesses had to start small. A Chico, California tortilla maker rented a little storefront to sell fresh corn tortillas. A tamale maker in Bakersfield bought some used tables and chairs and opened a lunchtime restaurant. A former migrant in Milwaukee hired two friends to help him do odd lawn care and clean-up jobs. Within a year, he had hired two more people and had a full-time landscaping service.

Krissman recounts how some farm workers maneuvered their way into positions of income and authority by cooperating with both employers and members of their home communities. A Mixtec *indocumentado*'s engaging personality and zest for both work and adventure took him from being a crew member to a recruiter and foreman's assistant (*subjefe*). He acquired a van to transport workers to and from their job sites, established his home as a safe house and after gaining legal status under the amnesty provisions of Simpson-Rodino, he purchased land in his home community in Oaxaca.

Another migrant gained his apple grower employer's confidence and rose from being a "private" to having a salary, a cottage, and a truck to drive. After the Simpson-Rodino Act went into effect, he corralled thirty or more countrymen to come to Washington to work and provided each of them with certification that would enable them to legalize their status.[29] Soon he had *subjefes* working for him and was making winter trips back to his birthplace in Michoacán, where he contributed to renovations to the town plaza and the Catholic church.[30]

Not all immigrants wanted to return to Mexico but many did. As a teenaged *indocumentado*, Cliserio Mercado worked as a bellhop in a Rawlins, Wyoming hotel. He spoke no English but realized that he needed to learn in order to get better tips. A local teacher offered to help him enroll in Western Wyoming Junior College "but you have to pay your own way," the teacher insisted. Mercado returned to Mexico fully bilingual and now is a successful Cabo San Luis entrepreneur and much sought after Rotary Club speaker.

Others, like Elías Mora run multifaceted businesses on both sides of the border. When the U.S. House of Representatives passed the immigration control bill in 2006, Mora whipped out letters asking "Who is going to pick our lemons, oranges, grapes, tomatoes, lettuce, peaches, cucumbers? Who is going to mow your garden? Who is going to wash dishes and do the dirty work at the Restaurants at the Ski Resorts? Our Congressmen? They never worked a day in their life, I am not [going to do that work], I am too busy running my business, my son is not, he graduated from SDSU as a Mechanical Engineer and works for a high tech company."[31]

While most legal and undocumented Spanish-speaking immigrants retained financial and sentimental ties to the country of their birth, their English-language children often merged into the dominant culture, only to discover later, as Pacific Gas and Electric accounts representative Roberto Martinez, did, "from my younger days spent at home in a Spanish-dominated environment to my English language- and culture-dominated elementary and high school days to an environment where, with my involvement with Hispanics from all over the state, I began to take pride in my Spanish language, my parents' music, the history of my ancestors—in general, the culture neglected during my early schooling years. It was a beautiful rediscovery of part of my identity that added tremendously to my self-esteem and personal development.

"Fortunate best describes my struggle through sixteen years of school and graduating the way I started, as a bilingual-bicultural person."[32]

"It's the Law!"

HERE THEY COME!

"As a teenager working in Butte County, California's peach and olive or-chards, Gridley resident Marcelino Rodriguez witnessed a yearly ritual," Leslie Layton kicked off an article on migrant laborers in the August 14, 1997 *Chico News & Review*.

"'We'd see a plane over the fields,' Rodriguez said, describing how the Immigration and Naturalization Service would round up illegal farm workers in the 1970s. 'Everybody would run and hide. Every single year, immigration would be there—just a day or two before the season was over. [They] always let you finish the crop.'"

After the low flying aircraft located the pickers, INS ground agents would load all of those without documentation on buses, drive them to Tijuana and turn them over to Mexican authorities. Meanwhile, legal res-idents in the farming areas would pick up the paychecks owed the de-ported workers and mail them to their families.

Neither workers nor farmers doubted that the INS intentionally timed their sweeps to accommodate agricultural production. Peaches, olives, and almonds had to be harvested quickly during a two- or three-week period; the growers massed as many workers as they could to get every-thing off the trees while the weather was right and the fruit was neither too green nor too ripe. Losing workers to a raid—even a suspected raid—not only could wipe out a grower's profits it could bankrupt him and the growers in California, like farm owners throughout the South and Mid-west, had political pull.

The migrants, of course, had none. Clearing them away after the crops were in could be considered a social service. No longer were they needed and neither growers nor law enforcement wanted them cluttering up the countryside.

Deporting undocumented immigrants was great sport throughout the 1970s. Mexican-American activists told newly elected President Jimmy Carter in 1977 that Spanish-speaking communities lived "under a virtual state of siege."[1] Even though Carter appointed a descendant of Mexican immigrants, Leonel Castillo, to head the Immigration Naturalization Service (INS), the rate of deportations continued to increase, reaching 950,000 by 1978 and nearly 2 million in 1985.

The U.S. government urged Mexican officials to take steps to prevent— or at least slow down—the number of immigrants trying to cross the border but according to long-time Tijuana political activist José Ruiz López the Mexican police were more interested in collecting bribes than preventing *paisanos* from leaving the country. A former *indocumentado* describing his deportation said the Border Patrol delivered him and several others to a Mexican police *caseta* in Tijuana. The Mexican police searched them and demanded $50 from each of them for what they called a "repatriation processing fee." They took from those who couldn't pay the $50 what valuables they had, then released all of them.

That the federal government paid individual cities and counties for housing undocumented immigrants in their jails stimulated local law enforcement to apprehend and hold *indocumentados*. But the money being spent was taxpayer money and apprehending and deporting *indocumentados* was costing the federal government $42 billion dollars a year by 1998, or more than $4,000 for each illegal entrant sent back across the border, more than many of them earned during their brief stays in the United States.

By law (as defined by INS regulations in the late 1980s and by the Mexican government) Central Americans apprehended as illegals couldn't be dumped back into Mexico but had to be held at their point of entry until diplomatic paperwork could be completed to return them to their home countries. By 1988, agents had so many Central American *indocumentados* waiting for processing in Harlingen, Texas, that they couldn't house or control them. The *aprehendidos* were sleeping in the streets or squatting in downtown buildings. Things got so bad, Tina Rosenberg reported that "the cops finally shut down the town's INS office." [2]

"MIGRA, MIGRA, PINCHE MIGRA, DÉJAME IN PAZ!"[3]

Apprehended after Border Patrol SUVs intercepted his column of semi-concealed *pollos* and forced them back into the hands of Mexican authorities, a *coyote* identified only as "Bermudas" countered accusations that dealing in human contraband was among the most despicable of crimes by spitting toward the *migra* and snapping, "You created me! If it were not for you, I wouldn't exist!"

By the mid-1970s, when a young Guatemalan *indocumentado* decided that becoming a *coyote* would be more profitable than being led across the border by one, organized crime—the so-called "Mexican Mafia"—had become a major player in the *indocumentados* game. Already experienced in putting all the pieces together to acquire, convey and sell marijuana, heroin, and cocaine, *mafiosos* found it relatively simple to recruit and transport would be workers from Mexico into the United States.

That it was a vicious business the young Guatemalan, Cedric Calderón, learned quickly. Those who couldn't afford to pay, or who were robbed before they could contact a *coyote*, became "street garbage." Women who wanted to cross the border were set up with contacts at the Hotel Montejo in Tijuana's Zona Rosa but instead of encountering guides they encountered procurers who set them up for a night—or nights—of rapes. Many times, Calderón noted in *Contabando Humano de la Frontera*, these women neither made it across the border nor returned to their homes in Mexico but became prostitutes, or went crazy from the violence committed against their persons, or they became drug addicts and victims of venereal disease. He added, almost ingenuously, "When the Mafia believes they know too much, they physically eliminate them and incinerate their bodies, leaving no traces."[4]

According to Calderón, *aspirantes* pouring into Tijuana and other border towns wanting to get to the Land of Money provided the raw material and employers in the United States provided the demand side of supply and demand. Hours after *migra* sweeps routed *indocumentados* off the fields or out of sweatshops, the labor contractors or owners would call the labor suppliers on the Mexican side of the border and the *coyotes* would round up and transport new batches of migrants.

The *coyotes*, Calderón noted, not only had to get their *pollitos* across the border, but had to deliver them to the places they were going to work. Usually that meant smuggling them past INS checkpoints on the major highways. The less a migrant looked like a migrant, the better chance he or she had of not being stopped. As noted in the second chapter, Luis Muñoz' *coyote* had him dress like a young businessman and fly from Ontario to Chicago.

Since Border Patrol agents were much more likely to stop older vehicles with dark complexioned drivers, some *coyotes* hired gringo-looking chauffeurs to drive through the checkpoints in new cars with their well-dressed *pollitos* in the passenger seats. Some younger women whose relatives in

Oakland had paid for their passage rode past the San Clemente check-point in a newer model station wagon fluttering banners announcing their initiation into a popular university sorority. An immigrant named Alvaro Gonzalez told me in San Francisco that his guide driving a late-model sta-tion wagon followed an old delivery van toward the San Clemente check-point on Interstate 5. The *migra*, detecting passengers in the back of the van, stopped that vehicle and waved the station wagon through, not re-alizing that the van's driver was in cahoots with the driver of the station wagon. All the passengers in the van were legal and after being checked were sent on their way. The station wagon with its cargo of *indocumenta-dos*, meanwhile, was barreling toward Los Angeles.

During the 1970s, some smugglers hired Marine dependants at Camp Pendleton to escort *indocumentados* through the base and deliver them to transportation waiting on the other side of the San Clemente checkpoint. Calderón on several occasions outfitted groups of young *aspirantes* in ath-letic sweat suits monogrammed with the name of a local junior college and for several days had them jog through early morning winter rain and fog along the highway near Temecula. On the fourth or fifth day, waving toward the officers, they jogged past the checkpoint onto a side road and hopped into a waiting truck for transportation to Los Angeles.

Some subterfuges like those worked, others did not. Border Patrol agents often claimed they could "sniff out" scams and/or had a "sixth sense" about where and how migrants were going to try to cross.[5] Calderón noted that the *migra*, equipped as they were with implements of modern warfare—helicopters, motion detectors, radar, audiphones, and high-caliber pistols and rifles—had a distinct advantage over the *coyotes*, who were unarmed and "with their valor and knowledge of the terrain, like real coyotes" were trying to slip through and evade them.

All forays past the Border Patrolled frontier were risky and the *coy-otes* knew that prison awaited them if they were caught. Many *coyotes* rented residences on both sides of the border and identified themselves as "importers" when asked what businesses they were in. They knew ev-ery roadway, every ditch, every underpass, every abandoned rail line and drain pipe and creek bed in the areas they crossed.

The seemingly endless supply of *aspirantes* enabled *coyotes* like Calderón to live in luxury. Like many, however, he stumbled and was caught and arrested on the U.S. side of the border. He was deported as a criminal and hauled to prison in Mexico City and never was able to re-turn to his *coyote* life of excitement and luxury.

The *coyote* who managed Luis Muñoz' border crossing was a former Oaxacan *indocumentada* living in Tijuana's Colonia Libertad, a popular gathering place for *aspirantes*. Periodically, S. Lynne Walker wrote in the Sacramento *Bee*, hapless migrants would knock on her door begging for food or shelter.

"First she gave the men tacos. Then she started loaning blankets. Then she gave them a place to sleep. One day she decided to help them get across the border ... Now she and her husband run a well-organized smuggling ring ... [and] live in a carpeted three-bedroom house at the top of the hill. A housekeeper works in their modern kitchen while [their] children watch a thirty-inch color television set."[6]

Like most *coyotes*, the couple who helped Muñoz hired young men to lead the actual border crossing trips, although the former *indocumentada*'s husband would take the *pollitos* from the pickup point northward if he couldn't find other drivers.

That immigrant smuggling operations are gang-organized, high tech, and *mafia* controlled is disputed by many immigrants who successfully employed *coyotes* to help them enter the United States. Many smuggling operations are one- or two-person or family-run units like that which helped Muñoz get from Michoacán to Chicago. A 1976 Comptroller General's report acknowledged that 92 percent of the smuggling rings in one sector had three or fewer members. After interviewing both *indocumentados* and coyotes, Grace Halsell concluded, "Smuggling, then, must be a business somewhat like prostitution: For every one that is part of a highly organized ring, there are a thousand or more who are individual entrepreneurs."[7]

Calderón admitted that some *coyotes* extorted money from their *pollitos* or abandoned them instead of guiding them safely into the United States. Those who did that, however, lost the support that *coyotes* like Calderón got from affiliates on both sides of the border. By the 1980s, people smuggling had become a complicated business requiring a large amount of logistical support: safe houses on both sides of the border and also in the destination cities, cars especially modified to secretly carry passengers and to indulge in high speed chases, larger transportation vehicles, recruiters in Mexico, "heels" and scouts and lookouts. Even in the late 1970s and early 1980s immigrants paid up to $1,500 apiece to be conveyed from their point of origin in Mexico to their destination in the United States. For every one who got caught at least ten slipped through successfully.[8]

The prosperous *coyotes* "know everybody and everything," a former *indocumentado* named Ramiro Flores told me while I was doing an article on Amnesty for a Los Angeles publication. A *coyote* who helped his sister arrive safely in L.A. put her and Flores in contact with someone who could provide them with green cards, social security cards, and other documents. Flores said he spent over a thousand dollars on visas that turned out to be worthless counterfeits.

He was only one of thousands—perhaps hundreds of thousands—who fell for scams involving fake or stolen documents or social security numbers. One San Diego woman posed as an INS officer, rented a motel conference room in Anaheim, interviewed and offered to process paperwork that would allow those acquiring her services to become legal residents. If they complained about her fees or delays in processing the purported paperwork, she threatened them with deportation.

Other *indocumentados* "rented" social security numbers from legal immigrants. The latter enhanced their unemployment and pension benefits by having the *indocumentados'* earnings credited to their accounts and the *indocumentados* benefited by having a document that would help them get a job.

The paperwork was important because neither the Border Patrol nor their parent organization, the INS, had access to computerized social security or naturalization applicant files during the 1970s and 1980s and most employers were satisfied to be shown any document that made a worker seem hirable. But during the economic downtown when Ronald Reagan was president, the Republican administration began to blame *indocumentados* for taking employment away from U.S. citizens. "Project Jobs" authorized INS raids on farms and workplaces. One of these raids, Earl Shorris reported in *The Nation* in 1989, swept through a Sacramento business owned by a Vietnam veteran of Mexican ancestry. He complained to the agent in charge of the Sacramento INS office and the official told him, "We can enter a property without a warrant if we see Mexicans in plain view from the street."[9]

Throughout the United States, but particularly on the West Coast, agents boarded city buses, swept through housing camps, and interrupted dances looking for "wets" and "tonks" as INS documents identified Spanish-speaking immigrants. (The description "tonk," according to an INS agent named Larry Moy, was "the sound of a flashlight hitting somebody's head.")[10] An immigrant relative of my friend Jose Mata's wife described trying to evade a *migra* intrusion into a Las Vegas bar-pool parlor by ducking into the men's bathroom. Two agents cornered him there and forced him to kneel over an unflushed commode. "What do you see?" they asked him, then insulted him, "It's a mirror. What you see there is what you are!"

Predictions that legal action against employers who hired undocumented workers would close businesses and deter immigration never materialized after the passage of Simpson-Rodino, in part because the administration found that "closing the border" was a more popular political maneuver. Neither Republicans nor Democrats wanted criminal actions taken against the hundreds of thousands of employers who were campaign contributors. Instead, the INS focused on more equipment, more agents, more detainments at the border. They added mounted patrols to go after *aspirantes* caught in the beams of helicopter lights and profiled vehicles that might be transporting *indocumentados*: delivery vans, pickups, or trucks riding low on their axles, LTDs, and other high-horsepower sedans rolling along on silicon-filled tires. INS helicopters sprayed phosphorescent materials over areas being traversed by attempted border crossers, making the *aspirantes* "glisten like bits of radioactive material" a caller to a San Diego radio talk show reported.

High speed chases resulted in several fatal accidents, including one that killed agent John McCravey near Calexico in 1987 and another in Riverside County when a car being pursued by the Border Patrol swerved out of control and crashed in front of a school, killing four students and two passengers. The INS advised its units not to proceed in chases "where the danger posed to the public is greater than the benefit of apprehending the suspect" but that didn't prevent agents in California's Carmel Valley, California from jeopardizing the lives of both motorists and children waiting for a school bus as the *migra* swerved around curves and fired a pistol at suspected *indocumentados* shortly after that edict was issued. Two of the pursued vehicle's three occupants were deported as illegals after they abandoned their car and tried to escape on foot but the incident illustrated the extent to which individual INS agents regarded *indocumentados* as criminals to be pursued and if necessary killed.

Mount Pleasant-area residents in Washington, D.C., rioted after police shot a handcuffed immigrant they were attempting to arrest. Angry Mexicali residents staged marches and demonstrations after a Border Patrol agent shot a fifteen-year-old trying to scale the fence that separates Mexicali from Calexico, California. The agent claimed he fired because the youth was going to throw a rock at him, which drew angry responses not only in Mexico but from Mexican-American groups in the United States. They said witnesses denied that the youth was going to throw anything and, further, that even if he had had a rock, to shoot and try to kill him was a clear over-reaction and an absolutely unnecessary use of force. Calexico police later arrested two Mexican consular employees for trying to bribe a Calexico police employee to reveal the agent's name.

The Mexican consulate in Nogales, Arizona in 1998 protested that Border Control agents pursued three migrants who fled on foot after being stopped on their way toward Phoenix and beat them so badly that one was taken to a hospital in critical condition. The consul spokesperson, Roberto Burgos, indicated that the migrants were unarmed and afraid and did not present a physical threat. But in the eyes of the agents, the *aspirantes* were lawbreaker criminals who could and should be apprehended with the same force that would be used against murderers, armed robbers, or rapists.

Many Border Patrol agents were ex-U.S. Marines and soldiers and responded to terms like "the battle for our borders" and "the war against illegal aliens." When twenty-three-year-old Jesús Ibarra tried to escape being captured after he crossed the frontier near Calexico the arresting *migra* "taught him a lesson," by brutally beating him, then forcing him to hold a sign reading *Yo respaldo a la Patrulla Fronteriza* ("I respect the Border Patrol") while they laughed and took photos of him.[11]

That many *migra* were of Mexican descent, the sons or grandsons of migrants and *indocumentados*, chagrined and perplexed both Mexican authorities and deportees who had been maltreated and humiliated. However, agents in Texas, where approximately three-fourths of those employed by the Border Patrol are of Mexican ancestry, contended that they didn't see major contradictions between their ethnic backgrounds and their work.

"It's a matter of the law," one of them told *La Jornada* correspondents Jim Cason and David Brooks.[12] "It's a job that's interesting and has variety, it's not the same day after day." Then he added, "It's a game, one can't take it too seriously, because if one did it would drive him crazy if he believed that it was possible to stop this flow [of immigrants coming across the border]."

As the Border Control effectively closed off the most frequently used entry points, more and more migrants and their *coyotes* opted for more difficult—and dangerous—places to cross. "Operation Guardian," which began in 1994, forced would-be immigrants away from Tijuana and Otay Mesa onto the torrid deserts along the Arizona border. The number of deaths from sunstroke and hypothermia increased dramatically. Both the California Rural Legal Foundation and the Civil Liberties Union begged Mary Robinson, in 1998 the international high commissioner of the U.N.'s human rights branch, to investigate the way that Operation Guardian "deliberately is giving those crossing illegally a sentence of death."[13] Robinson severely criticized U.S. policy and later was forced to resign her position due to extensive pressure against the U.N. from U.S. diplomats.

Human rights organizations in the Tijuana-San Diego crossing areas documented over 400 instances of physical abuse against immigrants related to Operation Guardian, including five *indocumentados* shot to death by inexperienced border patrolmen. A teenager lost an eye to a *migra*'s bullet in 1986 and customs agents at San Ysidro beat and tried to drown a would-be immigrant in July of that same year. The director of the Centro de Apoyo al Migrante affirmed that all such abuses were a "cruel and inhuman" consequence of the xenophobia and discrimination created by Operation Guardian.[14] Derechos Humanos, based in Tucson, Arizona, reported a notable increase in incidents of corruption, physical abuse, sexual assault, and fatal shootings by the Border Patrol after that entity was put under the administration of Homeland Security in 2003. Agents were not called to account for verbal or physical abuse, leading them to understand that there were few limits on what they could and could not do. The "tonks" trying to cross the border were criminals and needed to be dealt with harshly.

With five times as many agents patrolling the area, and an expenditure of more than a billion dollars, Operation Guardian reduced the undocumented immigrant flow by only 1 percent between 1994 and 2000. At the same time the death rate of those attempting to get past the border rose 600 percent.

"In other words," Joseph Nevins wrote in the *Christian Science Monitor*, "the billions of dollars spent over the past ten years to gain control over the southern boundary has achieved nothing of the sort. Instead, they have only resulted in increased human suffering."[15]

Hipólito Acosta, head of INS' Mexico office, denied that Operation Guardian was responsible for any of the deaths and laid the blame on *coyotes* who "take advantage of those seeking to enter the United States ... They are the principal reason why migrants try to cross in dangerous places."[16] Nevertheless, he admitted that over 1,000 persons a day were trying to navigate the frontier into Arizona and that none of the Border Patrol's efforts had been able to mitigate the flow.

The deaths, and reports of the brutal way some *aspirantes* were being treated by the Border Patrol, prompted the Mexican government to form Grupo Beta, a federal force designed to protect and aid *aspirantes*. Grupo Beta spaced ten solar-operated lighthouses along the Mexican side of the frontier that could be seen from ten kilometers away to guide migrants crossing the desert at night. Each lighthouse contained tanks of potable water. Beta agents did not openly discourage *aspirantes* from trying to cross but they did detail the dangers and difficulties of trying to safely make it across the desert.

Some of the advice they gave came from a booklet published by Mexico's National Institute of Migration. It offered practical suggestions for migrants trying to cross the desert, like following transmissions lines or railroad tracks to keep from wandering in circles, rationing water by not drinking either too much or too little and what to do in case of injury or snakebite. It also advised migrants what to expect and how to react in case they were apprehended by U.S. authorities. Almost immediately anti-immigrant advocates, particularly Arizona representative J. D. Hayworth and Colorado Congressman Tom Tancredo, denounced the booklet's publication as "aiding and abetting the illegal invasion" of the United States.[17] The Mexican government withdrew distribution of the booklet, leaving emigrants to their crossings without helpful advice.

The Mexican state of Baja California inaugurated its own border assistance program in 2001 by setting up patrols to warn immigrants about the dangers of trying to cross through the La Rumorosa Mountains between Tecate and Mexicali. With the conventional routes across Otay Mesa and around Mexicali blocked off, more migrants were attempting to work their way into California through the steep, jagged, treeless ridges. Mexican gangs ambushed groups along the way, robbing them of all of their possessions and sometimes killing them. Periodic gunfights erupted between Beta agents and these *asaltantes* with casualties on both sides.

To the chagrin of U.S. authorities, the Mexican patrols were not trying to stop emigrants from leaving their country. (It is not illegal to leave Mexico without papers, just as it is not illegal to leave the United States without a passport. According to international law, it is up to the receiving country to determine what documentation is necessary for entry.)

Although the Border Patrol criticized the aid Beta gave to would be border crossers, most *migra* agents felt a certain kinship with the Beta agents since, as border patrolman told me, "We're cut from the same stripe."

"I DON'T LIKE THE WAY YOU LOOK"

"Some people think these smugglers are latter-day Robin Hoods, but that's a myth," asserted Virginia Kice, a spokeswoman in the southern California field office of the Bureau of and Immigration Customs Enforcement (ICE) which supplanted INS as the Border Patrol's overlord agency.[18] She claimed that every year more criminal organizations were getting involved, and their operations not only were on a larger scale but also more violent. Not only did they include transporting workers from as far away as Ecuador to cities throughout the United States and Canada, they enticed teenaged girls with promises of work as housekeepers or nanas to cross with them, then turned them over to brothel keepers to work off what they owed for their passage.

Federal agents discovered over a hundred *indocumentados*, most of them Central Americans, locked into a small house in Watts, in Los Angeles County "living shoulder to shoulder amid rotting piles of food and debris as they waited for family members to pay ransom to the smugglers who had led them across the border."[19] The *coyotes* had conveyed the immigrants in separate groups across the Arizona desert, then driven them to the house in a run-down Watts neighborhood. All apparently were to be flown or bussed to East Coast cities once fees from $1,500 to $9,000 had been paid by their U.S. contacts. The *Post* went on to quote an ICE special agent, "They had no idea where they were, or how long they had been there."

The *Post* attributed to unnamed "federal officials" an admission that the Operation Guardian crackdowns had forced *aspirantes* and their *coyotes* to attempt much more difficult—and costly—forays through Arizona. No longer was a trip across the border something that a Tijuana *mamá* could coordinate with her sons and nephews. To cross in Arizona, then move immigrants to L.A. before dispersing them to East Coast locations, the *coyote* entrepreneurs needed more drop houses, more drivers, more supplies, more vehicles, more food and water, and more guides desperate enough, or adventurous enough, to make trips that could result in death by sunstroke, dehydration, or starvation. They needed more money up-front and bigger payments afterwards.

"The smugglers lie to them [the *aspirantes*]," Border Patrol agent Charles Griffin told a writer from England's *Guardian Newspapers*.[20] "These people have no idea what they are going into. They run out of water on the first or second day of a five- or six-day walk." *Coyotes* herding groups unable to keep up the pace abandoned them on the desert, other agents claimed, citing instances of groups of from fifteen to thirty men, women, and children knocking on ranch house doors near Arizona City, seventy-five miles from the border, and being picked up by the agency's search, trauma, and rescue teams over hundred miles from Phoenix thinking they only were a three-hour hike away.

The Border Patrol station in the once thriving copper mining town of Douglas, Arizona, absorbed much of the increased activity after Operation Guardian forced *aspirantes* eastward onto the desert. Buses from the interior ran to Agua Prieta, on the Mexican side of the frontier, and old mining and ranch roads make crossing by automobile relatively easy in places along the border. By 2004, Douglas agents were hauling in over 600 *indocumentados* a day, many of whom tried to sneak into Douglas from Agua Prieta by hacksawing through the ten-foot high fence or vaulting over it from the roof of a vehicle. Agent T. J. Bonner told the *Guardian*, "I have apprehended the same people four times in one shift."[21] All of those detained were locked in the Border Patrol station's holding cells until their nationality was corroborated and a records check showed that they didn't have criminal records in the United States. Then they were bussed back to Agua Prieta.

Operation Guardian preceded Operation Rio Grande in Texas by a year but both pushed the same Clinton administration policies: more manpower, more technology, more money to restrict illegal immigration. Operation Rio Grande diverted *aspirantes* toward dangerous crossings upriver from the popular entry locations near Brownsville and McAllen. By 1998, over 700 agents were patrolling the 280 mile stretch along the river between those two cities day and night. Armed *migra* monitoring special infrared night vision cameras set up by the Border Patrol along the river could detect any human movement a mile away and the officers could rush to almost any site along the river before a "bandit" could pull himself onto the bank. Despite the increased manpower and millions of dollars worth of equipment, the number of apprehensions per month and per year along the Rio Grande remained much the same. Border Patrol spokespersons explained that the statistics indicated that Operation Rio Grande was discouraging attempts to cross but shied away from explaining why the number of deaths along the river had increased.

Similar to what was happening with Operation Guardian on the California and Arizona border, immigrant crossings in Texas moved away from the heavily guarded stretch along the lower part of the river to the area around Eagle Pass, Texas, 300 miles away. So visible were activities in Piedras Negras, the town on the Mexican side of the Rio Grande, that border agents pointed out individual "river rats" to *La Jornada* correspondents Jim Cason and David Brooks during a July 2002 visit by those journalists to the border city.[22] ("River rats," the agents explained, were small-time smugglers not worthy of the designation *"coyotes."*) *Indocumentados* clustered on the Mexican side of the river waiting for nightfall. Border patrolmen watched and waited, some high above the river monitoring signals from the cameras and movement sensors. As soon as they detected something, they radioed the patrol nearest the attempted crossing point. Cason and Brooks described the camera images of three *indocumentados* attempting to cross the river as "ghosts across the eye of the infrared beam."

The *migra* were prohibited by law from making house-by-house searches through individual neighborhoods, although they had the right to drive or walk onto any land within forty miles of the border. Many residents were openly hostile toward the Border Patrol and according to

Cason and Brooks had taught their dogs to bark only at agents and not at anyone else passing near their residences.

Brooks and Cason reported an average of a hundred detentions every twenty-four hours in Eagle Pass alone; possibly that many more *indocumentados* managed to evade the *migra*'s grasp during the same period of time. Those led across by river rats were easier to catch; those who hired *coyotes* had a better chance to get through, since the organized smugglers, like their counterparts in California, knew how and where the Border Patrol operated, where it had sent up the motion detectors and cameras and what parts of the river were easiest to ford. An estimated 20 percent of the *coyotes* operating on the Texas frontier were U.S. citizens and owned property in both countries that served as shelters and jumping off points for transportation to cities further north.

The Texas equivalent of the Arizona desert was the barren scrubland northwest of Eagle Pass. There one found few roads and fewer ranch houses, few places with fresh water and miles of barbed wire fences. Some ranch owners, tired of having their fences cut or broken, built stiles so immigrants could cross them without causing damage. But the fences were minor obstacles compared to the lack of potable water and brutal summer temperatures. Agents told Cason and Brooks that during the summer "there's often a death a day—sometimes more." The *migra*'s detection and apprehension teams also were rescue teams, with their helicopters and river speedboats hauling half-dead migrants to landing spots where patrol cars could take them to processing centers via the nearest McDonald's take-out for hamburgers and soft drinks.

Not all those crossing illegally into Texas were jobseekers, however. Armed drug smugglers used some of the immigrant routes and they created a different situation for the *migra*, for the drug smugglers neither were docile nor afraid. The agent Cason and Brooks interviewed told them, "When one approaches immigrants they'll usually start to run in all directions. But the *narcotraficantes* stand their ground because they don't want to lose their merchandise." The agent showed the correspondents from *La Jornada* where drug smugglers had shot and killed one of his coworkers and told them, "Just about every day we detain one type of *narcotraficante* or other."

The *Washington Post* reported in 1996 that the area between Eagle Pass and Del Rio, further northwest, "is a frontier under siege."[23] They described armed drug traffickers using night-vision devices and walkie-talkies fording the Rio Grande with military-like precision as they "pushed tons of marijuana, cocaine, heroin, and amphetamines into the United States with virtual impunity." Ranchers reported destroyed fences and missing livestock and told interviewers they were afraid to leave their homes after dark. Although the Border Patrol was seizing an average of over 5,000 pounds of marijuana a month from smugglers, the Drug Enforcement Agency (DEA) admitted that the seizures amounted to less than 15 percent of what probably was coming across the border.

DEA special agent Donald F. Ferrarone described the drug smuggling operations as a highly sophisticated coordinated effort among Columbian suppliers, Mexican intermediaries and U.S. distribution centers.[24] Landing strips or little-used country roads on isolated Mexican ranches near the border allowed planes from the interior to land and unload their cargo. Trucks hauled the sixty-pound bags of marijuana to the Mexican side of the river where, among thick mesquite and carrizo cane waiting porters—*mulas*—unloaded it and forded the river to load it on other trucks bound for Houston, San Antonio, Dallas, and other cities further north. Witnesses reported seeing Mexican federal police escort the trucks to the river fording places and ranchers in that part of Texas claimed the smugglers came through their property equipped like "soldiers" with AK-47s, cell phones, and night-vision goggles.

That the cartel smugglers were better equipped than the law enforcement units trying to stop them wasn't lost on either the Border Patrol or area ranchers. The latter often were the most critical.

"They like to go out and larrup the wetbacks," one rancher told a San Antonio radio talk show host, "but they're scared of drug smugglers. They don't want anything to do with them." A Maverick County rancher told Douglas W. Payne of the New York *Times Magazine* that many border patrolmen "seem like they're just ridin' around, waiting for their shift to end."[25]

According to the DEA, most of those involved in the smuggling operations either were citizens or legal residents of the United States. The tightly organized cartels paid well but couldn't trust any phase of their operations to amateurs, even portering the marijuana across the river, and they couldn't afford to have any of their people picked up as *indocumentados*. The violence between competing cartels on the Mexican side of the river, resulting in killings and payback killings, heightened the perception in the United States that anyone crossing the river illegally not only was a criminal but a dangerous criminal. Discrimination and retaliations against the Spanish-speaking community increased.

The creation of the Homeland Security agency after the September 11, 2001 attacks on the World Trade Center in New York and Pentagon building in Washington, D.C. added an "anti-terrorist" element to border security, despite the fact that there was no evidence to indicate that *indocumentados* had anything to do with past or potential terrorist attacks. The Immigration and Naturalization Service became the Bureau of Customs and Border Protection in 2003 and was charged with more aggressive law enforcement than the older INS. In August, 2003, the agency rescinded the limitation put on agents from pursuing or arresting suspected *indocumentados* in nonborder areas. As agents throughout the United States interpreted the policy change, they had gained the right to stop and question anyone who *might be* an *indocumentado*.

Among those stopped for looking Hispanic and having Hispanic last names were four students especially selected by their Phoenix high school for achievement. With five others students from Wilson Charter High School, they had earned a trip to Niagara Falls, New York to enter a solar-powered boat they designed in international competitions being held there in June, 2002. Their teacher asked Border Patrol officials if the students could use their high school IDs to sightsee for a few hours in Canada. Immediately the agents detained the students, even though they had not actually tried to cross the border. The *migra* supervisor told them they were interrogated solely because of their appearance. Several of the agents, the students reported, jeered while they were being held and addressed them using ethnic slurs. The students appealed the deportation ruling after they were sent back to Arizona and were allowed to remain in the United States until the appeal was processed. Three years after their detainment a Phoenix immigration judge cancelled their deportation orders, noting that the agents had violated the students' constitutional rights against illegal search and seizure. Irate ICE lawyers immediately notified the court that they would appeal the ruling, an action that would cost the federal government hundreds of thousands of dollars. Apparently, for ICE and Homeland Security, any expense was worth getting rid of undesirable aliens, even if those aliens were brilliant students who'd lived in the country since childhood and had won international awards.

A senior patrol agent in San Diego, Tomas Jimenez, told the Los Angeles *Times* that the Border Patrol was stopping, interrogating, and arresting persons based solely on their appearance at Hispanics.[26] In San Diego in 2003, they targeted the Mexican consulate and detained and interrogated persons coming from and going toward the building. The consulate issued a vigorous protest but it had little affect on the aggressive new BCBP policies.

Migra raids targeted *indocumentados* in Portland, Maine, Dade City, Florida, Chicago, and Houston. No other excuse was given for the sweep through Portland's low-income areas than that Spanish-speaking migrants lived there. In Chicago, a series of December 2002 raids dubbed "Operation Tarmac" sent Department of Homeland Security personnel through Chicago's Midway and O'Hare airports, into businesses that supplied the airport and into the homes of airport workers. The agents arrested over 800 persons whom, they said, lacked proper documentation. A spokesperson for the Justice Department commented that no longer could employers be guaranteed that they could hire "illegals" and get away with it. He did not note, however, that it was only the workers—not the employers—who were arrested.

Homeland Security also targeted specific workplaces, including Wal-Mart. Night raids on more than sixty Wal-Marts around the country netted over 250 undocumented janitorial personnel during October 2003.

How far Homeland Security personnel would carry the right to stop and question anyone about his or her immigration status was answered when agents purportedly looking for an *indocumentado* with a criminal record awakened immigrant Jose Luis Aguilar in his San Diego home one morning in March, 2004. Aguilar was not the man they were looking for but they demanded to see documentation. They then spread their search through the neighborhood and carted off twelve to fourteen residents in ICE-marked vans. The same month San Diego-based agents began boarding buses and demanding identification from people who appeared to be Hispanic. They arrested over 200 after "interviewing" several thousand.[27] According to witnesses, the arresting agents did not permit those being detained to contact family or friends.

At approximately the same time, agents stopped passengers who appeared to be Hispanics as they were leaving the JFK International Airport and Newark Liberty Airport terminals and arrested over 160. In May, agents in San Francisco entered the Sunrise Hotel to arrest a resident who had violated immigration orders. They took him into custody—and stopped everyone who might be of Mexican or Central American ancestry walking through the lobby. The raid resulted in eight more arrests and "voluntary" deportations.

This raid, according to *In These Times* contributor R. M. Arrieta, drew the ire of city officials.[28] The San Francisco Board of Supervisors responded by passing a resolution requiring that anyone detained by ICE be provided with access to legal counsel and access to hearings. ICE officials reacted coldly. Arrieta quoted deputy field office director Tim Aiken saying, "This notion that we can't question people about their immigration status because they weren't the ones we're looking for is complete nonsense. We have a right to do our job and we are enforcing the laws that Congress gave us."[29]

A Border Patrol sweep through San Bernardino and Riverside counties in June 2004 waylaid "suspected illegals" driving to work, leaving grocery stores, and chatting in front of their apartment complexes.[30] All those questioned, reported an irate Abel Medina, the director of *Hermandad Mexicana Nacional* in Ontario, were "people with brown skin" and he added, "This is harassment and totally aggressive." Persons processed and deported, without right to appeal, included a twenty-year-old whose wife was pregnant and the single father of two young children. During the same month agents raided workplaces and Spanish-speaking neighborhoods in Modesto, in California's San Joaquin Valley, and in Yakima, in the valley of the same name in Washington, areas in which local agriculture depended heavily upon migrant workers. Federal spokespersons reacted against the terminology "sweeps" and "raids" and denied that any increase in seeking out undocumented aliens was taking place. Nevertheless they retained their right to stop, interrogate, and detain anyone with Hispanic colorings or features wherever they might encounter them, including in their workplaces and residences.

They also assumed the right to define as "criminal actions" any help given to *indocumentados* by non-immigrant U.S. citizens. On July 9, 2005, border patrolmen arrested two members of the volunteer group No More Deaths because they were taking three migrants who'd collapsed on the Arizona desert to Tucson for emergency medical care. The Border Patrol and the federal attorneys who pressed charges against the two insisted that the transporting of *indocumentados* was a federal offense even if it were being done for humanitarian reasons. Patrol spokespersons declined to answer if they would have arrested Minutemen or other border vigilantes had they been hauling *indocumentados* to Tucson to turn them over to immigration authorities. Proposition 200, passed by Arizona voters in November 2004, criminalized any efforts by state employees to provide social services to *indocumentados*.

The Immigration and Customs Enforcement raid on an Arkansas poultry plant in July, 2005, followed the same pattern as the sweeps in California. Over twenty-five armed agents blocked entrances and demanded to see the identification documents of each of the nearly 600 workers employed at the plant. They arrested seventy female and fifty male workers for possessing counterfeit, invalid, or stolen social security cards, loaded them in vans, and hauled them off. Over half of those arrested had children in school or day care and were unable to contact them. "They didn't know why Mommy and Daddy didn't come to pick them up," the mayor of nearby Arkadelphia complained to the Arkansas *Democrat-Gazette*.[31]

ICE spokesperson Temple Black claimed the agents "interviewed" each of those arrested but Clark County Sheriff Troy Tucker blasted the supposed interviews and told the *Democrat-Gazette* that ICE conducted the raid without notifying local law enforcement. If there were interviews, he indicated, they were conducted in such a threatening and hostile manner that those being arrested refused to respond for fear their children would be picked up and jailed with them.

Many of those seized were deported within twenty-four hours according to ICE spokespersons in Dallas. The others were jailed until their processing was completed.

These militarized tactics showed a notable deviation from the way the replaced Immigration and Naturalization Service had treated undocumented immigration. United States justice granted rapists, murderers, and pederasts—even those who bomb federal buildings—the rights to lawyers, court appearances, appeals. But a thirty-seven-year-old mother of three trying to support her children by working forty-eight hours a week at minimum wage was handcuffed, separated from her family, and herded into a crowded detention center not much different from a World War II concentration camp, then without trial dumped across the border. According to Joel Wendland, "The Bush administration has made no gestures to the Latino community except to deny an increase in operations and to insist that the panic and fear in those targeted communities is simply in the imagination of the people living there."[32]

ARMIES OF THE NIGHT

Lynching Mexicans, noted historian Rodolfo F. Acuña, "is as American as apple pie."[33] Throughout the Western expansion, but particularly after the discovery of gold in California, the English-speaking occupiers of the newly acquired territories dealt with the lands' formers owners and settlers as inferiors with few if any rights. Individual accounts of the shooting and hanging of Mexican miners, traders, and cowhands filtered through history but no statistics were kept, just as no statistics were kept about the slaying of Indians. The lynching tradition continued into the twentieth century with fewer deaths but the same anti-Mexican discrimination. According to a Tina Rosenberg article in *The Washington Monthly* a south Texas rancher named C. K. Miller shot eleven workers gathered to complain about the low wages they were being paid.

"'I didn't shoot *at* them,' he later corrected a television reporter, 'I shot *them.*'" [34]

Miller never was indicted for the May 30, 1975, shootings but ten years later his son Chet was convicted of firing at four immigrant trespassers, one of whom drowned trying to escape.

"I'll-shoot-'em-if-I-want-to" attitudes were shared by anti-Hispanics throughout the country. In 1976, the Douglas, Arizona Hannigans—rancher George and his sons Patrick and Thomas—ambushed three *indocumentados* who were looking for work, stripped them, branded them with hot pokers, dragged them across the desert, and shot them with buckshot. The local judge declined to issue warrants for the Hannigans arrest until pressured into doing so as news about the attacks spread throughout the United States and Mexico. A local jury acquitted the three men but three years later a federal grand jury indicted them for violating a provision of the interstate commerce act.

Several *indocumentados* were shot and killed near San Diego, including a twelve-year-old crossing a field past the apartment building in which an avowed gun enthusiast lived. In 1996, in Arizona Glenn Spencer began organizing cohorts to repel immigrants under the banner of "American Patrol." Three years later rancher John Barnett of Douglas and his two brothers detained a group of nearly twenty-five immigrants and marched them into town to deliver them to the Border Patrol. The Barnetts claimed the *indocumentados* had trespassed on their property. Neighbors of the Barnetts formed "Concerned Citizens of the U.S.A." to notify Border Patrol agents where migrants were hiding or what routes they were taking. In Texas, an anti-immigrant activist named Jack Foote also organized and sent out patrols. When members of one of his groups caught two Central Americans they accused of being criminal invaders, they pistol whipped one of them.

Like many ranchers and landowners along the border, the Barnetts felt justified in taking the law into their own hands because, they claimed, the Border Patrol was too out-manned to protect their property. "If the government refuses to provide the security, then the only recourse is to provide it for ourselves," a group of Arizona ranchers wrote President Clinton in 1999.[35]

By the late 1990s, the "Tucson Sector" between Nogales and Douglas had become the most popular place to try to enter the United State from Mexico. Agua Prieta, a dusty little border town of less than 30,000, quadrupled in size in less than ten years. Quickly-built hotels provided shelter for would be emigrants. Thousands crowded into streets and *coyote* safe houses or camped amid scrubby desert growth outside of town. As many as 1,000 a day crossed the border and spread across ranchlands, often breaking fences and water lines, frightening livestock, tromping down gardens, and littering the countryside with empty plastic water bottles, ripped apart shoes, clothing, and other debris.

Some ranch families near Douglas complained so bitterly—and so often—about these intrusions that the Border Patrol installed twenty-four-hour cameras and underground sensors around their homes. One resident, Theresa Murray, told *U.S. News and World Report* correspondent Carol Morello that her home had been broken into more than twenty-five times. Concerned Citizens organizer Larry Vance Jr. insisted, "We need the military ... we need helicopters and more surveillance. If we can control Kosovo's borders, why can't we control out own borders?"[36]

Violence against immigrants wasn't confined to the border states, however. Two Farmingdale, Long Island residents, pretending to be labor contractors, ferried two "illegals" to a supposed work site, battered them with shovels and cut them with knives. The instigator, a twenty-nine-year-old that *Christian Century* writer David L. Ostendorf described as "bedecked from neck to ankle with racist tattoos" was sentenced to twenty-five years in prison for attempted murder but like the Millers and the Hannigans was considered a hero by many locals for defending Farmingdale's "quality of life."[37] Other anti-immigrant groups like Voices of Citizens Together and American Patrol made violence against immigrants seem patriotic. Radio talk show hosts from California to the East Coast incited anti-immigrant behavior by condemning legal and undocumented Hispanics for everything from "robbing jobs from decent Americans" and "getting free rides on the welfare system" to spreading AIDS and "infecting our children with drugs." According to the Anti-Defamation League, one such host, Hal Turner in New Jersey, directed his listeners to "kill every single one of these invaders."[38]

It was not killing that Jim Gilchrist had in mind when he formed the Minuteman Project. What he did have in mind was organizing civilian border patrols, an amplification of what the American Patrol and Concerned Citizens U.S.A. already were doing on the Arizona border. Gilchrist told radio listeners that the ultimate object of the Minuteman Project would be to expel twenty-two million illegal aliens from the United States so the nation could again return to a state of law.

Volunteers from throughout the United States responded to the ex-Marine's "gigantic neighborhood watch." Some Minuteman backers claimed over 1,000 patrollers participated during their April 2005 expedition but Border Patrol spokespersons relayed a figure much lower than that. California governor Arnold Schwarzenegger praised their "patriotism" while human rights groups and the Border Patrol held their breath, hoping for a minimum of violent confrontations.[39] Press coverage during the first days of their "service" greatly exceeded that given to either Iraq or Afghanistan and the Minutemen responded with militaristic talk and anti-immigration testimony. A Texas participant insisted, "Maybe twenty years ago the illegals were innocent, hard-working people. Not any more. Now they're extremely dangerous. They mean violence."[40] The Minuteman web page urged taking action to prevent "a tangle of unassimilated squabbling cultures" from taking over the country. The Minuteman patrollers notified the Border Control of the presence of various "Mexican intruders" then disbanded well satisfied with their efforts.

Minuteman's foray had little effect on curbing the flow of attempted entries through Arizona. Governor Janet Napolitano sent a scathing letter to Homeland Security Secretary Michael Chertoff in August, 2005, assailing the department's "bewildering resistance" to cooperating with Arizona's Department of Public Safety.[41] She berated ICE's "inattention to Arizona" and pointed out that the Phoenix ICE office had not had a permanent chief since the agency was created over two years before. Her chief of staff, Dennis Burke, noted that Phoenix police officers waited for hours to get assistance from the Border Patrol for incidents involving undocumented immigrants and sometimes were told that ICE agents were too busy to help, including one case that involved a killing at a drop house.

In August, 2005, both Napolitano and the governor of neighboring New Mexico, Bill Richardson, declared a state of emergency along the border with Mexico. The declarations allowed the two states to spend $1.5 million each to shore up law enforcement in counties most affected by *indocumentados* but neither they nor ICE dedicated any funds—or consideration—to addressing the situation except by marshalling more forces to continue to try to restrict an immigrant flow that billions of dollars spent every year for nearly three decades has barely been able to dent.

A Pox on Both Your Houses!

EASY SOLUTIONS

Solving illegal immigration problems didn't seem difficult to U.S Attorney General Griffin B. Bell. In April 1977, he announced in San Diego that the Carter administration's investment of $90 million not only would stop 90 percent of the *indocumentado* traffic but "dry up narcotics at the source."[1]

Nearly thirty years and billions of dollars later the governors of Arizona and New Mexico declared states of emergency to curb what they called an invasion of unprecedented proportions. Despite an average of over a million deportations a year, undocumented aliens continued to risk their lives crossing deserts, suffocating in closed vans and locked freight cars, fording rivers and canals, and fleeing from delinquent bands of rapists and robbers to eat and sleep in squalid housing, and work at less than minimum wage. Those crossing the border in 2004 included a high percentage of young women with children. Less than 1 percent of those entering from Mexico had criminal backgrounds of any kind.

Bell based his optimism on the belief that with proper force one can stop anything, even though ten years of increasing cost and increasing force had failed to stop the Communist takeover of Vietnam. Successive administrations from Ronald Reagan through George W. Bush have adhered to a philosophy of more border agents, more walls, more arrests, more incarcerations, and more deportations. Despite studies that demonstrated that poverty in the sending countries, exacerbated by the political and economic policies of the United States and other industrial nations, provided the impetus for the migrations, few U.S. government officials took notice. The belief in force was paramount: With a big enough hammer one can crush anything.

Bell seemingly accepted without question the versions of the illegal immigrant problem given him by the attorney generals of the four border states: *Indocumentados* were responsible for rising crime rates; they were becoming increasingly violent and they were a drain on community services, particularly welfare and law enforcement. Bell advocated going light on employers who hired undocumented aliens since it was difficult for employers to know whether a person was in the country legally or not. California Attorney General Evelle J. Younger countered, "Many people here knowingly hire illegal aliens. There wouldn't be many clean bedrooms in Beverly Hills if this weren't the case."[2] And New Mexico's Anthony Anaya added, "Those who employ illegal aliens know what they're doing. Many, in fact, are involved in smuggling them in."[3]

Needing a scapegoat for rising unemployment in 1973–1974, state and federal legislators and union leaders accused *indocumentados* of taking jobs away from U.S. citizens by accepting lower wages and lower standards of living. President Gerald Ford asked the Mexican government to impede the flow of immigrants and announced that, in his opinion, the best solution would be to expel the six to eight million persons that were interfering with our economic prosperity.

Immediately growers, farmers, and agricultural processors told the president that crops would rot in the fields if it weren't for the temporary workers. California Republican governor George Deukmejian announced, "California agriculture hires about 300,000 more workers during the harvest season, of which 50–70 percent are undocumented workers. Interruption in this supply of these workers could cripple the agriculture industry."[4]

Nevertheless, apprehensions and deportations increased. The cities of San Diego and Los Angeles instituted programs requiring that employers replace deported workers by hiring U.S. citizens. Thousands of jobs went unfilled; many others went to workers who only lasted a few days or few weeks. In most cases the jobs paid only minimum wage—or less where piece work was involved—and many included undesirable or repugnant tasks like cleaning toilets and hospital rooms, handling chemicals or degutting seafood, chickens, and others animals.

Texas onion growers, faced with losing their 1977 harvest, petitioned for and received permission to hire non-resident Mexican pickers. Griffin Bell's Justice Department granted the request over the objections of the Department of Labor, whose representatives insisted that the onion growers hadn't done enough to solicit non-immigrant workers.

The following year the federal government granted even more requests for temporary agricultural workers, citing the potential loss of harvests

throughout the South and Southwest that a shortage of farm laborers might cause. At the same time, the Border Patrol was deporting *indocumentados* at an accelerated rate. Griffin Bell and the Carter administration continued to advocate fortifying the border, deporting those without papers and sanctioning employers because of the negative impact that *indocumentados* were having on the economy, particularly by taking jobs away from unemployed legal residents. Nevertheless, the administration approved emergency measures to import harvest workers because of the scarcity of available labor.

This schism between word and deed continued during Ronald Reagan's first presidential term. Reagan personally assured Mexico's president José López Portillo that immigration reform was a U.S. priority but Reagan, in line with his conservative supporters, favored a "guest worker" program that would bring specific numbers of workers into the United States for clearly defined employment—in other words, a modified *bracero* project tightly controlled by the federal government and corporate employers. Reagan's backers insisted that such a project not only would convey workers to jobs when they were most needed but return them to Mexico when they weren't. Some agribusiness and industry titans, true to capitalistic philosophy, argued for totally open borders, reasoning that when employment was available workers would cross the border to perform it, then sift back to Mexico where the cost of living was lower when they were laid off.

Most labor unions opposed instituting a guest worker program. They felt that guest workers would diminish the unions' abilities to recruit and organize and would lower overall wages and salaries. AFL-CIO president George Meany and his successor Lane Kirkland advocated amnesty for undocumented workers already living in the United States and a stringent no-admittance policy for anyone attempting to enter. By granting legal residency and work permits to those already in the United States, Meany and Kirkland believed that the unions could recruit them and help bring what they earned up to a standard equitable with what other workers were making.

Republican Congressman Peter W. Rodino of New York began pushing for sanctions against the employers of *indocumentados* as early as 1973 but never was able to rally enough support from his colleagues to get a bill through the House of Representatives. His proposed legislation put the onus on the hirer, not the worker, dictated fines and/or jail terms for employing nondocumented workers and for anyone falsifying or counterfeiting passports, visas, work permits, or social security cards.

Both Republican and Democratic Congressmen from the states facing the Mexican border opposed Rodino's insistence on sanctions against

employers. Levying fines, they feared, would shut down businesses and increase unemployment. They pointed out that many employers simply would deduct the amount of their fines from their profits (or their workers' wages) and continue to hire *indocumentados*. And they noted that the threat of fines would force employers to become even more secretive about the way they operated and the way they treated and paid their workers.

New Mexico's Senator Joseph Montoya proposed a bill that would establish what amounted to a "new and better" *bracero* project by setting up a national commission to oversee immigrant farm employment but he was unable to convince enough colleagues to support it.[5] Texas' Senator Lloyd Bentsen and Representative Henry Gonzalez pushed the idea of creating a development fund that with the cooperation of the Mexican government would establish job-producing industries in that country but that too failed to garner sufficient support.

Contentions that *indocumentados* were a drain on social services proved to be fallacious. A 1979 study showed that 75 percent of *indocumentados* paid federal income tax and social security taxes but those paying lacked the legal right to the services for which the money was being deducted.[6] Few of these workers filed income tax returns, although the vast majority had money owed them by the federal government. Less than 2 percent received food stamps and less than 4 percent collected unemployment when they were laid off. A 1976 survey in San Diego showed that *indocumentados* contributed twenty-four dollars in taxes for every dollar they received in services.[7]

Ten years later California Governor George Deukmejian commissioned a survey to back up his Republican administration's claims that immigrants who'd just been granted amnesty were burdening the state financially. But his own state agencies reported that an overwhelming majority of newly legalized residents held jobs and rarely used government assistance. Less than 3 percent were receiving food stamps and less than 1 percent receiving welfare. President Reagan's Council of Economic Advisors reported that same year that immigrants paid more to the federal government annually through income and social security tax than they received in benefits.

That farmers and growers kept labor costs down by paying *indocumentados* sub-minimum wages (and often deducting such things as the cost of meals, housing, and transportation from those wages) helped keep the prices of agricultural products at a lower level, thus acting as a deterrent to inflation. Often, in both agriculture and industry, the lower wages paid meant higher profits for employers and middlemen. That these workers

could be dispensed with at the end of a job and not retained year-round on a payroll made employing them even more attractive.

GET LEGAL OR GET OUT

In the mid-1960s Cesar Chavez was able to organize some farm workers and effectively boycott the producers of certain agricultural crops, particularly grapes and lettuce. At its peak, Chavez's organization, the United Farm Workers, numbered nearly 80,000 members and included Chicanos, legal immigrants, and *indocumentados*. Chavez's energy and direct non-rhetorical language at a time when the major television networks were vying for on-the-spot news coverage made him a cause celebre. Chavez was praised, listened to by politicians, and accused of being a pinko, a labor agitator and a racist by his detractors.

While he claimed to represent *La Causa*—and the Mexican-American culture—Chavez never intended that the UFW be other than a labor union which could give its members "the power to control our own destinies."[8] That California at the time had liberal union laws, a legislature dominated by Democrats and a profarm workers governor gave Chavez the backing he needed to forge collective labor contracts between the UFW and grape growers. Thousands of *indocumentados* participated in *La Causa* and through their association with Chavez and the UFW gained some stability and earning power. Chavez and the UFW aligned themselves with the liberal wing of the Democratic Party and with the AFL-CIO.

Although the boycotts organized by the UFW included a significant percentage of *indocumentados*, most of the scabs hired by owners to circumvent the UFW also were *indocumentados*. Many within the UFW urged Chavez not to take a stand against undocumented workers but at the same time the AFL-CIO pushed the farm workers' leadership to adopt an orthodox union stance: Strikebreakers were strikebreakers and could destroy the union if not dealt with. Chavez and the UFW opted to go with the AFL-CIO, Griffin Bell and the Carter administration. The *indocumentados* were on their own.

Although the UFW boycotts were the most publicized—and most successful—farm worker interventions, they weren't the only labor disputes that included *indocumentados*. During the early 1970s, many non-legalized residents were involved in strikes against the food producer Tolteca, a firm founded by Mexican capital but sold to an international conglomerate, and against Farrah, a manufacturer of men's jeans. In May 1975, melon workers in the Rio Grande Valley broke with Chavez and the UFW and started a summer-long strike. UFW officials chastised their

Texas counterparts for violating the nonviolent spirit of *La Causa* and the Texans formed their own Farm Workers Union. They urged *indocumentados* in the Valley not to become *esquiroles* ("squirrels," i.e. scabs) and not to believe the farm owners and labor contractors who were trying to get them to work in spite of the strike.[9]

In November of the same year, some 310 workers, of whom over 85 percent were *indocumentados*, walked out and picketed California Originals. The clothing manufacturer countered by replacing the strikers with Vietnamese refugees who had just arrived in Los Angeles. INS agents called by the firm's owners arrested twenty-five of the Mexican *indocumentados* and the National Labor Relations Board refused to recognize the workers' union and declared the strike illegal. The company fired all of the strikers and reopened without altering either working conditions or salary scales.

Also deported were farm workers who struck the Arrowhead Ranch in Arizona. Law enforcement battalions swept in and apprehended and deported nearly 280 *indocumentados* but the strikers persisted and after three weeks of edgy confrontations achieved their goal and signed a contract guaranteeing fair wages.

Despite increased deportations and the construction of the so-called "Tortilla Curtain" to restrict immigrants from entering El Paso, President Carter tried to engage in friendly contact with Mexican presidents Echeverria and López Portillo over immigration issues. His successor, President Ronald Reagan, met with López Portillo but Reagan's administration was much harsher in its determination to resolve the "problems of illegal immigration."[10] In 1986, after nearly fifteen years of vacillation, debate, and political tugs-of-war, Reagan's Republican-dominated Congress passed the Simpson-Rodino Immigration Reform Act. It included many provisions presented in previous proposals, including the granting of permanent resident status to *indocumentados* who had been living and working in the United States for a set period of time and increasing funding for the Border Patrol. It also made hiring anyone who lacked legal documentation a crime punishable by fines and by jail terms for repeat offenders.

According to the bill's authors and supporters the act would create an immigrant work force that would satisfy the need for low-cost labor in agriculture and industry. Once passed, the act would reinforce border security, thus cutting off the entrance of noneligibles, and enable law enforcement to deport those who didn't qualify for residency. Punishing those who hired *indocumentados* would constrict the flow of newcomers: If there were no jobs there no longer would be a reason to cross the border illegally to look for them. Those with papers would stay in the United States and work; those without would leave voluntarily or would be deported.

Response to the amnesty provisions was slow at first, primarily because most *indocumentados* did not trust dealing with INS. Nongovernmental groups, including immigrant organizations and the Catholic Church, formed task forces to pass out application forms and guidelines and to explain what documentation would be needed. The INS issued preregistration cards to applicants that they could show to border patrolmen or other law enforcement officers to prevent apprehension or deportation.

As registrations picked up, so did optimism within the immigrant society. The prospects that three million immigrants could gain legality stimulated at least twice that many more to emigrate in hopes that they too could obtain residency benefits. Despite discrimination, racism, low paying jobs, and the Border Patrol, the granting of amnesty under the Simpson-Rodino Act made the United States seem like a land of opportunity to millions in Mexico and Central America. The long delayed legislation to resolve the problem had done the opposite of what it had been intended to do.

Unfortunately for those who demanded restrictive immigration policies, the framers of the Simpson-Rodino bill relied on outdated information and made incorrect assumptions about the *indocumentado* population. While it basically was true during the *bracero* period and the early 1960s that most immigrants were single men between the ages of fifteen and thirty-nine who entered the country for periods of three to eight months, worked in agriculture, then returned to Mexico during the off seasons, by 1985 a large percentage of *indocumentados* no longer went back and forth. They lived among relatives and acquaintances in communities much like the communities they had lived in in Mexico. Each year these communities added new members as individuals brought their brothers, sisters, cousins, nieces, neighbors, and/or friends to join them in the United States.

An estimated 40 percent of new arrivals were women. Many had children and the majority had no homes nor jobs to return to in their native land. Those ineligible for amnesty did not, as the bill's originators had anticipated, leave voluntarily. Whether they had documents or not, the majority of them considered themselves permanent residents—or at least as long-term temporary residents—of the towns and cities in the United States in which they had settled.

A 1990 survey conducted by the Center for Agricultural Business at California State University, Fresno revealed that one-third of the agricultural workers in that area admitted they were *indocumentados* (although most had papers of some kind), leading the surveyors to conclude "employer sanctions don't seem to have much effect."[11] They also noted that there had been seven times as many farm worker applicants for amnesty than could have been eligible under the guidelines, indicating that some growers were verifying employment that hadn't existed. A 1991 Commission on Agricultural Workers report called the Act's seasonal agricultural worker concept fundamentally flawed and plagued by widespread document fraud.

By 1991, over three million former *indocumentados* had gained amnesty—1.6 million of them in California. But though legalized they were not necessarily better off financially. Farm employment remained seasonal and many of those granted amnesty only had primary school educations, making it difficult for them to do anything but field work or basic manual labor. That unauthorized immigration continued to increase contributed to an overabundance of workers in many areas. With so many workers to choose from, farm employers had little incentive to improve work or living conditions or pay higher wages.

Farm Bureau spokespersons noted that the Simpson-Rodino Act hadn't caused nearly as many problems as growers had expected, except to create a "paperwork jungle" of record keeping, document checking, and reports.[12] Hundreds of thousands of applicants waited for years before receiving even temporary documents from INS. *USA Today* reported that spouses of legal immigrants waited up to seven years to receive their own green cards—a procedure that only should have taken months. "Many immigrants," the journal editorialized, "find overwhelming the temptation—and need—to work during these waits."[13]

Monica L. Heppel and Sandra L. Amendola of the Center for Immigration Studies commented that Simpson-Rodino hadn't stopped the flow of illegal immigrants but had "created a fraudulent documents industry."[14] Immigrants who had gone back and forth between the two countries, or who had left all or some of their children with relatives in Mexico, qualified for amnesty but their children did not. Parents who qualified for amnesty and could go back and forth between the two countries legally often could not bring children born in Mexico back to the United States with them.

In a case reported by the Sacramento *Bee*, INS ordered the five-year-old daughter of a twenty-nine-year-old working mother of four deported because, due to a legal technicality, the child neither qualified for amnesty nor legal residency. Her mother and three sisters, however, did. Appeals to INS brought an acrid response from the acting director of the San Francisco INS district. "It seems like we reward people who smuggle other people into the country," he made clear that he considered the mother a criminal.[15]

California Assemblywoman Marguerite Archie-Hudson estimated that over 100,000 cases of families split into legalized and nonlegalized members existed in California in 1993. Many, like the five-year-old described above, had appealed INS decisions—part of a "huge backlog" that California Senator Dianne Feinstein claimed was aggravating that state's illegal immigrant problem.[16] Feinstein indicated that *indocumentados* were manipulating the appeals system to stay and work in the United States instead of being deported. Appeals cases often involved bureaucratic errors and false reports, including the filing of inappropriate documents by swindlers who claimed to be immigration consultants. Catholic Church volunteers who helped applicants fill out amnesty requests in Riverside County told INS paper handlers that many of the immigrants they were involved with could barely read and write, much less understand complicated legal ambiguities.

More than half of Mexico's population in the 1980s was under twenty years of age. Every year during the 1980s and 1990s, two million more young Mexicans were ready to enter the work force. Once across the border they could earn in a day what it would take them more than a week to earn in Mexico. The great failure of Simpson-Rodino "was to criminalize a moral and human compulsion," insisted Father Gregory Boyle of Los Angeles' Dolores Mission Catholic Church.[17] The law "made it illegal to pursue the basic human right to work."

The Act "seems only to have succeeded in transforming a seasonal flow of temporary workers into a more permanent population of settled legal immigrants . . . thus transforming Mexican immigration from a seasonal and predominately male flow of rural, undocumented workers going to a handful of states into an urbanized population of settled immigrants."[18]

Although employers no longer could dangle the threat of deportation over the heads of intransigent workers, they could assume a "take it or leave it" stance: "You don't like working here, get out. I'll find someone else." The United Farm Workers' Dolores Huerta asserted that in less than eight years "the cost of living has gone up about 25 percent but wages for many farm workers stayed exactly the same."[19] Joseph Velarde, a consultant to *La Cooperativa Campesina de California*, insisted, "Most farm workers are worse off today than plantation field hands before the Civil War."[20]

"Government regulators seem powerless to protect farm workers from being cheated, kept in squalid housing, injured, and exposed to dangerous pesticides," concluded a December 1991, *Sacramento Bee* special report on farm labor.[21] Worse yet, the report added, "They rarely even try."

The *Bee* quoted the district director for the U.S. Labor Department admitting that investigation of migrant work and living conditions was largely "a symbolic effort." Regulators "just don't do their jobs," insisted State Senator Nicholas Petris.[22] Statistics for investigating minimum wage violations from 1985 to 1991 showed only twenty-eight investigations in seven years despite what probably were thousands of violations. There would have been more investigations, federal officials claimed, if the agencies responsible for them weren't understaffed and if the documentation for proving liability weren't so demanding. Labor contractors in particular were slippery. If a worker was paid in cash, or accepted illegible or inaccurate pay stubs, he or she couldn't prove that he or she had been cheated.

It was a regulatory system designed to please the "know nothings in Congress," a former California Employment Development Department claims adjuster, Guillermo Albañez, told me in 1988, not "to achieve any equality between employer and employee." He cited instances where workers had finished their jobs, been paid, and moved on before the Department of Labor showed up to certify that the jobs in question couldn't be filled by U.S. citizens. The crops needing harvesting simply couldn't wait that long, and neither could the growers.

The 1982 Migrant and Seasonal Agricultural Worker Protection Act gave laborers the right to sue employers for violating federal or state agricultural laws. But investigations declined from slightly over 800 in 1986 to less than half that in 1990. Employers routinely appealed DOL fines and the cases disappeared into a four-to-five year backlog that rendered any sanctions moot.

The Commission on Agricultural Workers warned Congress in 1993 that working and living conditions for farm workers was deteriorating badly. Overall wages had declined 5 percent between 1989 and 1991 and in some states, including California, they were lower than they had been eight years before. The commission attributed the decline to the surplus of job-seekers aggravated by a barely reduced flow of undocumented workers, although the UFW's Huerta, a commission member, criticized the conclusion by insisting "the agribusiness industry, which exploits the workers for profits, with no regard to their human condition"[23] was primarily to blame.

Like many studies sponsored during the 1980s and 1990s, the Commission on Agricultural Workers report was praised for its perspicacity and accuracy by members of Congress and their aides—and then ignored.

In 1992, both the Democratic and Republican candidates for the U.S. Senate from California advocated deporting criminal aliens to serve time in prisons in their countries of origin. The winner of that Senate race, Democrat Diane Feinstein, urged using the Army and Navy to help close off the U.S.-Mexico border. California and other states passed legislation to inhibit the use of tax dollars to educate *indocumentado* children, to require doctors and hospitals to report suspected "illegals" they had seen or treated, and to deny workers' compensation benefits to *indocumentados* even though their injuries were caused by employer carelessness or neglect. California billed the federal government for 1.5 billion dollars that it claimed the state was owed for social, health, and prison services spent on immigrants and refugees.

But, during that same time period, California's Industrial Relations Unpaid Wage Fund—uncollected money owed to migrant workers—accumulated nearly ten million dollars that belonged to *indocumentados*. The money was turned over to the state but never used to counterbalance expenditures the state claimed *indocumentados* had cost California.

Now and then, Congressional committees would make noises about providing health care to immigrants, regulating exposure to pesticides, and supplying adequate housing, but few measures were passed and regulation of those in effect was tepid or nonexistent. In 1991, a U.S. General Accounting Office report to Congress noted that the Environmental Protection Agency seldom took action against growers who misused pesticides. Labor Department investigations the same year reported grossly inadequate housing for farm workers and distressing sanitation problems.

Some cities and counties with high immigrant populations created bilingual programs and Spanish-immersion classes in which Spanish-speaking students were taught primary level skills such as grammar and mathematics first in their own language, then in English. But, anti-immigration groups besieged both state and federal legislators to force through "English-only" education despite the highly positive results the bilingual and immersion programs were achieving. The result was to impede even children of legal residents whose native language was Spanish from keeping up with their classmates and to increase the dropout rate of children from Spanish-speaking families.

Fifteen years after Attorney General Bell's optimistic promise that a 90 million dollar package for fortifying the border would reduce 90 percent of *indocumentado* traffic into the United States, President George Bush's Attorney General, William Barr, told a San Diego audience that the administration's fiscal year 1993 appropriation of $1.07 *billion* dollars for more agents, more fences, more vehicles, more helicopters, and more sensors would significantly reduce the flow of undocumented immigrants. A portion of the appropriation, Barr noted, would be devoted to hiring temporary workers to help process a backlog of over a million immigration applications.[24]

Barr didn't mention that the Border Patrol had apprehended and deported over 1.1 million *indocumentados* during 1991 without significantly diminishing the number of new immigrants looking for work in California and elsewhere in the United States. Newly elected U.S. Senator Dianne Feinstein of California advocated stiffer penalties for people smuggling—ten–twenty years in prison and fines as high as $250,000. She also proposed to stop "financially sound people" from coming to the United States and receiving medical care at taxpayer expense, to enlarge the border processing stations, to add at least 600 more Border Patrol agents, and to charge fees for all those entering the United States with day passes or white cards.[25] This tough anti-immigration posture coming from a Democrat was a factor in newly elected President Clinton's backing away from Border Patrol budget cuts and endorsing the hiring of the 600 agents in August, 1993.

Even liberal officeholders like California Senator Barbara Boxer, also a Democrat, and Congressman Richard Lehman from Fresno jumped on the anti-immigration bandwagon, Boxer suggesting National Guard deployment on the border and Lehman the issuance of noncounterfeitable national work identification cards. In October, as joblessness continued to increase throughout the United States, the House of Representatives rejected a bill that would have extended unemployment benefits because it contained a clause that would have given aid to blind, disabled, and elderly immigrants. "Americans and taxpayers first!" expounded Texas Representative Bill Archer, not "welfare for aliens over unemployed American workers."[26]

Despite the rhetoric the proposals weren't different in kind—only in quantity—from those of ten, twenty, and thirty years before. In the eyes of Congress, the only way to solve the problem was to swing a bigger hammer not clamp down on employers who made jobs available to *indocumentados*. Employers would continue to hire those they could pay little or nothing until deterrents against that practice were stringent enough.

Feinstein's stance, like that of many elected officials during the early 1990s, was in part a response to increasing pressure being exerted by nongovernmental anti-immigration organizations like the Federation for American Immigration Reform (FAIR). Founded by John Tanton and led by Alan C. Nelson, a former INS commissioner, FAIR played on "silent invasion" fears. A 1986 Tanton memo described the threat that a higher birth rate among Spanish-speaking immigrants could have on the United States. He wrote:

"Will the present majority peaceably hand over its political power to a group that is simply more fertile? . . . perhaps this is the first instance in which those with their pants up are going to get caught by those with their pants down!"[27]

Nelson refuted claims that FAIR was racist by delineating between legal immigrants and illegal immigrants and insisted in 1993 that more and more Hispanics favored tighter immigration laws. While admitting that causes like FAIR sometimes attracted fringe groups and kooks, he insisted that FAIR was a middle-of-the road organization anchored in strong traditional values of equality and prosperity. He claimed to be concerned not only about the effect that "unchecked illegal immigration" was having on the United States but for the immigrants themselves.

"From a dollar point of view they might be making more, but what about their quality of life?" he asked Sacramento *Bee* writer Marcos Bretón in 1993.[28] "Oftentimes it's worse, and they are living a shadowlike existence being exploited by unscrupulous employers. You also have to ask the question, 'Is the child better off here?' The child might not be better off here than in Mexico."

Nelson was one of the principal organizers of California Proposition 187—ballyhooed as the "Save Our State" initiative—which would have denied social and health services to *indocumentados* and denied them access to public education. California Republican Governor Pete Wilson, hoping that an antiimmigrant stance would help ferry him to the White House, publicly campaigned for its passage. He put the blame for much of the state's financial adversity on *indocumentados* for draining social service programs and claimed that the measure's passage would generate significant savings and defuse the state's budget crisis.[29]

Proposition 187 publicity depicted immigrants as leeches who'd come to California to get welfare benefits and to take jobs away from American citizens. Its proponents claimed that immigrants significantly lowered the quality of education by using resources that should have gone to educate the children of legal residents. In November 1994, California voters passed Proposition 187 by a 59–41 percent margin. The dean of Valparaiso University School of Law, Edward McGlynn Gaffney Jr., called the claims made by Proposition 187 advocates a lie. He traced California's budget crisis to a severe downturn in the economy and the cap put on property taxes by a 1978 voter-approved measure, Proposition 13.

"Undocumented aliens form California's hidden economic infrastructure.[30] They mow the lawns in Pasadena. They are the nannies of Beverly Hills. And they pay taxes on virtually everything they buy . . . if attendance diminishes, the schools will lose some of their revenues from federal subsidies predicated on student count... Proposition 187 was a racist distraction from the real budget issues."

Proposition 187 was declared unconstitutional for bumping against a 1982 Supreme Court decision that overturned a Texas law that would have allowed authorities to expel the children of undocumented aliens from public school. But, the antiimmigrant feelings it generated didn't go away.

A 1995 University of California study refuted claims made by Governor Wilson and other Proposition 187 backers by concluding that during a fifteen-year span Spanish-speaking immigrants were learning English and becoming citizens at three times the rate that they had fifteen years before. Patrick J. McDonnell, writing in the Los Angeles *Times*, summarized, "the results clearly indicate that many immigrants are embracing the much-idealized American Dream more quickly than casual observers and policy-makers might conclude."[31]

Anti-immigration spokespersons vehemently disagreed. A huffy Glenn Spencer of Voice of Citizens Together told the *Times* that the question wasn't assimilation, "It's annexation by Mexico!"[32] Immigrants in his view had no right to weasel their way into what belonged to WASP America.

SLUSH FUNDS

If estimates made during the 1970s are correct, *indocumentados* sent 30 to 40 percent of what they were paid to family and relatives in Mexico. Not only did these remittances provide the major source of income for hundreds of thousands of men, women, and children in towns throughout the country, they enabled the Mexican government to bypass spending on social programs. These wire transfers coming in, these cashier's and personal checks, the cash brought back in wallets or sewed into clothing or tucked into boots provided investment-free income; the only thing that either the Mexican private or public sector had to do was allow it to be spent. Mexican presidents from Miguel Alemán to Ernesto Zedillo acknowledged U.S. complaints about illegal immigration but weren't about to take any definite steps to deter it. Why? The cash and wire transfers and checks—$50, $100, $400 at a time—brought the country more dispensable income than any other activity or industry except oil.

It has been impossible to accurately compute how much immigrant workers in the United States actually sent or brought back to Mexico. The totals provided by financial institutions from wire transfers and checks included sums sent by nonimmigrant relatives of Mexican families and business transactions between individuals in the two countries. They did not include cash that individual migrants carried home with them, nor cars, televisions, or other "big ticket" items that the returning workers brought into the country. According to the Bank of Mexico, in 1970 remittances topped twenty-one million dollars. The amounts rose to 51 million in 1975, 108 million in 1978 and over 225 million dollars in 1979.[33]

Twenty-five years later, in 2004, immigrants and their descendants in the United States sent 16.6 *billion* dollars home to Mexico. Official Mexican government estimates showed remittances topping oil revenues for the rest of the decade, with a minimum of twenty billion expected each year. Some of the checks and wire transfers now were larger, but few topped $1,000. Simple math indicates that a majority of the estimated twenty-four million U.S. residents of Mexican birth and/or Mexican descent remitted money regularly to relatives south of the border. Little wonder that there's been so little enthusiasm on the Mexican government's part to cut off emigration!

Throughout the 1970s and the decades that followed families throughout Mexico considered becoming an *indocumentado* a viable way for a family member to earn an income. (In many parts of Mexico it became the expected way for him or her to do so.) Emigration increased dramatically during the 1960s as agriculture and industry in the United States boomed during the Vietnam War. Mexican president Gustavo Diaz Ordaz tried to negotiate guest worker agreements with the U.S. government throughout his six-year term from 1964–1970 but he could not get American negotiators to guarantee fixed quotas nor guaranteed incomes. Many American growers and industry owners were lukewarm to the idea of a rejuvenated *bracero* program which would require them to provide government-inspected housing and detailed payroll documents. They preferred to hire *indocumentados*, pay them as little as possible and not have to deal with bureaucratic red tape.

Diaz Ordaz' successor, Luis Echeverría, pushed for even more beneficial terms, including allowing guest workers to remain in the United States and not be required to return to Mexico. But in October 1974, he abruptly reversed course. He told U.S. President Gerald Ford that Mexico no longer wanted any kind of guest worker accord. He explained that his government was deeply concerned about the escalating emigration from the interior to the border cities. A new guest worker arrangement would accelerate that flow, with the result that the thousands of migrants unable to gain guest worker status either would remain on the border or try to emigrate illegally into the United States.

Echeverría was lying. Or at best concealing what the Mexican government finally had realized: The several million undocumented workers who'd migrated to the United States not only were bolstering Mexico's economy with millions of dollars of remittances every year but they also had relieved a severe unemployment problem within the country itself. They cost the government nothing; they used none of their country's material resources yet they contributed over 30 percent of their earnings to families living in Mexico. The National University of Mexico reported in 1996 that immigrants comprised 3.6 percent of the U.S. labor force and that over 15 percent of Mexico's economically active population was immigrants working in the United States.[34]

Echeverría and his successors refocused their rhetoric to "the necessity of creating more sources of employment in agriculture and industry to prevent the loss of workers to the United States."[35] For the next twenty-five years Mexican diplomats would echo those clichés and insist on "fair and humane treatment" of their countrymen by the Border Patrol, the U.S. courts and rural law enforcement but any structuring of national policy to restrict or control emigration—the rights of Mexican citizens to choose where and how they traveled—was dead.

There was, however, another side to the coin. Many formerly active and industrious pueblos virtually had become ghost towns. "The economic impact also can be measured in the loss of human resources—young men, bold and capable, who on emigrating cause tremendous social problems. On the one hand, one sees family disintegration and on the other the unjust work conditions in a system where the *indocumentado* has no legal rights and is used when needed, then deported when he's no longer useful."[36]

Early reports after the Congress of the United States passed the Simpson-Rodino Act in November 1986, indicated that as many as two million *indocumentados* would be shoved back into Mexico in less than four months, creating catastrophic unemployment and depriving the country of millions of dollars in remittances. Members of the Mexican Senate and Camera de Diputados denounced the deportation provisions of the Act as "outrage against human rights" and a "unilateral" action that violated the principles of international law. They expressed their incredulity that the United States would stifle the production of its own ranchers, farmers, factories, and workshops that depended almost entirely on the inexpensive manual labor that Mexican immigrants provided.

What they failed to note was that deportations already were at an all-time high (1,600,000 in 1985) and the amnesty provisions of Simpson-Rodino would act as a magnet for many who did not qualify for amnesty or who had not yet emigrated. In April 1987, shortly after the act went into effect, I asked an *indocumentado* if he weren't afraid of being deported. He gave me a "you-must-be crazy-look" and laughed. "I've already been

deported six times." Then, more sagely than many of the creators of legislation in either Washington, D.C. or Mexico City, he added, "There are
millions of us. There only are thousands of them [the *migra*]. How can they
expect to control us?"

The year after the passage of the immigration act, the director of programs of Mexico's *Conapo* (National Council of Population) estimated that
16 percent of the small industries in the state of Jalisco (the capital of which
is Guadalajara) had been funded by migrants. At least one out of ten Mexican families depended upon remittances from the United States for the
majority of their financial support, *Conapo* data indicated, and those who
received help from emigrants were 60 percent better off financially than
those who didn't. *Conapo* put the number of Mexican nationals in the
United States at 6.6 million, a figure probably more accurate that higher
U.S. government estimates.[37]

Jorge A. Bustamante told *La Jornada* readers in April, 1997 that the
United States did not want to close the border but wanted to guarantee
cheap labor for agribusiness and industry in order to continue to dom-
inate world markets.[38] Illegal immigration was essential to the United
States and the persecution and maltreatment of *indocumentados* guaranteed that, as criminals, they had no rights to seek better wages, to strike,
or to improve conditions where they worked or lived. The more intolera-
ble their situations became, the more the established society would reject
them, mistreat them, and discriminate against them. Legalizing their presence by established guest worker programs or government controls over
wages and work conditions would alter that dynamic. The Border Patrol
fit into this scenario by making it so difficult for migrants to reach job sites
that the *indocumentados* would suffer work and pay abuses in order not to
be arrested and deported.

Many Mexicans felt betrayed that U.S. Presidents Carter and Clinton
backed away from their initial sympathies toward immigrant workers.
They also did not understand that nothing motivates political opinion
more than having an "enemy" that needs to be conquered. Few of us can
remember a time when the United States hasn't had to contend with some
oppressive force: Germany and Japan, then Russia, Korea, Vietnam, not to
mention the "War on drugs" and various other "isms" and threats from
foreigners, longhairs, African-Americans, bureaucrats, and IRS tax collectors. If playing to the masses and bashing immigrants will get votes, politicians will play and bash.

Mexico's ex-chancellor of foreign affairs Santiago Roel admitted that
Mexico had little or no way to stem emigration except by creating enough
employment inside the country to make staying more attractive than

leaving. But the signing of the 1994 North America Free Trade Agreement (NAFTA) with the United States diminished the possibility that Mexico could develop labor-intensive agribusiness or industry. NAFTA was designed to open foreign markets to U.S. products by eliminating tariffs and other trade barriers. It made U.S. manufactured goods and farm products less expensive than those produced locally, increasing un- and under-employment and costing millions of *ejidarios* (small landowners) the ability to continue to support themselves. Every year since January 1, 1994, when NAFTA took effect, more Mexicans have slid below the poverty level and more Mexican entrepreneurs have joined the ranks of the world's multi-billionaires. And every year more Mexicans view emigration as their only economic choice.

Mexican journalist Juan Manuel Magaña scored the governments of presidents Carlos Salinas de Gortari and Ernesto Zedillo for failing to do more to defend the rights of the *indocumentados*, particularly those reportedly beaten or those who had lost their lives trying to escape the *migra*.[39] According to his figures over 100 *indocumentados* died at the hands of the Border Patrol between 1989–1995. The brutal beatings of a Mexican couple by Riverside County deputy sheriffs on April 1, 1996, which was televised throughout Mexico, and a fatal crash of a truck trying to escape pursuit, also in Riverside County, five days later triggered an outpouring of public resentment, much of it fomented by the media describing handcuffed deportees thrown face-down on detention center floors and left there for hours, Ku Klux Klan threats against the Mexican consul in Los Angeles, roundups at workplaces where workers as young as fourteen and fifteen were manhandled and cursed.

These sensationalized accounts diverted focus from descriptions of extortion that many migrants experienced at the hands of Mexican police and the harsh treatment accorded Central American *indocumentados* when they were apprehended by Mexican immigration authorities.

While acknowledging the failure of his country to provide sufficient employment to keep the migrants at home, Magaña insisted that NAFTA and neo-liberal economics were making Mexico increasingly dependent upon the United States for everything from corn to tractors. In the early 1990s, more than 15,000 Mexican industries closed, exacerbating unemployment. Droughts, the lack of good-paying jobs, unpayable debts, constantly rising prices, overcrowding, deteriorating public health, and escalating crime forced more and more Mexican citizens northward.

While Pete Wilson was ranting about the failure of the courts to let him implement the provisions of Proposition 187 and the Clinton administration was responding to Senator Feinstein and others in the Senate and

House of Representatives by increasing manpower and materiel on the border, the Mexican government was laying off and firing federal employees. Three thousand five hundred Pemex workers were given their walking papers; the National Lottery dispatched 150. The Zedillo government's inability to allocate budgeted money during the first trimester of 1996 triggered 200,000 layoffs in related employment. No figures exist to indicate how many of those who lost jobs headed for the United States but the ripple effect from lost employment, unpaid debts, and diminished purchasing power obviously stimulated migration.

Most of Mexico's Catholic hierarchy berated the government's inability to provide employment and control crime. Yet few of them offered solutions, other than to urge authorities to deal more effectively and severely with crime and human rights abuses. Zedillo's government had dedicated the bulk of the nation's gross national product to paying interest on the country's enormous foreign debt. That more than three million immigrants were remitting more than three billion 500 million dollars annually provided internal income and purchasing power the government couldn't afford to lose. The country's diplomats would continue to make what Magaña called "tepid protests" to Washington for deaths, deportations, and arrests but do nothing to impede continuing migration.

As prices being paid for oil exports declined in 1997 and 1998, Zedillo's government adjusted expenditures and raised taxes on fuel, telephone service, and rents. Reconfigured electricity rates eliminated subsidies for users who lived in areas where summer heat was the most oppressive, doubling and tripling many consumer bills. The added taxes, coupled with industry layoffs and rising prices for consumer goods, accelerated emigration, particularly from areas that previously had not provided large number of *indocumentados*. The government denied that its policies caused workers to leave the country. Sub-secretary of Immigration Fernando Solís told *La Opinión* in December 1998, that the Zedillo administration was "oriented to increased social spending on the most vulnerable sections of the population" and that emigrants left because they were receiving "offers of work" in the United States.[40] However, most of those "offers" were sub-minimum wage in agriculture and industry where workers had no rights and lived in constant fear of deportation.

MORE OF THE SAME?

Proposals for a revived "guest worker" program have been popular on both sides of the border but neither country has been able to ascertain that such a program would work successfully. The *bracero* program stimulated rather than curtailed illegal immigration. The Simpson-Rodino Act that was supposed to solve "the immigration problem" by legalizing longer term *indocumentados* and securing the frontier encouraged new arrivals despite making entry more difficult and work places less safe. More immigrants are crossing the border than every before, many from as far away as Brazil and Ecuador; "sealing the border" only has succeeded in making the crossings more dangerous. Mexico and the other sender countries still need their remittances and growers and restaurants and sweat shops and grain elevators and poultry producers in the United States still need their low-cost labor. Guest workers might satisfy some needs but the mere existence of such a program wouldn't retard those not getting guest-worker status from trying to cross the border illegally.

What the solutions should be are obvious—how to attain them is not. If Mexico could provide adequate employment, millions of jobseekers wouldn't be leaving the country. If U.S. agribusiness and industry could do without low-cost labor to produce food, clothing, and services there would be no need to recruit or hire nonlegals.

Using Senator Feinstein as an example, since she was the epitome of hard-nosed unreasonableness and ethnic prejudice to many Mexicans, Bustamante proposed selecting from the list of her largest campaign contributors the names of those companies that did the most extensive business with Mexico and boycotting them. As long as the boycotts were organized by nongovernmental groups and not the Mexican government such boycotts would be legal. He suggested that more than one officeholder could be pressured at a time by researching what businesses most heavily supported anti-immigration candidates. As Cesar Chavez did with his grape boycotts, the organizers would plead for public support and continue the boycotts until the officeholders were forced by their donors to soften their ramp.

Whether such a boycott would work is debatable. It's difficult to go anywhere in Mexico and not encounter someone who has relatives in the United States, or someone who worked for years in the United States, or someone who depends upon remittances from the United States. Urban shoppers purchase a variety of U.S.-made products, from soft drinks to car batteries to computer components. Many—probably a majority—view more American-made movies on television and in theaters than they do those made in Mexico. Those who can afford it go to Disneyland for vacations, or Las Vegas. Others save up money to shop in Los Angeles and San Antonio. They root for the Dallas Cowboys and the San Diego Chargers, they baptize their children with names like Erika, Dennis, and Jonathan, they know much more about the United States than most Americans know about Mexico. And they know that a significant percentage of the United States's twenty-four million residents who are first- or second-generation Mexicans are materially better well off than they are.

Most second- and third-generation Mexican-Americans who live in the United States support higher wages and better living conditions for immigrants but on the whole the Chicano population has been more passive than active politically. Nevertheless, Pacific News Service associate editor Gregory Rodríguez noted a distinct turnaround in Latino voter participation in 1998.

"Sheer self-defense has pushed Latino civic- and political-participation to all-time highs. Lingering fear and anger engendered by Proposition 187 and the partial denial of government benefits to legal immigrants have spurred foreign-born Mexicans to apply for citizenship at historically unprecedented levels."[41] In 1994, Republican Pete Wilson campaigned for reelection riding antiimmigrant sentiments. In 1998, California's Republican Party went out of its way to woo Latin voters.

But neither as a voting bloc, nor as a unified cultural force, have U.S. Hispanics unified behind specific legislation. Mexicans tend to "rely heavily on family and other informal social networks to negotiate daily life," Rodríguez observed. And in both the United States and in Mexico he noted "a strong distrust of government" and "a cultural tendency to turn to each other for help." Despite an outcry over immigrant use of public services, Spanish-speaking immigrants underutilize health facilities and have the lowest rates of persons on welfare of any ethnic poverty group. This reliance on family, and on interactive family-formed communities, has proved to be a strong survival tool but has weakened the ability to forge a political or social identity.

Coupled with guest worker proposals have been suggestions that the United States grant amnesty to *indocumentados* working in the country. While doing so would acknowledge the reality of their presence it wouldn't per se alter their living or working conditions. The last mass granting of amnesty (Simpson-Rodino) stimulated even greater emigration from Mexico and Central America. Farm wages in the United States declined; living and working conditions worsened; border crossing became more dangerous and accounting, bookkeeping, and regulatory activities foundered. Billions spent annually "securing the border" didn't keep the immigrants out and supposed employer sanctions didn't deter the hiring of the millions of *indocumentados* who fought their way across rivers, deserts, and freeways to work for minimum wage or less.

Congress' attitude toward illegal immigration has been no different from its attitude toward illegal drugs: Go after the supplier and ignore the market. Capitalism is based on making the most profit possible for the least expenditure. If there were no jobs, poverty-driven immigrants wouldn't flock across the border to fill them. The *chiste*, as they say in Spanish, is to regulate employers, not to beat up the people they want to hire.

How can that be done? (Perhaps a better question is, Can it be done?) It could, but it would take an enormous bureaucratic effort and expenditure of personnel. It would make checking employer records—hirings, firings, payroll, housing, benefits—the principal preoccupation of the Border Patrol. It would mean amplifying the social security system through Internet access so that an inspector could check the actual earnings of each worker to make sure that he was who he claimed to be, that he had been paid what he was supposed to have been paid, and that all of his documents were authentic. Employers would have to check by Internet with Social Security each time they hired someone new to ascertain that the card number that he or she presented was legitimately his or hers.

It could mean utilizing closed military bases as barracks-type migrant housing for which residents would pay a set amount to cover upkeep, maintenance, supervision, and clerking. Inspections would have to be made weekly in agriculture and at least every fifteen days for construction and industry. Fines levied against nonconforming employers could offset some of the costs; so would diverting *migra* from their border hunts. There would additional employment for computer programmers, administrative help, and equipment repair people.

It could be done but would the cost be worth it? (Of course one also could ask, "Are the billions being spent to non-secure the still leaky border worth it?") Some costs could be defrayed by the formation of worker cooperatives which could supply employers with prescreened qualified personnel. (Some might want to define "worker cooperatives" as "labor unions.") Instead of an employer-hired contractor whose job it was to squeeze both work and money out of vulnerable *indocumentados* one would have the equivalent of a union shop steward who would determine who worked when and where. (One also could have a rerun of union-employer relations that resulted in corruption, briberies, outsourcing, and a flood of cheap foreign goods.)

The prices that consumers would pay for agricultural products would go up and probably there would be fewer strawberries, less asparagus, fewer tomatoes, and fewer chickens in markets a longer distance away from the producing areas as growers cut back on their production. Some growers, small industries, and sweatshop manufacturers might decide that it would more profitable to move their production south of the border to take advantage of lower labor costs and less government interference.

The other obvious alternative would be to create reasons for workers not to leave Mexico to seek work elsewhere. If the billions spent over the last three decades to keep *indocumentados* out of the United States had been invested in Mexican agriculture and industry many of the problems connected with illegal immigration would have been mitigated. But obstacles against such investment were (and are) huge. Even though Mexico's last four presidents have embraced neo-liberal economic polices, the country's government has remained highly defensive about its "sovereignty." Strong internal opposition to outside investment in gas and oil production and in the generation of electricity has thwarted substantial involvement by outsiders in those industries.

For more than half a century a flow of workers crossing the border without documentation to work where and how they could and sending remittances back to Mexico has benefited both countries. Fifteen percent of Mexico's active labor force works in the United States, legally or illegally, for U.S. employers. Growers, ranchers, housing and construction contractors, grain warehouses, poultry plants, clothing manufacturers, and service industries—janitorial, domestics, garbage—make profits they couldn't otherwise make by hiring immigrants and *indocumentados*.

The Border Patrol, with its fences, helicopters, electronic devices, and immigration sweeps has kept the system in balance by apprehending and deporting approximately a million *indocumentados* a year while another million slip through and find work somewhere in the United States. The ongoing threat of deportation that the Patrol holds over the heads of migrants has kept them frightened, undemanding, and thankful for the minimum-wage or sub-minimum-wage work that they can get. Enough find work to encourage more to keep coming and the surplus provides employers with an unending supply of cheap labor.

Should anti-immigration activists be successful in braking immigration and deporting the majority of immigrants now in the United States, thousands of businesses, particularly those connected with agriculture, would collapse. The potential revolution spared Mexico by the safety valve could fester and break out with dire consequences for U.S. oil imports, grain sales, and other NAFTA-enabled industries. As the status quo exists, the United States needs its cheap labor and Mexico needs the out-of-country contributors to its economy. Despite all the rhetoric from both sides of the border, the system seems to be functioning.

The question is: Can it continue to do so?

Most probably the answer is: No.

World population growth prohibits a return to an idyllic America WASP America, just as it prohibits a return to an all-Anglo Great Britain or an all-Catholic France. The changes can't be wished away. Nor can they be blindered away by protesting the eyesores that poverty has caused. To solve a problem one first needs to define and understand what caused it. In politics, as in matrimony, no solution is ideal. And in politics, as in matrimony, no solution is permanent. Those based on dealing with reality rather than politics, prejudices, or dreams have the best chance of succeeding.

Don't Kill the Cash Cow

NOTHING SUCCEEDS LIKE FAILURE

They had much in common, these two newly elected presidents, Vicente Fox and George W. Bush. Both had grown up in relative wealth, both had strong entrepreneurial backgrounds, both had adopted a Marlboro man image and each had replaced the leader of an opposition party in the presidency. Each manifested to be religious, conservative, anti-big government and proprivate enterprise. And each, while he campaigned for office during the year 2000, promised to resolve the thorny problems of undocumented immigration.

Fox pushed for an early "summit conference" to forge an accord. He made much of his association with his *"amigou"* Bush and invited the U.S. president to his ranch in Guanajuato. Bush, cordial but noncommittal, agreed to meet with Fox to work out the details of a guest worker agreement that would ease border tensions and give immigrant laborers better working conditions.

Media coverage of Border Patrol pursuits and arrests had aroused *antiyanquismo* feelings south of the border that Fox felt his friendship with Bush would mitigate. Mexico's economy was stagnant and though exports were rising so was unemployment. Nearly half of the country's business was being conducted informally—i.e., under the table, untaxed, and unregulated. During the 1990s, the real purchasing power of wages plummeted more than 20 percent and was continuing to slide downward after Fox's election. While hourly compensation for U.S. production workers averaged nearly $18.00, in Mexico the average was $1.50 an hour. An immigration accord that would assure the continued flow of worker remittances to Mexico and that would authorize those workers' presence in the United States would help solidify an unstable situation and put Mexican workers—and Mexican residents—on more equal footing with their northern neighbors. Border restrictions would be eased, goods could flow back and forth more easily and the economic package that Fox planned to present to his countrymen would open petroleum and energy industries to U.S. and foreign investors.

After what Fox's government considered foot-dragging on the part of the United States, a date for the Fox-Bush summit was confirmed for mid-September 2001. Despite his popularity with voters the year before, Fox's star already had started to tarnish. Squabbles within his cabinet had dulled public approval and opposition to his proposed economic reforms, which included taxing food and medicine, had pushed him into a corner. Though he'd won the presidency his *Partido Acción Nacional* (PAN) held a minority of seats in both the Senate and Chamber of Deputies, curtailing his ability to push through any kind of legislation.

The meetings between Fox and Bush never took place. The September 11 terrorist attacks on New York's twin towers and the Pentagon in Washington, D.C. cancelled the summit and requests by Fox's government to reinstitute the talks failed to get U.S. approval. Amnesty and guest worker accords no longer interested Bush's neo-conservative government. The administration reformed INS as a strictly law enforcement agency under the new Homeland Security Department and stepped up border vigilance and *migra* raids.

"The northern frontier no longer is the same," reported the Mexican weekly *Proceso* a month and a half after the attacks. "Tightened control, massive layoffs, businesses at the point of bankruptcy for the lack of sales, tourism paralyzed ..."[1] During the two weeks following the attacks, El Paso suffered an estimated fifty million dollars worth of business losses and Ciudad Juarez *maquiladoras* discharged more than 60,000 workers. Commuters waited for up to two hours to cross the border from Tijuana to San Ysidro, California, forcing many green card holders to remain in the United States sleeping in their cars rather than be late for work. Government officials and business groups throughout Mexico braced for a massive exodus of displaced *indocumentados*, much as they had after the passage of the Simpson-Rodino Act in December 1986.

For a few months over the winter of 2001–2002 border apprehensions dipped, an indication that fewer *aspirantes* were trying to cross the frontier, and a greater flow of traffic southward indicated that some *indocumentados* were returning to Mexico. But as the restrictions against local vehicular and pedestrian movement between the United States and Mexican border cities eased, commuters and shoppers resumed their work and spending habits and thousands of Mexican and Central American men, women, and children again converged on Agua Prieto, Mexicali, and Piedras Negras in order to attempt new crossings.

Deaths in the desert increased as more migrants and their *coyotes* tried to avoid the *migra* by detouring through areas "that even rattlesnakes wouldn't live in," as a member of the Mexican migrant support organization *Grupo Cuauhtémoc* described the western Arizona desert. By July 2005, over 130 known deaths had been recorded in six months in Arizona alone.[2] Many of those who died were women; most of the deaths were heat related. The Latin American Working Group noted that the area is so rugged and vast that only a percentage of bodies were being found.

A sizeable number of those trying to enter the United States were from countries other than Mexico. In May 2002, Mexican authorities arrested thirty Brazilians in Hermosillo, Sonora. The same month a U.S. Coast Guard vessel intercepted an Ecuadorian freighter in international waters with over 500 *aspirantes* stacked in its hold. It was the third such vessel bound from the South American country to Cabo San Lucas, in Baja California, that had been apprehended in less than a year. All told, the Border Patrol apprehended over 150,000 non-Mexican immigrants in 2005, over triple the number from two years before. Mexican immigration reported the arrests of Pakistanis, Chinese, Peruvians, and natives of various African countries, most of whom were trying to use Mexico as a trampoline to get into the United States, and Arizona "Civil Homeland Defense" vigilantes claimed to have caught natives of twenty-four countries, including Poland, and turned them over to the Border Patrol.

Complaints against Mexican immigration and federal and local police escalated as emigrant traffic from Central America through Mexico increased. Deportations of Central Americans by the Mexican government topped 140,000 in 2003 and 200,000 in 2004 and has continued to escalate. Half of those apprehended never made it past the border state of Chiapas and 15 percent were women. Nearly 4,000 of those detained by Mexican authorities were children traveling without their parents.[3] Many who weren't deported claimed they were shaken down repeatedly by Mexican authorities who considered their activities to be no more than a "toll road charge" that they levied as these "tourists" passed through on their way north. But worse than the police were the *Mara Salvatruchas*— Central American gangs that had originated among the immigrant population in southern California and operated in southern Mexico.

For years *indocumentados* who'd managed to sneak across the Guatemalan border into Mexico but who couldn't afford to pay *coyotes* had hitched rides on the freights that ran northward through the Isthmus of Tehuantepec and along the eastern slopes of the mountains to Veracruz. The immigrants would hide along the right of way then, as a train pulled out of Tapachula they would race to clamber on board, clinging to whatever they could—roofs, couplings, ladders. But by the year 2000, armed gang members were going from car to car to assault, rob, and rape. A train mechanic, Óscar Muñoz, told *Proceso* writer Alejandro Gutiérrez, "Those who resist being robbed they kill and those who have nothing to be robbed of get thrown off the train while it's moving."[4] He claimed to have made trips with as many as 800 *indocumentados* hanging onto the freight cars at one time. Many who slipped and fell trying to board or to escape the gangs lost their lives or their limbs under the freight's grinding wheels.

"For the traffic in illegals by the mafia to thrive, it's definitely necessary to have collaboration from [law enforcement] authorities," stated a 2001 report by the *Centro de Investigación y Seguridad Nacional* (CISEN—Mexico's equivalent of the FBI).[5] The same network of safe houses, drivers, documents, and bus and airline tickets was needed to cross Mexico from its southern border to the United States as it was to cross into the United States. Some immigrants who were able to pay for *coyotes* flew to Mexico City from Tapachula; others went as passengers in delivery vans or in trucks transporting coffee or bananas or even in ambulances or in tour buses. Still others tried to evade the Mexican *migra* checkpoints by edging along the coast in boats to Mazatlán.

The United Nations Commission on Migrants' Human Rights censored Mexico in 2003 for the "existence of apparent complicity among *coyotes*, the delinquents who assault the migrants and law enforcement agents who extort them."[6] It criticized the crowded conditions of detention centers and the lengths of time that *indocumentados* were held in custody. It noted that the *Plan Sur* forced those entering the country from Guatemala to take routes through hazardous mountains and dense jungles in order to evade Mexican immigration authorities who had set up barriers and twenty-four-hour-a-day patrols along the more accessible routes. (The *Plan Sur*, implemented in 2001 with U.S. backing, was modeled after tactics used by the United States on Mexico's northern border.)

Despite his failure to achieve a guest worker or other immigration accord with the Bush administration, Vicente Fox continued to make emigration—or rather emigrants—a political priority. By 2005, Mexico's unemployment rate had reached more than 1.6 million persons and 40 percent of those working could not rise above the poverty level. In addition, 2.4 million Mexicans left the country during Fox's six-year term to seek employment in the United States. In his reports to the nation, sluggish production and inflation were offset by the "unprecedented" amounts of remittances being sent by those "national heroes" working in the United States.[7] He set up a "Three-for-One" program to court money for municipal projects in Mexican cities, offering federal contributions of three dollars for every dollar received from immigrants in the United States for specific construction, remodeling, or water purification ventures.[8]

In addition, Mexican consulates began issuing immigrant identity cards which some U.S. banks accepted for opening accounts that included debit cards. Family members in Mexico could draw money off the accounts by using the cards, thus eliminating the expenses of wire transfers. According to Bank of Mexico statistics, Mexican residents in the United States sent over 14 billion dollars in individual remittances to their families south of the border in 2003, $16.6 billion in 2004, more than $20 billion in 2005 and an estimated $25 billion in 2006. Halfway through his six-year term, Fox made a point of confirming that the $14 billion sent by expatriates in 2003 exceeded the federal government's total 2003 appropriation to education, agriculture, and rural development, and "to great measure has reduced the poverty in Mexico."[9]

That Fox's portrayal of the Mexican economy wasn't shared by many within that country became more and more evident as border crossings increased dramatically in 2004. "It's non-stop madness," an acting supervisory agent in Yuma complained about his sector's inability to contain the flow that included more and more women and children and an ever-increasing percentage of Central Americans.[10] T. J. Bonner, the president of the National Border Patrol Council, predicted that "the strategy of trying to regain control of the border inch by inch" would continue to fail until the country put "teeth in the sanctions" that prohibit employers from hiring undocumented immigrants.[11] The lure to earn ten times what one could earn in Mexico or Central America was just too great, particularly since some researchers estimated that 95 percent of those who made it into the United States successfully found work.

"It is obvious from the Border Patrol's own figures that the current strategy has done nothing to either reduce or control migration," the *Arizona Republic* quoted the Reverend John Fife of Tucson, who organized a project to reduce the number of deaths among immigrants trying to cross through Arizona.[12] Mexican consuls in various border cities continued to file protests for individual cases of maltreatment by U.S. authorities but Fox's government left uncontested the right of Mexican citizens to emigrate and the right of the U.S. government to establish its immigration policies. This "right," noted economist Miguel Pickard, derived in part from the fact that Mexico and other sender countries "really do want to get rid of *campesinos* with ties to the land who often create an obstacle to the sale of communal lands and natural resources."[13]

Although U.S. President George W. Bush didn't include Fox in his suggested "opening the doors to debate" over immigration reform in January 2004, he did reactivate many old immigration clichés by proposing "earned legalization" for current workers and an extended guest worker program that would grant temporary residency to immigrants for up to three years. He made no mention of reducing Border Patrol pursuits and apprehensions, nor of changing what Sean Garcia of the Latin American Working Group called an "inhumane and ineffective" border blockade.

"It has failed to reduce undocumented migration, it has redirected migrants to their peril, and it has led to an increase in civil rights violations by a dangerously inexperienced Border Patrol force. Despite these failures, the deadly policies continue, with a proposed budget of $6.2 billion for border enforcement in 2005 alone."[14]

The federal Government Accounting Office (GAO) reported in 2005 that the administration was failing in its efforts to stop the traffic of immigrants because of bureaucratic stumbling and duplication of efforts by federal agencies. It characterized the Department of Homeland Security as disorganized and ineffective and criticized the lack of coordination between ICE and the Bureau of Customs and Border Protection. A Border Patrol report obtained by the Associated Press acknowledged that only 6 percent of the immigrant smugglers the agency apprehended actually were prosecuted during 2004. AP quoted T. J. Bonner complaining that the lack of prosecutions is "demoralizing the agents and making a joke out of our system of justice."[15]

Proposals for earned legalization and guest worker authorizations generally omit mention of employer responsibilities for anything besides paperwork. Many immigrants who achieved amnesty under the Simpson-Rodino Act of 1986 continued to work sporadically, to earn less than minimum wage and to contend with shop and field conditions detrimental to their safety and health. Though some became UFW (United Farm Workers) members, and others became members of various restaurant and service unions, most found themselves at the mercy of those who hired them. Garcia insisted that "immigration reform should ensure that temporary workers have the same labor protections that U.S. workers receive."

Current labor laws offer built-in protections but they cannot be enforced by a federal government that continually cuts back on inspections, manpower, and administration. The Pew Hispanic Center reported in December 2005, that although 95 percent of new immigrants were working, 38 percent were unemployed for thirty days or more during the previous year. This lack of permanent employment caused UFW's membership to decline. Many UFWs moved and took on non-UFW jobs, or found work in the restaurant or construction industries, or returned to Mexico. Others lost their jobs to *esquiroles* that employers surreptitiously hired. One UFW organizer that I talked to described agricultural workers as "a fluid mass" without union experience and the ability "only to see one dollar at a time."

President Bush's proposed "opening the doors" to immigration debate never got past the threshold. Criticism from election year Republicans pushed it aside and the administration, instead of opting for worker accords, increased border security and ICE raids on undocumented workers. The prolonged conflict in Iraq took precedent as Bush, running for reelection as a "get tough" commander in chief, needed clear-cut issues for his campaign. Neo-conservative backers insisted that the "War on Terror" was the primary issue for most Americans. Heather MacDonald of the ultra-right Manhattan Institute summed up neo-con thinking by advising, "Washington should allocate the resources to detain and deport illegals and should start enforcing long-standing laws against employing alien lawbreakers. A deafening roar of 'racism' will result—but with the country at war, pandering to the race advocates must give way to protecting American lives."[16] How criminalizing *indocumentados* would save the life of even one American she didn't explain but the philosophy speaks for itself: Scapegoat those who can't fight back.[17]

Not all conservatives agreed with the neo-con position, however. In a strong criticism of spending billions on "a three-tiered replica of the Berlin Wall," Daniel T. Griswold of the Cato Institute noted that sealing the border "would not have kept a single September 11 terrorist out of the United States."[18]

Many of Bush's reelection managers felt that worker accords and amnesty for *indocumentados* would "soften" that get-tough image even though they wanted to appeal to Hispanic voters. Since neither agribusiness and nonunionized industry was anxious for changes that would diminish the supply of cheap labor, immigration reform could be set aside, particularly since anti-immigration initiatives were on the ballot in Arizona and Colorado. According to Tom Barry, policy director of the Inter-hemispheric Resource Center, at least thirty groups in other states, most of them receiving logistical assistance and in some cases funding from FAIR and other national anti-immigration organizations, were preparing to sponsor and collect signatures for new state referendums to be introduced in 2005 and 2006.

Popular support for these initiatives proved easy to manipulate. Practically all of the *indocumentados* who've entered the country in the last four years are living in poverty even though the vast majority of them are working. Every year two million more young Mexicans enter—or try to enter—the work force in that country. Over 15 percent of them will be working in the United States if the current situation continues without change. Many of them may wind up camped in canyons, or locked in deteriorating trailers, or huddled on levee banks blighting what otherwise might be pastoral landscapes. Or they will wedge into city barrios that offer little or no space for them, forcing an overflow into neighboring areas. They become easy scapegoats for problems not of their making—crime, drugs, social disintegration, higher taxes, and the spread of communicable diseases.

Ironically, the provisions in most of the initiatives on state ballots would worsen these problems by denying them legitimate work opportunities, driver's licenses, and minimal health benefits. "As immigration restrictionists advance their agenda, the very act of assimilation that they demand of immigrants will become increasingly impossible."[19]

Even when initiatives like California's Proposition 187 are declared unconstitutional, they push those in elected office to approve stronger anti-immigration policies. Cities and towns in what formerly were non-immigrant areas have passed ordinances prohibiting taco stands, renting to *indocumentados*, conducting business in Spanish and even sitting on front porches "because that's what Mexicans do." Even though a summer 2006 Gallup Poll revealed that acceptance of immigration is at an all-time high, the Southern Poverty Law Center reported a dramatic increase in what they call "hate groups."[20]

Arizona's Civil Homeland Defense vigilantes, who claimed to have turned 2,000 "illegals" over to the Border Patrol every year since they began patrolling in 2002, insist that those who hire *indocumentados* are guilty of treason. Their founder, Chris Simcox, editorialized in his *Tombstone Tumbleweed*, a rabid anti-immigration journal, that President Bush's "hands off" immigration policies are the result of an unwillingness to displease agribusiness owners, most of whom contribute heavily to Republican causes.

On this issue Simcox and his gun-wielding followers were in agreement with such genteel intellectuals as Samuel Huntington and Samuel Francis. Tom Barry labeled Huntington and Francis "paleoconservatives"— a designation not necessarily to their liking—in noting that they, too, argued that corporate America had lost its allegiance to the United States as a country that must take care of itself. The fundamental issue involving immigration, Francis attested, is "who we are and what sort of nation we want to be."[21] He, like Huntington, described an

America-that-never-was, Protestant, moral, with high ethical standards and an appreciation for culture. However, the America he pictured with reverent nostalgia is not the America described by writers throughout the eighteenth, nineteenth, or early twentieth centuries: Melville, Dana, Hamlin Garland, Theodore Dreiser, Frank Norris, William Attaway, Langston Hughes, Faulkner, and James Baldwin. In contrast with Simcox, many "paleoconservatives" favored small over big business, expressed doubts about economic globalization policies and opposed the U.S. involvements in Iraq and Afghanistan.

In a sweeping four-part series published in December 2003, the *Palm Beach Post* detailed the lives and work experiences of migrants brought to Florida to work in citrus and other agriculture. Individuals described a five-year-old child dying in her mother's arms as they crossed the Arizona desert, a baby dying of cold in an unheated shack, a twenty-year-old forced into sexual slavery to pay off her debt to a *coyote*, a sixteen-year-old run over by the truck carrying him to a work site.

The report showed that most of the contractors were themselves Spanish-speaking immigrants who had purchased the workers from the *coyotes* who had brought them to Florida. The *indocumentados* owed the *coyotes* money; the labor contractors paid off their debts on condition that the immigrants pay those same debts off with their earnings. Not only did some of these contractors fail to pay for all of the hours worked, they brought the migrants back from the job sites and locked them in crowded trailers so they couldn't escape. Even women who had passports and work permits reported that they were kept in jail-like restrictions and paid less than half of what they had been promised. A fifteen-year-old who escaped from the contractors who'd brought her from Mexico to Florida recounted being promised work in child care but instead was forced into prostitution.

Many of the contractors, the *Post* noted, were being squeezed by owners and consequently they squeezed workers. Some would dismiss migrants the day they paid off their debts and bring in others who still owed money to their *coyotes*.[22] Since the contractors had to provide transportation, they often carried workers to and from job sites in dangerously crowded and poorly maintained vans and pickups. They provided *indocumentados* with false IDs and social security cards and often pocketed deductions taken out for social security and workmen's compensation. As the *Post* explained, the growers needed their fields gleaned at the instant the crops were ripe and the contractors had to get the workers to the fields to fulfill their contracts with the growers and the migrants had to send money to their families in Mexico and Guatemala, so the abuses passed down the line. The *Post* reported that migrants said Florida was the worst state in the union as a place to work.

"Agribusiness in Florida, California, and Texas profits hugely from migrant laborers," labor consultant Joseph A. Kinney told the *Post*.[23] "But those large companies and the farmers who sell their fruits and vegetables to them don't have to pay the hidden costs incurred by the exploitation of those workers, most of whom remain in the United States long after they stop working in the fields."

Many migrants shift from agriculture to constructions jobs, or to work as resort maids, gardeners, and dishwashers, in order to continue to have an income after the last crops are harvested.[24] Many—if not most—live in fear of deportation. Cuts in school funding cripple their children's ability to learn—and consequently to improve their future incomes. Many farm workers in Florida, Texas, and California are third-generation migrants who barely earn one percent of the retail prices of the crops they plant, weed, hoe, and harvest.

"Taxpayers of Florida, California, Texas, New York, and the other states that absorb most of agriculture's throwaway people will pay the price for decades more" unless the system is changed, Kinney told the *Post* then asked who was going to step in and effect the changes: "Poor farm workers who came from worse poverty across the border who are here illegally? Giant companies piling up profits? The consumer who appears to be getting bargain-priced fruits and vegetables?"

Miguel Pickard concluded a 2005 review of migratory trends, "To reverse the flow of poor migrants, an alternative worldwide economic program is needed, one that emphasizes economic growth, the domestic market, and the national priorities of poor countries. Without major changes, the coming decades will bring increasingly unstoppable displacement of the uprooted poor of the South, marching toward the prosperous citadels of the North."[25]

There's another side to the coin, however. A 2005 study by the American Farm Bureau Federation concluded that a crackdown on immigrant labor could cause U.S. agriculture to lose from $5–12 billion dollars annually. "The size, concentrations, and tight margins of industrial farm production have fueled a continuous demand for cheap labor to keep the pipeline running."[26]

By 2006, nearly one out of every five families in Mexico counted remittances from the United States as their major source of income. Percentages may be even higher in Guatemala, Honduras, and El Salvador. For them migration has become a way of life—almost the only way of life. "Small self-employed producers cannot generate enough value from what they produce and sell [to compete] ... with multinational corporations as the latter invade their markets."[27] One of the conclusions that emerged from the three-day Cuernavaca conference in 2005 warned that "international migration has been silently incorporated into government strategies, generating an economic model that distorts the concept of development, basing it on the export of workers and capture of remittances."[28] In other words, the "national heroes" are too important to the sender countries to be lost.

The neon-con viewpoint that migration is a criminal activity parallels in an odd way Lyndon Johnson's "guns and butter" attempts to win both the "War on Poverty" and the war in Vietnam. The Bush administration, like the Democratic and Republican administrations before it, is committed to a domination of world trade engineered, in part, by international banking loans and restrictions. To achieve this domination the United States must be the principal exporting country and the country with the most material resources, including both agricultural and manufactured products. NAFTA and the recently devised CAFTA and other tariff-breaking accords guarantee the flow of U.S. products and the ability to acquire, with few restrictions, needed raw materials.

One of these raw materials is cheap labor. A free flow of disposable cheap labor—like the corresponding flow of exported products unimpeded by tariff or import restrictions—enables the producing country to keep costs below those of its competitors, including Third World nations that no longer protect their economies by restrictive tariffs. As William I. Robinson points out, "free trade agreements, privatizations, the contraction of public employment and credits, the breakup of communal lands, and so forth, along with the political crises these measures have generated has imploded thousands of communities in Latin America and unleashed a wave of migration, from rural to urban areas and to other countries, that can only be analogous to the mass uprooting and migration that generally takes place in the wake of wars."[29] If the United States would adhere 100 percent to avowed free trade policies it would permit worker migration and focus law enforcement on actual criminal activities, including fraud, workplace violations, and domestic violence.

"It makes no sense for the United States to treat workers as criminals," insists the director of the Americas Program of the International Relations Center, Laura Carlsen. "It makes no sense for Mexico to consider out-migration an acceptable economic strategy ... Our current immigration policy not only split the two nations but has pitted members of the same communities against each other by calling out shameful subcurrents of racism and xenophobia in our culture."[30]

In the hallowed halls of Harvard, the theory of globalization may work well but at the factory, farm, migrant, policeman level its application gets messy. The labor needs of agriculture and industry fluctuate and the labor force that arrives is poor, dependent, and often untrained. As the supply of this raw material—cheap labor—increases, the value of each entity diminishes. No longer is it necessary to pay a prevailing wage, or provide benefits, because entity Mariano will work for less than entity Leo who will work for less than entity Rubén and more entities will keep coming who will work for less than any of them.[31]

Because the employment of *indocumentados* remains outside the law, employers do not have to take responsibility for what happens to their unauthorized workers once they are laid off, injured, or quit. Krissman insists that many labor-intensive industries such as those in U.S. agriculture purposefully maintain substandard conditions for their workers in order to keep prices down and profits up.[32] Meanwhile, the consumer public, while complaining about residual costs and eyesore living conditions, pays affordable prices for everything from tuxedos to grapefruit and chicken wings.

Even while they are employed, these raw material worker groups do not contribute heavily to local economies since much of their earnings are being remitted to their countries of origin.[33] The more raw material workers that the country of origin permits to emigrate, the more money it receives and the less its government has to dedicate to social services. Its participation in globalization is to produce and send the raw material, not to determine how it is used or to limit its production.

However, governments heavily influenced by a voting populace have to do more than please the major beneficiaries of free market globalization. In order to get elected—and reelected—to public office, politicians have to coattail popular sentiments, whether they be anti-war, anti-immigration, defense against terrorism, or urban beautification. Aligning unauthorized immigration with protecting the county against terrorist invaders inflamed anti-immigrant feelings throughout the United States. With a conservative majority in control of the Republican Party, this anti-immigrant mood culminated in December 2005, with the House of Representatives passing a stringent anti-immigration bill which not only increased the size of law enforcement's hammer but made unlawful entry a felony. A more moderate Senate proposal did not include the felony provisions but did include "sealing off the border" with hundreds of miles of wall construction and with machinery to enable many of the approximately eleven million *indocumentados* living and working in the United States to legalize their status.[34]

Despite President Bush's urgings, the differences between the House and Senate proposals couldn't be reconciled during the 2006 Congressional year nor was Congress able to pass President Bush's urged immigration legislation in 2007. The 2006 House Bill in particular aroused antagonism throughout Latin America and among immigrants within the United States. On May 1, 2006, millions of demonstrators marched in Los Angeles, Chicago, Denver, New York, and other cities to protest anti-immigrant legislation. Seventy-two thousands students walked out of classes in Los Angeles.[35] Businesses that relied on immigrant labor closed their doors for the day, and boycotts limited purchases of both agricultural and manufactured goods.[36]

The administration responded by softening its anti-immigrant rhetoric and emphasizing that the legislation it proposed would provide a "pathway" to legalization for workers who had demonstrated "productive behavior." Nevertheless, to appease anti-immigration elements within the Republican Party and to end what advisors detected was vacillation on the federal governments part, Bush announced in May 2006 that he was authorizing the deployment of National Guard units to the U.S. side of the border with Mexico. He insisted that the 6,000 guardsmen would be performing logistical and support duties, not hunting down *indocumentados*, a declaration that did nothing to mitigate an angry response from south of the border.[37]

With Congressional elections in the offing in November of 2006, many of President Bush's advisors urged a pulling away from the tough House stance. Although they continued to endorse border security measures, which had popular support throughout the country as a defense against terrorism, they resuscitated the idea of a "guest worker" program that would legitimize a certain amount of immigrant labor but restrict unauthorized entry. In part to appeal to Hispanic voters and to moderates in both parties without alienating big business, Bush urged passage of the proposal, which had been floating around Washington since 2002. Could something be in place before the Congressional elections the immigration issue would not divide the Republican Party.[38]

This guest worker proposal was first aired by the Essential Worker Immigration Coalition (EWIC), an association of industries that relied heavily on emigrant labor, and the ultra-conservative Cato Institute. "When Bush unveiled his immigration reform plan in January of 2004, it was taken almost word for word from the Cato Institute report and the EWIC recommendations."[39] Opposition to the guest worker and legalization provisions of the proposal forced delays in passing the legislation before the 2006 recesses of the Senate and House, with the leadership of the latter still determined to oppose any legalization.[40]

The fact that immigrants can't vote gives them with little or no political influence but immigrants formed into organized blocs can effect decisions, particularly those made by employers. But as long as immigrant workers can be defined and treated as criminals they are unlikely to organize because, by organizing, they emerge from invisibility and make themselves subject to deportation. Since employers can't manipulate the deportations themselves, they require law enforcement even though paying for law enforcement diverts some of the profits. Nevertheless, as long as the flow of human raw materials exceeds the demand for it in the United States, law enforcement's "chase, capture and deport" of would-be workers doesn't affect production.

Since 2004, ICE progressively has stepped up raids throughout the country. The early failures to coordinate sweeps with local law enforcement prompted ICE to formulate new strategies that include not only local units but the social security administration office of the inspector general and federal marshals. Reports from the Immigration News Briefs list 3–12 raids weekly, with most of those apprehended being deported within twenty-four hours.[41] As of September 2006, ICE had forty-five fugitive operations teams scattered around the country and had arrested more than 24,000 persons in the ten months between October 2005 and August 2006. Even so, this represents a very small proportion of the estimated twelve million *indocumentados* living in the United States.

During the three decades after World War II, the U.S. economy prospered by expanding its consumer base. Mass production and unionization drove working-class salaries upward; government employment at all levels increased; VA and FHA loans made home purchases possible; credit unions provided financing for vehicles and equipment. Labor unions enabled workers to negotiate with employers—or the unions shutdown production by striking.

The unions also wielded political clout. Candidates wanting to get into office in various parts of the country had to court them despite the fact that some, like the United Mine Workers, were dictatorially run. Gradually, however, the unions lost both membership and influence, in part the result of Republican-engineered legislation, particularly during the presidencies of Richard Nixon and Ronald Reagan, and partly because, after the merger of the two major unions, the AFL and CIO, the unions devoted more energy toward protecting their existing membership than widening their influence. Today the private work force is slightly under 7 percent unionized, contrasted with 25 percent in 1980.

Unions have no real place in free market planning and execution. Like a too strong or too meddlesome government, they interrupt the raw material-production flow. By pushing salaries upwards, they drive prices higher and reduce profits, just as governments, by taxing to pay for social services, take away money that otherwise would go into infrastructure or corporate bank accounts.

What would affect production and the free market flow would be:

(1) Organization of the human raw material into a cohesive body that could dictate some of its own terms;
(2) The cutoff or diminishment of the human raw material flow from the sender countries; and
(3) Closing the border so tightly and effectively that the raw material flow no longer could enter the country.

There are some jokers in the deck. One involves competition from foreign countries. If China, India, or Brazil, for example, begins to consistently undersell the United States citrus—or any other—industry then layoffs, diminished production, perhaps even bankruptcies result. The pool of raw material then becomes a wallow—there is no place for it to flow. Not only do unpaid workers lose their sustenance, they lose their mobility and the entire economy suffers.

It also suffers if industry undergoes a dramatic change such as a severe shortage or disruption in oil production. Layoffs and firings could strand millions of immigrant workers whose only choice then would be to scrape out some kind of livelihood or return to their country of origin.[42] Should they return en masse, the country of origin would be unable to cope with their needs. (Ironically, the anti-immigration activists and militant neo-cons succeed in ridding the country of undocumented workers they would create greater problems than now exist, for the United States not only would lose its cheap labor but would lose markets as well and have a festering cauldron just south of its border that could boil over into full scale revolution. The United States then would have to spend trillions of dollars and thousands of lives to repress the uprising and repatriate the millions of refugees it would create.)

Solutions to the current "silent invasion" lie with employers. Some already have realized that it is more productive in the long run to pay prevalent wages, keep accurate books and provide adequate housing or access to it at reasonable cost. Many have found that, except in construction and heavy industry, women equal men in productivity and that workers whose families live with them are more reliable than those whose families have remained in their countries of origin. Congressman Peter Rodino correctly assessed the situation over forty years ago: If there are no jobs there is no illegal immigration. Since he first proposed legislation to limit the employment of *indocumentados* somewhere between nine and fifteen million Spanish-speaking immigrants have found work in this country. The jobs have been here. The jobs still are here. And the immigrants, despite the barriers and hardships imposed by attempts to close the border, still are coming.[43]

At various times over the past 150 years, federal and state governments have attempted to regulate employment practices, often because situations in various industries had become so scandalous that intervention was necessary: slavery, child labor, conditions in the mines of the West and the slaughterhouses in Chicago and other Midwestern cities, prostitution, the Dust Bowl. Minimum wage and overtime regulations, equal employment for women and minorities, social security deductions, and a variety of worker safety rules emerged to benefit workers without over-penalizing those who hired them. Compliance often has depended upon the government's ability and willingness to enforce its regulations.

The much discussed guest worker program's proposed 300,000 authorizations fell far short of industry's and agriculture's needs. Those qualifying would have garnered better wages and, presumably, better working and living conditions but employer-*indocumentado* experiences over the past sixty years indicate that unless there is strict and constant enforcement many employers will continue to hire *indocumentados* and many *indocumentados* who do not qualify as guest workers will continue to emigrate to seek jobs.[44] In the Bush-urged proposal funds for enforcement were dedicated to the build up of border security, not to internal regulation.

Although the description of guest worker eligibility seems straightforward enough at first glance, it would very likely create another paperwork nightmare. Many agricultural employers in the 1960s and 1970s hired *indocumentados* precisely because they were *indocumentados*—they came to work, got paid, and left with a minimum of signatures, verifications, or reports. Given the changed migration patterns since the end of the *bracero* program, it no longer can be assumed that workers—whether authorized "guest workers" or unauthorized *indocumentados*—conform to a circular migratory system or that they would be willing—or for that matter able—to return seasonally to their places or origin. Escobar Latapí as his co-authors note that there may be "less seasonality in many of the labor markets in which Mexican-born workers are employed than is assumed, making it difficult to expect or enforce the worker rotation implicit in non-immigrant guest worker programs."[45] A 2005 *Consejo Estatal de Población* survey in Chiapas revealed that one out of three families in that state, Mexico's poorest and the state furthest from the U.S. border, depended upon remittances from immigrant workers and that nearly 80 percent of those emigrating from Chiapas did not return.[46] In addition, the possibility that a guest worker program would prompt employers to create low-wage positions to replace higher paying ones is not lost on many observers.[47]

While the conservative government of Vicente Fox advocated a guest worker program, it did not necessarily envision the same guest worker program proposed by the EWIC and the Cato Institute. "Mexico would like any bilateral guestworker to be large enough to substitute legal for unauthorized labor migration, to ensure that both Mexican workers and U.S. employers participate in the program, and to protect the legal and work place rights of legal migrant workers," Escobar Latapí and his co-authors explain. "A program agreed to by the U.S. would aim to admit only workers needed to fill legitimate labor shortages, and to ensure that foreign workers do not adversely affect similar U.S. workers. In addition the U. S. would require that migrant workers remain legal non-immigrant workers, and leave when their terms of employment end."[48]

A government that embraces free market concepts isn't likely to undertake regulatory efforts that curtail producing the necessary exports.[49] If there is to be regulation it is going to have to come from those whom regulation will benefit the most: the workers themselves. Cesar Chavez's temporary successes with UFW walk offs and boycotts proved that some such steps can be effective. But to be effective there needs to be leadership, there needs to be cooperation between worker groups and with organized labor. Perhaps it only can be done, as Chavez started to do, by boycotting one agricultural crop, one industry, at a time: strawberries, then prunes, then poultry, then resort hotels, with each step relying on support from non-governmental organizations, unions, prominent media, entertainment, and political figures. Eventually such a movement might force most employers to pay prevalent wages and narrow and/or define the employment market.

It would not, however, take care of everyone. Only by outreach into the sender countries can unrestricted emigration be abated. The danger of the free market economy, with its free flow of manufactured and agricultural products outward and flow of human raw material inward, is that the raw material collecting within the producing country can become combustible. Combustion happened forty years ago in Watts, in Philadelphia, in Washington, D.C. It has happened more recently in France. "Creating war-like conditions on the border could all too easily become a self-fulfilling prophecy," warns Laura Carlsen of *This Week in the Americas*.[50] One hopes the leaders who emerge from this increasingly desperate human mass today are Martin Luther Kings and Benito Juarezes.

Not Spartacuses. Or Pancho Villas. Or worse.

Notes

INTRODUCTION

1. Bryan R. Roberts, Reanne Frank, and Fernando Lozano-Ascencio, *Ethnic and Racial Studies*, Vol. 22, No. 2, March 1999.

2. Fred Krissman, "Apples and Oranges," Center for U.S. Mexican Studies, University of California, Santa Cruz, 2002.

3. Ángel Manuel Castillo, "Migraciones en el hemisférico," CEPAL No. 37, Centro Latinoamericano y Caribeño de Demográfica," Santiago, Chile, May, 2003.

4. Wayne A. Cornelius, and Marc R. Rosenblum, "Immigration and Politics," The Center for Immigration Studies, University of California, San Diego, October 2004 and Luin Goldring, "Continuities in Transnational Migration: An Analysis of Nineteen Mexican Communities," CERLAC Colloquia Paper Series, May 2005, Toronto.

5. Cornelius and Rosenblum, op. cit.

6. Jeffrey H. Cohen, *The Culture of Migration in Southern Mexico*, University of Texas Press, 2004

7. Wayne Cornelius, Phillip L. Martín, and James F. Hollifield, *Controlling Immigration*, Stanford University. Press, 1994. Cornelius sees migration as a strategy for residents of states that lack other forms of social insurance to achieve basic economic well-being.

8. Roberts, et al., op. cit. The authors distinguish among temporary systems like those that primarily involved agricultural workers, permanent systems in which the participants opt to move permanently to the U.S. and transnational systems based on the interrelationship of opportunities in places of origin and places of destination.

9. Roberts, et al., note that rural and small-town residents are much more likely to participate in transnational systems than urban emigrants who lack the strong family and neighborhood ties that characterize the former.

10. Cornelius and Rosenblum call Simpson-Rodino the "classic example of inefficient legislative design." Op. cit.

11. Agustín Escobar Latapí, Philip Martín, Gustavo López Castro, and Catherine Donato, "Factors that Influence Migration," U.S. Commission on Immigration Reform, 1998.

12. Cohen, op. cit. "... although a push-pull model based in labor market demand tells us something about one force behind migration, it cannot explain the variations encountered among migrants, their households, and their communities."

13. Escobar Latapí, et al. op. cit.

14. Elizabeth Fussell, and Douglas S. Massey, "The Limits to Cumulative Causation," *Demography* No. 41, 2004.

15. A majority of workers develop a desire for improving their work and living conditions while the demand for unskilled labor in both agriculture and industry remains the same, creating a constant need for new immigrants to fill bottom level jobs. Escobar Latapí, op. cit.

16. Douglas S. Massey, Rafael Alarcón, Jorge Durand, and Humberto González, *Return to Aztlan*, University of California Press, Berkeley and Los Angeles, 1987.

17. Almost invariably the companies involved benefit financially from these raids. Workers deported within 24 hours do not collect wages due to them. If ICE arrests and deports 30 *indocumentados* eight days into a pay period the arithmetic shows: 30 x 8 hours per day = 240 hours a day x 8 days = 1920 hours x \$12.00 an hour = \$23,400 that the company doesn't have to pay out for work already done.

18. Krissman, op. cit.

19. Escobar Latapí, op. cit.

20. Ibid.

21. The term *coyote* commonly is used in Mexico to describe any go-between hired to perform a service involving business or government, such as legalizing documents, importing cars or purchasing property. They rely on contacts and know how to shortcut the bureaucracy. Since most undocumented immigrants do not consider themselves criminals, they look upon hiring a guide to transport them safely across the border as both practical and a necessity.

22. "Unauthorized migrants have several packages of services available, and several options to pay for the cost of illegally entering the U.S., including working in a coyote-provided or coyote-arranged job in the U.S. to repay smuggling costs." Escobar Latapí, et al., op. cit.

23. Castillo, op. cit.

24. Ibid.

25. Ibid. "The condition of being an *indocumentado* permits the proliferation of abuses: inferior salaries, fiscal evasion, precarious work conditions, threats and obstacles to organizing, aggressions, and physical abuse, among others."

26. Escobar Latapí, et al., op. cit.

27. Manuel Roig Francia, *Washington Post*, April 17, 2006.

28. Frank D. Bean, and Robert G. Cushing, "The Relationship between the Mexican Economic Crisis and Illegal Migration to the United States," University. of Texas at Austin, Institute of Latin American Studies (undated).

29. Escobar Latapí, et al., op. cit.

30. This has been true not only of Mexico and Central America but of European sender countries during the late nineteenth and early twentieth centuries. Comments during those years included, "What is Ireland's principal export?" Answer: "Irishmen." Similar jokes were told about Italians, Scandinavians, Chinese, and other nationalities.

31. Cohen, op. cit.

32. Cohen op. cit., contends that each dollar sent by immigrants in the United States to Mexico increases that country's gross national product by $2.90.

33. Ibid.

A PLACE TO WORK, A PLACE TO LIVE

1. Luin Goldring, "Continuities in Transnational Migration: An Analysis of Nineteen Mexican Communities," *CERLAC Colloquia Paper Series*, May 2005, Toronto.

2. Ernesto Galarza, *Merchants of Labor: The Mexican Bracero Story*. McNally and Loftin, Santa Barbara, 1964.

3. Fred Krissman, "Apples and Oranges," presented at the forum, *Indigenous Mexican Migrants in the U.S.*, University of California-Santa Cruz, October 11–12, 2002.

4. Margulis and Tuiran, quoted by Agustín Escobar Latapí, Philip Martin Gustavo López Castro, and Catherine Donato, "Factors that Influence Migration," U.S. Commission on Immigration Reform, 1998.

5. *Sacramento Bee*, December 8, 1991.

6. Monica Verea, *Entre México y Estados Unidos: los indocumentados*. Ediciones El Caballito, México: D. F. México, 1982.

7. Douglas S. Massey, Rafael Alarcón, Jorge Durand, and Humberto González, *Return to Azlan*, University of California Press, Berkeley and Los Angeles, 1987.

8. Ibid.

9. Recruitment of this kind was not confined to Spanish-speaking immigrants, but was typical of arrivals from Europe throughout the nineteenth century. Cities throughout the U.S. featured ethnic ghettoes, many with their own services, newspapers and local bosses. The same was true in the West, where ethnic groups worked specific mines. Cornish immigrants were called "Cousin Jacks" because, invariably when an opening at a mine occurred, one of the Cornishmen would pipe up, "Me Cousin Jack, now, he be the man ye want."

10. Escobar Latapí, et al., op. cit.

11. Massey, et al., op. cit.

12. An estimated 45 percent of Mexico's manufacturing and business even today is "informal"—what in the U.S. would be called "under the table"—cash only, no benefits, no adherence to minimum wage or occupational safety laws.

13. Roberts, et al., op. cit.

14. Jorge Durand, Douglas S. Massey, and Emilio A. Parrado, "The New Era of Mexican Migration to the United States," *The Journal of American History*, September 1999.

15. Ibid.

16. Ibid.

17. *Sacramento Bee*, June 8, 1990.

18. *Sacramento Bee*, December. 8, 1991.

19. Norma Iglesias, *La flor más bella de la maquiladora.* D. F. México: SEP/Centro de Estudios Fronterizos del Norte de México, 1985.

20. Conversation with a Sr. Santos in the Mexico City airport, 1986.

21. E. H. Hutchinson, commentary after the author's presentation on undocumented immigration at California State University-Chico in 1983.

22. Verea, op. cit.

23. Jeffrey H. Cohen, *The Culture of Migration in Southern México.* University of Texas Press, Austin, 2004.

THROUGH HELL AND HIGH WATER

1. Monica Verea, *Entre México y Estados Unidos: los indocumentados.* Ediciones El Caballito, México, 1986.

2. Valencia described his experiences during conversations with the author in Hamilton City and Chico, California in 1987.

3. Mexico City *Excelsior.*

4. Phone conversation, 1983.

5. Agustín Escobar Latapí, Philip Martin, Gustavo López Castro, and Katharine Donato, "Factors that Influence Migration," U. S. Commission on Immigration Reform, 1998.

6. Manuel Ángel Castillo notes that in some cases coyotes are not paid professionals but persons from communities in the receiving country who use network contacts to bring new arrivals into the country. *"Migración en el hemisferia,"* Centro Latinoamericano y Caribeño de Demografía, Santiago, Chile, May 2003.

7. Quoted in Krissman, "Apples and Oranges," Center for U. S. Mexican Studies, University of California Santa Cruz, 2002.

8. Verea, op. cit.

9. Marcelo Cerrutti, and Massey, Douglas S., *Crossing the Border,* New York, Russell Sage Foundation, 2004.

10. *Atlas World Press Review,* August 1979.

11. Conversations with Luis Pulido in Corning, California, 1979.

12. *Sacramento Bee,* June 8, 1990.

13. The Cato Institute reported in 2002 that one out of six Mexican *indocumentados* first entered the country legally. Daniel T. Griswold, "Willing Workers," Center for Trade Policy Studies, October 15, 2002.

14. Wayne A., Cornelius, "Death at the Border," *Population and Development Review,* December 2001.

15. *El Fronterizo,* Ciudad Juárez, November 1986.

16. Ibid.

17. *El Sol de México,* October 27, 1986.

18. *Prensa Libre* (Guatemala), January 11, 1987.

19. Escobar Latapí, et al., op. cit.

20. Quoted in *La Opinión,* date and issue not available.

21. *Sacramento Bee*, Sep. 8, 1996.

22. Calderón R., Cedric, *Contrabando Humano en la Frontera*, Talleres de Litografías Moderna, Guatemala, Guatemala, 1983.

23. Fred Krissman, Center for Comparative Immigration Studies, University of California, San Diego, 2001.

24. Krissman, "Apples and Oranges," op. cit.

25. Cornelius, op. cit.

26. *Sacramento Bee*, September 22, 1997.

27. La Paz, México *Sudcaliforniano*, January 4, 2000.

28. Escobar Latapí, et al., op. cit.

MEXICAN FACES, AMERICAN DREAMS

1. Amelia Rodriguez, interview in Gridley, California, November 1989.

2. Emilio Maldonado, interview in Gridley, California, November 1989.

3. Telephone interview, 1989.

4. From notes taken after conversations with residents in 1983–84.

5. Douglas S. Massey discusses the establishment and functioning of migrant networks in a number of his works, noting "Migrant networks are sets of interpersonal ties that connect migrants, former migrants, and nonmigrants in origin and destination areas through ties of kinship, friendship, and shared community of origin." Massey's definitions, based on his research on Mexican communities in Michoacán, seem more cohesive than those evident in many U. S. communities, where immigrants from a variety of backgrounds, experiences and cultural values participate with various degrees of intensity in the subculture. See Douglas S. Massey, and Nancy A. Denton, *American Apartheid*, Harvard University Press, 1993.

6. From conversations at a forum in Austin, Texas in August 1978.

7. Enrique Leon, conversation in Austin, Texas in August 1978.

8. Chico (California) *News & Review*, May 4, 1989.

9. Chico *News & Review*, November2, 1989.

10. Associated Press, April 15, 1992.

11. *Sacramento Bee*, October 14, 1992.

12. Quoted by S. T. Rodríguez, who attended the forum in January, 1992.

13. *Sacramento Bee*, December 10, 1991.

14. Ibid.

15. Ibid.

16. Ibid.

17. *Sacramento Bee*, December 27, 1992.

18. Roberts et al., note that by 1999 an increasing number of *indocumentado* farm workers entered the U.S. intending to stay permanently. Bryan R. Roberts, Reanne Frank, and Fernando Lozano-Ascencio, *Ethnic and Racial Studies*, Vol. 22, No. 2, March 1999.

19. Wayne A. Cornelius, "Death at the Border," *Population and Development Review*, 2001.

20. San Francisco *Chronicle*.

21. Blog, *Damned Mexicans*, 2005.

22. *Sacramento Bee,* February 26, 1993.

23. Chico *News & Review,* August 5, 1993.

24. Chico *News & Review,* May 4, 1989.

25. Raúl Arroyo in a 1993 interview.

WHERE THE DOLLAR IS KING

1. Douglas S. Massey, Rafael Alarcón, Jorge Durand, and Humberto González, *Return to Aztlan,* University of California Press, Berkeley and Los Angeles, 1987.

2. Douglas S. Massey, and Jorge Durand, *Clandestinos,* Universidad Autónoma de Zacatecas, 2003.

3. Overheard during a radio interview in Oroville, California, in Fall, 1986.

4. Agustín Escobar Latapí, Philip Martín, Gustavo López Castro, and Catherine Donato, "Factors that Influence Migration," U.S. Commission on Immigration Reform, 1998.

5. Jorge, Durand, Douglas S., Massey, and Emilio A., Parrado, "The New Era of Mexican Migration to the United States," *Journal of American History,* Sep. 1999.

6. Andruw Korber, phone interview, September 1978.

7. Escobar Latapí, et al., op. cit.

8. Escobar Latapí, et al., note "The U.S. policy of permitting U.S. employers to write letters offering ex-*braceros* jobs enabled many to become legal immigrants with the right to unify their families in the U.S." Ibid.

9. Cruz Mora, during a May, 1989 interview in Chico, California.

10. Brian Krueger during a 1973 interview in Austin, Texas.

11. *Sacramento Bee,* December 8, 1991.

12. Greenwood and Tienda note that *indocumentados* seldom took jobs away from native workers. "The largest impacts of low-skilled migration from Mexico are on other low-skilled migrants from Mexico, because the two groups are good labor market substitutes." Michael J. Greenwood, and Marta Tienda, "U.S. Impacts of Mexican Immigration," University of Texas, Austin, 1998.

13. Krissman calls ethnic divisions "a unique weapon in the arsenal of management" and claims that "ethnicity can relegate all mestizos and all indigenous Mexicans into distinct camps, unwilling to cooperate even in mutual self-interest." Fred Krissman, "Apples and Oranges," Center for U.S. Mexican Studies, University of California, Santa Cruz, 2002.

14. *La Jornada,* May 29, 1997.

15. *Sacramento Bee,* December 9, 1991.

16. *USA Today,* July 1, 1992.

17. Ibid.

18. Nicolas Escalante, Mexican consul in Sacramento, press conference, June, 1992.

19. *USA Today,* May 8, 1991.

20. Rogelio Saenz and Cynthia M. Cready, "The Southwest Midwest Mexican American Migration Flows, 1985–1990," paper presented at the Rural Sociology Society meeting, Des Moines, Iowa, 1996.

21. *Los Angeles Times*, Aug. 17, 1996.

22. Greenwood, Tienda, op. cit.

23. Jill Esbenshade, "Emigrants and the Informal Economy," *Network News*, June, 2006. She adds, "We can see the informal economy working all around us: industrial homework; computer programming under the table; non-licensed garment shops; in-home catering services; domestic workers . . . "

24. Dr. Stephen McCurdy, University of California-Davis, presentation for the California Wellness Foundation.

25. Ibid.

26. Associated Press, October 20, 1997.

27. *Los Angeles Times*, August 17, 1996.

28. Cornelius, after noting the increases in *coyotes'* fees between the years 1990 and 2000 concluded "the U.S. economic boom of the 1990s increased the affordability of *coyote* services . . . the increase in smugglers' fees . . . has not been of such a magnitude that it would deter economically rational migrants from making the trip." Wayne A., Cornelius, "Death at the Border," *Population and Development Review*, December 2001.

29. An estimated 1.1 million farm workers achieved legal status through the Simpson-Rodino Act's SAW (special agricultural workers), although only half that many actually may have been eligible. Many employers, particularly in agriculture, did not keep accurate records and certified workers' applications without investigating them. See Douglas S. Massey, Jorge Durand, and Nolan J. Malone, *Beyond Smoke and Mirrors*, Sage, 2002.

30. Krissman, op. cit.

31. The son of an *indocumentado*, Elias Mora (no relation to Cruz Mora quoted earlier) added, "What we need is a way to expedite the legal crossing for temporary workers, that will eliminate the high cost 'Coyotes' . . . if they can easily cross back and forth they will not have to pay the abusive Coyotes and will be able to be with their families in Mexico or their country, instead of illegally taking their family to the United States"

32. Roberto Martinez, *Chico News & Review*, May 4, 1989

"IT'S THE LAW!"

1. *Sacramento Bee*, May 14, 1977.

2. *Washington Monthly*, April 1989.

3. Words from a popular *ranchero* ballad sung by Carlos Santana.

4. Calderón R., Cedric, *Contrabando Humano en la Frontera*, Talleres de Litografías Moderna, Guatemala, Guatemala, 1983.

5. The "cat and mouse game" between *la migra* and *coyotes* included the hiring of informants by the Border Patrol. A 1976 Comptroller General's report called these informants a highly efficient resource.

6. *Sacramento Bee*, September 9, 1996.

7. Grace, Halsell, *The Illegals*, Stein & Day, New York, 1978.

8. Mexican *aspirantes* and their families spent an estimated $380 million dollars on *coyotes* in 1986. As unauthorized entry has become more difficulty this figure

has continued to rise. M. Cerrutti, and D. S. Massey, "On the Auspices of Female Migration from Mexico to the United States," *Demography* No. 38.

9. *The Nation*, May 8, 1989.

10. Ibid.

11. *La Jornada*, May 8, 2000.

12. *La Jornada*, July 30, 2002.

13. *La Jornada*, June 22, 1999.

14. *La Jornada*, April 22, 1998.

15. *Christian Science Monitor*, August 8, 2005.

16. *La Jornada*, April 29, 2000.

17. Miguel Pickard, Americas Program, Interhemispheric Resource Center, March 18, 2005.

18. *La Jornada*, July 30, 2002

19. *Washington Post*, April 23, 2004.

20. London *The Guardian*, June 21, 2004.

21. Ibid.

22. *La Jornada*, July 30, 2002.

23. *Washington Post*, April 24, 2004.

24. *Washington Post*, October 6, 1996.

25. *Sacramento Bee*, August 24, 1997.

26. *Los Angeles Times*, June 10, 2004.

27. Agent Jimenez' description of the demands for identification. Ibid.

28. *In These Times*, June 18, 2004.

29. In San Francisco the job they were doing drew comparisons with the job that Hitler's brown-shirted police did in the 1930s and the justification claimed by deputy field director Aiken was almost word-for-word identical to responses my father heard when he visited Germany shortly before the beginning of World War II.

30. *Los Angeles Times*, June 10, 2004.

31. Little Rock, *Arkansas Democrat-Gazette*, July 28, 2005.

32. *Dissident Voice*, August 12, 2004.

33. *ZMag*, June 20, 2005.

34. *Washington Monthly*, April 1989.

35. *USA Today*, July 21, 1999.

36. Ibid.

37. *Christian Century*, December 19–26, 2001.

38. *ZNet*, June 20, 2005.

39. Ibid.

40. *San Antonio Express-News*, February 21, 2005.

41. *Washington Post*, August 22, 2005.

A POX ON BOTH YOUR HOUSES!

1. *Sacramento Bee*, April 22, 1977.

2. Ibid.

3. Ibid.

4. *Sacramento Bee*, December 8, 1991.

5. Monica Verea, *Entre México y Estados Unidos: los indocumentados*. Ediciones El Caballito, México: D. F. México, 1982.

6. Vic Villapando, *The Center Magazine*, May-June 1979.

7. Verea, op. cit.

8. Arturo Santamaría Gómez, *La Izquierda norteamericana y los trabajadores indocumentados*, Universidad Autónoma de Sinaloa, Mazatlán, Sinaloa, México, 1988.

9. Ibid.

10. Verea, op. cit.

11. *Sacramento Bee*, August 24, 1990.

12. Bill Allison, Fresno County Farm Bureau, 1991 (telephone interview).

13. *USA Today*, August 6, 2001.

14. Center for Immigration Studies, 1991

15. *Sacramento Bee*, May 13, 1994.

16. *San Francisco Chronicle*, August 2, 1993.

17. *Sacramento Bee*, October 7, 1990

18. Jorge Durand, Douglas S. Massey, and Emilio Parrado, "The New Era of Mexican Migration to the United States," University of Indiana (undated document). Although Simpson-Rodino certainly encouraged permanency and added unauthorized immigration, the authors seem to overlook the fact that by 1985 there already were an estimated 4–5 million *indocumentados* living permanently or semi-permanently in the United States, many of them in Midwestern cities, particularly Chicago, Minneapolis, and Milwaukee.

19. Dolores Huerta, 1st vice-president, United Farm Workers, 1992 telephone interview.

20. *Sacramento Bee*, December 8, 1991.

21. Ibid.

22. Ibid.

23. Huerta, op. cit

24. In 2001 *Government Executive* magazine rated INS as one of the worst managed agencies in the federal government. With most of its $4.8 billion dollar budget being spent on border agents, cars, helicopters, and other equipment, it found itself incapable of handling a paperwork backlog that had increased from just over 100,000 unprocessed applications in 1992 to more than one million in the year 2000. Money for processing immigration cases remained unspent and appeals dragged on, untouched, for years.

25. *San Francisco Chronicle*, August 2, 1993.

26. *Sacramento Bee*, October 15, 1993.

27. *Sacramento Bee*, January 24, 1993.

28. *Sacramento Bee*, November 28, 1993.

29. "Immigration revealed its potency as a political issue in 1994 when California governor Pete Wilson found himself struggling for reelection ... He endorsed Proposition 187, a referendum to ban undocumented migrants from receiving public health, education, and welfare services, and made it his rallying cry ... Both the governor and the proposition were endorsed by a majority of the state's voters." Durand, et al., op. cit.

30. *Christian Century*, March 1, 1995.

31. *Los Angeles Times*, November 3, 1995.

32. Ibid.

33. Consejo Nacional de Población, México, *"La migración de mexicanos hacia Estados Unidos,"* 1996.

34. *Viva!* April 15, 1996.

35. Verea, op. cit.

36. Ibid.

37. Consejo Nacional de Población, *"La migración de mexicanos hacia Estados Unidos,"* 1996.

38. *La Jornada*, April. 24, 1997. Bustamante then was president of the *Colegio de la Frontera Norte* in Tijuana.

39. *Viva!* April 15, 1996.

40. *La Opinión*, December 7, 1998.

41. *Los Angeles Times*, January 11, 1998.

DON'T KILL THE CASH COW

1. *Proceso*, October 28, 2001.

2. *Immigration News Briefs*, New York, July 9, 2005.

3. Another 6,000 unaccompanied children were apprehended in the United States. In many of these cases, the children were attempting to join parents already living and working in the United States.

4. *Proceso*, August 11, 2002.

5. Ibid.

6. *La Jornada*, January 15, 2003.

7. Not everyone in Mexico agreed with Fox. *The New York Times* quoted Jorge Santibáñez, president of Tijuana's *Colegio de la Frontera Norte*, "For too long Mexico has boasted about immigrants leaving, calling them national heroes, instead of describing them as actors in a national tragedy. And it has boasted about the growth in remittances as an indicator of success, when it is really an indicator of failure." May 26, 2006.

8. *El Universal, Mexico City*, June 20, 2005.

9. *La Jornada*, November 12, 2003.

10. *Arizona Republic*, April 23, 2004.

11. *Los Angeles Times*, October 13, 2004.

12. *Arizona Republic*, April 23, 2004.

13. Miguel Pickard, "Mesoamerican Migrants Journey North," Americas Program, Interhemispheric Resource Center, March 18, 2005.

14. Sean Garcia, "The ABCs of Immigration Reform," Americas Program, Interhemispheric Resource Center, May 28, 2004.

15. Associated Press, May 18, 2006.

16. Americas Program, Interhemispheric Resource Center, June 17, 2005.

17. In October 2005 President Bush vowed to expel "every single illegal entrant, with no exceptions" but later backtracked and admitted that the massive deportations of over 11 million unauthorized immigrants was a task beyond U. S. law enforcement capabilities.

18. Daniel T. Griswold, "Willing Workers," Center for Trade Policy Studies, October 15, 2002.

19. Americas Program, Interhemispheric Resource Center, June 17, 2005.

20. *Christian Science Monitor*, July 19, 2006.

21. Americas Program, Interhemispheric Resource Center, June 17, 2005.

22. Thousands of *indocumentados*, contracted to do clean up work after hurricane Katrina devastated the U.S. Gulf Coast found themselves stranded and penniless after subcontractors failed to pay either wages or provide promised housing and food. *Salon.com* November 15, 2005. By suspending the Davis-Bacon Act, which requires contractors to pay the prevailing wage for work done, the Bush administration gave "a green light to Gulf Coast employers to take advantage of immigrant workers." *Dissident Voice*, October 28, 2005.

23. *Palm Beach Post*, December 9, 2003.

24. The Pew Hispanic Center estimated that 7.2 million *indocumentados* were working in the United States in 2005 (approximately 5 percent of the U.S. workforce). Twenty-four percent of U.S. farm workers were unauthorized, 14 percent of construction workers and 12 percent of food preparation employees. That construction hired unauthorized immigrants for the grittiest and least desirable jobs was evident from statistics indicating that 36 percent of insulation installers and 29 percent of drywallers were unauthorized.

25. Pickard, op. cit.

26. Reuters, April 26, 2006.

27. Rick Wolff, "Immigration and Class," *New Socialist*, June 2006.

28. CERLAC Colloquia Paper Series, May 2005, Toronto.

29. William I. Robinson, "The Struggle for Immigrant Rights in the U.S.," *América Latina en Movimiento*, April 2, 2006.

30. Laura Carlsen, Resource Center of the Americas, March 29, 1006.

31. Rick Wolff points out that "Such U.S. industries as agriculture, construction, tourism, restaurants and hotels, and hospitals—all industries that cannot readily outsource—have long recruited and supported the immigration of low-wage workers, legally or illegally. Immigration solves their competitive problems." Wolff op. cit.

32. Fred Krissman, Center for Comparative Immigration Studies, University of California, San Diego

33. Greenwood and Tienda consider the owners of capital and land the largest beneficiaries of immigrant Mexican labor, followed by lower consumer prices for goods processed or manufactured by their employers. However, they also note that the workers themselves benefit from higher earnings that they would have received had they not emigrated. Michael J. Greenwood, and Marta Tienda, "U.S. Impacts of Mexican Immigration," University of Texas, Austin, 1998.

34. The Senate proposal authorized 500 miles of vehicle barriers and 370 miles of three-tiered fences, plus the hiring and training of 14,000 agents over a five-year period. The House proposal authorized 700 miles of double-layer fences.

35. "The peaceful protestors who bore huge banners reading. 'We are America' were not taunting, demanding, or excluding anyone. They were simply stating a fact." Laura Carlsen, *This Week in the Americas*, April 13, 2006.

36. Cargill Inc., the U.S.'s second largest beef producer and third largest pork producer, closed all of its plants "because we share the concerns of many employees," Reuters reported.

37. *Proceso*, May 21, 2006 quotes Rafael Fernández de Castro, "To militarize the frontier is unpardonable and has sent an incontrovertible message: To try to cooperate and resolve problems diplomatically and bilaterally means nothing [to the Bush administration]."

38. Often omitted from discussions about "guest workers" is the fact that the U.S. issues some 800,000 legal work permits to foreigners, particularly in specialized fields such as electronics, education, and nursing.

39. David Bacon, "A Bracero Program for the Willing," *Network News*, Spring 2005.

40. The Cato Institute went further than just advocating a guest worker program. "Legalizing Mexican migration would, in one stroke, bring a huge underground market into the open. It would allow American producers in important sectors of our economy to hire the workers they need to grow." Griswold, op. cit.

41. For example, during the week ending September 23, 2006, ICE raids included a day laborer raid in Connecticut, a Colorado Air Force housing construction site, a Georgia curb and gutter company, a Washington industrial laundry, an Illinois Chinese buffet, a Florida roofing contractor, a Mississippi country club, and several locations in Michigan for a total of 291 apprehensions.

42. Noting the vast increase in the informal ("under the table") economy, Jill Esbenshade insists "the growing economic and social polarization which we are experiencing under the global economic order also promotes informal economic activities at both ends of the spectrum." Esbenshade, Jill, "Immigrants and the Informal Economy," *Network News*, June 2006.

43. Journalist Molly Ivins suggested, "If you want to stop Mexicans from crossing the border to work here, put Americans who hire them in jail." "More Immigrant Bashing On the Way," *Common Dreams*, July 6, 2006

44. A "guest worker" program essentially is a *bracero* program by a different name and, as pointed out in previous chapters, the *bracero* program created a huge magnet for unauthorized immigration. Escobar Latapí and his co-authors note, "a legal channel for Mexican temporary workers would probably add to rather than substitute for unauthorized workers..." Agustín Escobar Latapí, Philip Martín, Gustavo López Castro, and Catherine Donato, "Factors that Influence Migration," U.S. Commission on Immigration Reform, 1998.

45. Ibid.

46. *La Jornada*, December 24, 2005.

47. "By greatly expanding that number [of guest workers] the president's bill guarantees the creation of even more jobs 'Americans don't want.'" Barbara Garson, *ZMag*, August 27, 2006

48. Escobar Latapí, et al., op. cit.

49. The number of employers prosecuted for unlawfully employing immigrants dropped from 182 in 1999 to four in 2003 and fines declined from $3.6 million to $212,000." Tom Hartmann, *Common Dreams*, July 5, 2006.

50. Laura Carlsen, *This Week in the Americas*, January 30, 2006.

Bibliography

BOOKS AND DOCUMENTS

Cerrutti, Marcelo, and Massey, Douglas S. *Crossing the Border*. New York: Russell Sage Foundation, 2004.

Cohen, Jeffrey H. *The Culture of Migration in Southern Mexico*. Austin: University of Texas Press, 2004.

Escobar Latapí, Agustín, Martin, Philip, López Castro, Gustavo, and Donato, Katharine. "Factors That Influence Migration." U.S. Commission on Immigration Reform, 1998.

Galarza, Ernesto. *Merchants of Labor: The Mexican Bracero Story*. Santa Barbara, CA: McNally and Loftin, 1964.

Goldring, Luin. "Continuities in Transnational Migration: An Analysis of Nineteen Mexican Communities." CERLAC Colloquia Paper Series, May 2005, Toronto.

Greenwood, Michael J., and Tienda, Marta. "U.S: Impacts of Mexican Immigration." Austin: University of Texas, 1998.

Griswold, Daniel T. "Willing Workers." Center for Trade Policy Studies, October 15, 2002.

Halsell, Grace. *The Illegals*. New York: Stein & Day, 1978.

Iglesias, Norma. *La flor más bella de la maquiladora*. D. F. México: SEP/Centro de Estudios Fronterizos del Norte de México, 1985.

Krissman, Fred. "Apples and Oranges." Presented at the forum "Indigenous Mexican Migrants in the U.S." University of California-Santa Cruz, October 11–12, 2002.

———. "Them or Us." Center for Comparative Immigration Studies. San Diego: University of California, 2001.

Massey, Douglas, Alarcón, Rafael, Durand, Jorge, and Gonzalez, Humberto. *Return to Aztlan*. Berkeley: University of California Press, 1987.

Massey, Douglas S., and Denton, Nancy A. *American Apartheid*. Cambridge, MA: Harvard University Press, 1993.

Massey, Douglas S., and Durand, Jorge. *Clandestinos*. Universidad Autónoma de Zacatecas, 2003.

Massey, Douglas S., Durand, Jorge, and Malone, Nolan J. *Beyond Smoke and Mirrors*. New York: Russell Sage Foundation, 2002.

Saenz, Rogelio, and Cready, Cynthia M. "The Southwest Midwest Mexican American Migration Flows, 1985–1990." Paper presented at the Rural Sociology Society meeting, Des Moines, Iowa, 1996.

Santamaría Gómez, Arturo. *La Izquierda norteamericana y los trabajadores indocumentados*. Mazatlán, Sinaloa, México: Universidad Autónoma de Sinaloa, 1988.

Verea, Monica. *Entre México y Estados Unidos: los indocumentados*. D. F. México: Ediciones El Caballito, 1982.

MAGAZINES AND ON-LINE RESOURCES

Andreas, Peter. "U.S.-Mexico: Open Markets, Closed Border." *Foreign Policy*, Summer 1996.

Bacon, David. "A Bracero Program for the Willing." *Network News*, Spring 2005.

Carlsen, Laura. *This Week in the Americas*. January 30, 2006.

———. *This Week in the Americas*. April 13, 2006.

Castillo, Manuel Ángel. *"Migración en el hemisferia."* Centro Latinoamericano y Caribeño de Demografía, Santiago, Chile, May 2003.

Cerrutti, Marcelo, and Massey, Douglas S. "On the Auspices of Female Migration from Mexico to the United States." *Demography* No. 38.

Consejo Nacional De Población, Mexico. "La migación de mexicanos hacia Estados Unidos," 1996.

Cornelius, Wayne A. "Death at the Border." *Population and Development Review*, December 2001.

Coyne, Kevin. "A Place of Our Own." *Notre Dame Magazine*, Spring 1995.

Durand, Jorge, Massey, Douglas S., and Parrado, Emilio A. "The New Era of Mexican Migration to the United States," *The Journal of American History*, September 1999.

Esbenshade, Jill. "Emigrants and the Informal Economy." *Network News*, June 2006.

Gaffney, Edward McGlynn, Jr. "Immigrant Bashing." *Christian Century*, March 1, 1995.

Garcia, Sean. "The ABCs of Immigration Reform." Americas Program, Interhemispheric Resource Center, May 28, 2004.

Gutiérrez, Alejandro. "Frontera del Sur: El Sueño Roto." *Proceso*, August 11, 2002.

Hartmann, Tom. *Common Dreams*. July 5, 2006.

Ivins, Molly. "More Immigrant Bashing on the Way." *Common Dreams*, July 6, 2006.

Magaña, Juan Manuel. "Indocumentados, la Sangre que Lubrica el Mecanismo Político Estadounidense." *Viva!*, April 15, 1996.

Ostendorf, David L. "Workers, Go Home!" *Christian Century*, December 19–26, 2001.

Pickard, Miguel. "Mesoamerican Migrants Journey North." Americas Program, Interhemispheric Resource Center, March 18, 2005.

Roberts, Bryan R., Frank, Reanne, and Lozano-Ascencio, Fernando. "Transnational Migrant Communities and Mexican Migration to the U.S." *Ethnic and Racial Studies*, March 1999.

Robinson, William I. "The Struggle for Immigrant Rights in the U.S." *América Latina en Movimiento*, April 2, 2006.

Rosenberg, Tina. "Farm Workers Don't Have to Be Poor." *Washington Monthly*, April 1989.

Shorris, Earl. "Raids, Racism and the I.N.S." *The Nation*, May 8, 1989.

Wolff, Rick. "Immigration and Class." *New Socialist*, June 2006.

PERIODICALS CONSULTED

Atlas World Press Review
The Center Magazine
Chico (CA) *Enterprise-Record*
Chico (CA) *News & Review*
Christian Science Monitor
Ciudad Juarez *El Fronterizo*
Counterpunch
Dissident Voice
Guatemala *Prensa Libre*
Immigration News Briefs
In These Times
La Paz (Mexico) *Sudcaliforniano*
Little Rock (Ark.) *Democrat-Gazette*
London *The Guardian*
Los Angeles *La Opinión*
Los Angeles Times
Mexico City *Excelsior*
Mexico City *El Heraldo de Mexico*
Mexico City *La Jornada*
Mexico City *El Sol de Mexico*
Mexico City *El Universal*
Mexico City *Uno Más Uno*
Palm Beach Post (FL)
Sacramento Bee
San Antonio Express-News
San Francisco Chronicle
USA Today
Viva!
Washington, Post
World Press Review
ZMag

Index

Acosta, Hipólito, 111
Acuña, Rodolfo F., 120
AFL-CIO, 129
Agua Prieta, Mexico, 113–15, 121
Aguilar, Abraham, 35
Aguilar, Joel, 24
Aguilar, José Luis, 118
Aiken, Tim, 118
Albañez, Guillermo, 134
Ambulantes, 96
Amendola, Sandra L., 132
American Farm Bureau Federation, 158
American Patrol, 121–22
Amnesty, 45, 68, 145; children, 132–33;
    farm-workers, 132; registrations
    under
Simpson-Rodino, 131
Anaya, Anthony, 126
Angulo, Pablo, 29–30
Archer, Hill, 136
Arrieta, R. M., 118
Austin, Texas, 64–65, 73

Baca, Herman, 34
Bank of America, 100
Barnett, John, 121
Barr, William, 135–36
Barry, Tom, 155
Bell, Griffin B., 125–26

Bentsen, Lloyd, 128
Birds of passage, 25
Black, Temple, 120
Bonner, T. J., 113, 153–54
Border Patrol, 34, 40–41, 48, 50, 52–55,
    104, 106, 108–10, 112–17, 121–23, 127,
    130, 134, 146–47, 151; beatings,
    110–11, 142; checkpoints, 42, 50, 105-
    6; high speed chases, 50–51, 109;
    inexperienced agents, 154;
    shootings, 37, 109–11; sweeps, 119
Boxer, Barbara, 136
Boyle, Gregory, 133
Braceros, 3, 18–21, 79; backgrounds, 15;
    definition, 2; housing, 57–58,
    statistics, 17
Brooks, David, 88, 110, 114–15
Bureau of Customs and Border
    Protection (BCBP), 117, 154
Bush, George W., 149–50, 154–55, 161
Bustamante, Jorge A., 42, 47, 141,
    144

Calderón, Cedric, 49, 105–6
Calexico, California, 109
California Farm Bureau Federation,
    70
California Institute for Rural Studies,
    90

California Rural Legal Assistance, 70, 110
Carlsen, Laura, 159, 166
Carter, Jimmy, 37–38, 104, 130, 141
Cason, Jim, 88, 110, 114–15
Casteñeda, Alejandra, 77
Castillo, Gustavo, 76
Castillo, Leonel, 104
Castillo, Manuel Ángel, 10
Cat and mouse game, 33, 50–51
Catholic Church, 66–7, 131, 133, 143
Center for Immigration Studies, 132
Central Americans, 46–47, 68–69, 104, 113, 142, 151–53, 158
Cerrutti, Marcelo, 38
Chavez, Cesar, 129–30, 165
Chicago, Illinois, 63–64, 66, 95–96
Chico, California, 74, 100
Child labor, 83–85
Chula Vista, California, 40
Civil Liberties Union, 110
Cleveland National Forest, 52–53
Clinton, Bill, 136, 141; support of NAFTA, 9
Cohen, Jeffrey H., 5, 10, 28
Commission on Agricultural Workers, 132, 134
Concerned Citizens of the U.S.A., 121–22
Consejo Nacional de Población (Conapo), 141
Cornelius, Wayne A., 51, 72
Corning, California, 76–77
Cortés, José, 36 Coyotes, 7, 33, 35, 38, 41, 48–49, 53–54, 77, 104, 106–7, 110, 113, 157; arrests of, 39; fees, 72; gangland connections, 34, 105; inexperienced, 48; menus of prices and services, 55; in Mexico, 46, 152; taking risks, 52; in Texas, 115
"Crash of '81," 37–38

Department of Labor, 58–59, 126
Deportations, 103–4, 109, 125, 127, 136, 141, 147, 162; criminal aliens, 34; high school students, 117; by Mexican government, 151; statistics 27, 37
Deukmejian, George, 126, 128

Díaz, Maribel, 24, 42
Díaz Ordaz, Luis, 139
Douglas, Arizona, 113, 121–22
Drug dealers and smugglers, 47, 67–68, 72, 77, 105; in Texas, 115–16
Drug Enforcement Agency (DEA), 116
Durand, Jorge, 22–23

Eagle Pass, Texas, 114–15
"Earned legalization," 154
Echeverría, Luis, 130, 139–40
Encinitas, California, 69
"English only" legislation, 135
Escobar Latapí, Agustín, 4–7, 9, 19, 34, 83, 164–65

Farmworkers, 45–46, 83–93, 103–4, 157–58; injuries, 97–98, 132–33
Farmingdale, New York, 122
Federation for American Immigration Reform (FAIR), 136–37
Feinstein, Dianne, 132, 135–36, 144
Ferrarone, Donald F., 116
Fife, John, 153
Flores, Marco Antonio, 66–67
Foote, Jack, 121
Ford, Gerald, 126
Form H-II, 42–43
Fox, Vicente, 149–50, 152–53
Francis, Samuel, 156–57
Fuentes Ruiz, Alfonso, 39

Gaffney, Edward McGlynn, 137
Galarza, Ernesto, 16
Garcia, Sean, 154
Gerawan Ranches, 70
"Get tough" policies, 37–38
Gilchrist, Jim, 122
Globalization, 160
Goldring, Luin, 15–16
Gonzalez, Henry, 128
Goss, Porter, 91
Green cards, 42–43
Greenwood, Michael J., 95
Gridley, California, 61; Farm Labor Housing camp, 67–68
Griffin, Charles, 113
Griswold, Daniel T., 155

Grupo Beta, 111–12
Guest worker programs, 127, 139–40,
    143–44, 149, 165; Bush proposals,
    154,161, 164–65; qualifications, 11

Halsell, Grace, 107
Hannigan, George, 121
Harlingen, Texas, 104
Haworth, J. D., 112
Heppel, Monica L., 132
Homeland Security Agency, 116–18;
    formation of, 150, 154
Huerta, Dolores, 133–34
Huntington, Samuel, 156
Hutchinson, E. H., 27

Iglesias, Norma, 26–27
Immigration and Customs
    Enforcement (ICE), 6, 112, 117–20,
    123, 131, 154; fugitive operations
    teams, 162
Immigration and Naturalization
    Service (INS), 103–4, 108, 117, 132;
    paperwork backlog, 133
Informal economy, 81–82, 149
Ives, Edwin Mitchell, 92

Jara, José Vicente, 75
Jimenez, Tomas, 117

Keppel, Monica L.
Kice, Virginia, 112
King, Peter H., 95, 99
King's Beach, California, 71
Kinney, Joseph A., 158
Kirkland, Lane, 127
Korber, Andruw, 83
Krissman, Fred, 6, 16, 50, 101, 160

Labor camps, 57–62, 67, 70, 81, 87
Labor contractors, 36, 79–87, 89–92,
    105, 134, 146; buying workers,
    157
LaBouyer, Benigno, 38–39
La Causa, 129
La Pisca, 91
La Rumorosa Mountains, 112
Layton, Leslie, 103

Lehman, Richard, 136
León, Guanajuato, 24
Leon, Enrique, 66
Light, Ken, 25, 41
López Portillo, José, 37, 127, 130
Los Angeles, California, 96
Los Angeles Reader, 93–4, 96
Lucero, José, 30

MacDonald, Heather, 155
Magaña, Juan Manuel, 142–43
Maldonado, Emilio, 23, 61
Maquiladoras, 26–27; closings, 150
Mara Salvatruchas, 151–52
Martinez, Roberto, 66, 102
Massey, Douglas, 22–23, 28, 38, 80
Mata, Jose, 74, 80–81, 108
Matamoros, Tamaulipas, Mexico, 46–47
Maytorena, Felix, 30–31, 33, 86–87
McDonnell, Patrick J., 138
Meany, George, 127
Medina, Abel, 119
Mercado, Cliserio, 101
Mercado, Juan, 73–74
Mexican Mafia, 105, 107, 152
Michoacán, Mexico, 73, 99
Migrant networks, 18–19
Migration widows, 22
Miller, C. K., 120–21
Minutemen, 122–23
Molina, Uri, 91
Montoya, Joseph, 128
Mora, Cruz, 84
Mora, Elías, 101–2
Moy, Larry, 108
Muñoz, Carmelita, 61
Muñoz, Luis, 48–49, 51, 54, 105–7
Muñoz, Oscar, 152

NAFTA, 9, 159; effects on migration,
    141–42, 147
Najar, Joel, 98
Napolitano, Janet, 123
"National heroes," 153, 159
National Institute of Migration
    (Mexico), 111
Nelson, Alan C., 136–37
Nevins, Joseph, 111

No More Deaths, 119

Oakland, California, 73–74
Oaxaca, 92, 101
Occupational Safety and Health
    Administration (OSHA), 98
Operation Guardian, 110–11, 113–14
Operation Rio Grande, 114
Operation Tarmac, 118
Organ Pipe Cactus National Park, 37
Ostendorf, David L., 122
Otay Mesa, 34, 40, 50

Paleoconservatives, 156–57
Parrado, Emilio, 22–23
Payne, Donald W., 116
Permanent migration system, 4
Petris, Nicolas, 134
Pickard, Miguel, 153, 158
Piedras Negras, Mexico, 114
Plan Sur, 152
Playa de Muertos, 35
Portland, Maine, 117–18
Project Jobs, 108
Proposition 187 (California), 99,
    137–38, 145
Proposition 200 (Arizona), 119
Pulido, Luis, 39–41
"Push-pull theory of migration," 3–4,
    11

Quacinella, Lucy, 83

Raisin City, California, 71
Reagan, Ronald, 38, 127–28, 130
"Refugee Route," 46
Remittances, 10, 75–76, 138–40, 144,
    147, 152–53, 158–60, 165; statistics,
    153
Reno, Nevada, 98
Return to Aztlan, 18, 80
Rio Grande River, 35–36, 114–15
"River rats," 114–15
Riverside, California, 73
Robinson, Mary, 110
Robinson, William I., 159
Rodino, Peter W., 127–28, 164
Rodriguez, Amelia, 60–61, 67

Rodríguez, Gregory, 145
Rodriguez, Marcelino, 103
Roel, Santiago, 141
Romo, Lázaro, 74
Rosenberg, Tina, 104, 120
Rulis, María, 88

Sacramento, California, 96–97
"Safety valve," 147
Salgado, Jesse (Jesús), 87–88
Salinas de Gortari, Carlos, 9
San Antonio, Texas, 65–66
San Diego, California, 99, 117–18, 121,
    126, 128
San Francisco, California, 118
San Ysidro mountains, 52–53
Sanchez, Rafael, 100
"See-throughs," 64
Shorris, Earl, 108
Simcox, Chris, 156
Simpson-Rodino Immigration Reform
    Act of 1986, 4, 82, 133, 140, 144–45;
    legal actions against employers,
    108–9; passage of, 44–45, 130–31
Singer, Audrey, 28
Social Security, 98–99, 128, 145
Social security cards, 108; counterfeit,
    44
Solis, Fernando, 143
Sotelo, Felipe, 87
Spencer, Glenn, 121, 138
Spener, David, 35

Tahoe City, California, 71
Tancredo, Tom, 112
Tanton, John, 136
Taquerías Mi Ranchito, 100
Target earners, 15, 20, 28
"Three-for-One" Program, 153
Tienda, Marta, 95
Tijuana, 32–33, 53–54, 105–6,
    maquiladoras, 26
Torrington, Wyoming, 57–58
"Tortilla Curtain," 130
Trinity Knitworks, 97
Tucker, Troy, 120
Tucson Sector, 121
Turner, Hal, 122

United Farm Workers, 129, 133, 155

Valencia, Antonio, 31–33
Vance, David, Jr., 122
Velarde, Joseph, 133
Villa Guerrero, Jalisco, 75, 100–1

Walker, S. Lynne, 48–49, 107
Wal-Mart, 118
Washington, D. C., 94, 109

Watts, California, 113
Wendland, Joel, 120
West Los Angeles, California, 93–94
White cards, 42
Wilson, Pete, 99, 137–38, 142, 145

Younger, Evelle J., 126

Zacatecas, Mexico, 16–17
Zedillo, Ernesto, 138

About the Author

ROBERT JOE STOUT is a journalist who has worked as a magazine editor, newspaper reporter, copy editor and contributing editor. The author of *The Blood of the Serpent: Mexican Lives* (2003), he has published his nonfiction widely in magazines, journals, and newspapers, and he has also published a lot of short fiction and poetry. He currently lives in Mexico.